HISTORY
OF ECONOMIC
ANALYSIS

ECONOMICS INFORMATION GUIDE SERIES

Series Editor: Robert W. Haseltine, Associate Professor of Economics, State University College of Arts and Science at Geneseo, Geneseo, New York

Also in this series:

THE ECONOMICS OF MINORITIES—*Edited by Kenneth L. Gagala*

TRANSPORTATION ECONOMICS—*Edited by James P. Rakowski*

CONSUMER EDUCATION—*Edited by Terry A. Darveaux**

RUSSIAN ECONOMIC HISTORY—*Edited by Daniel and Vera Kazmer**

ECONOMIC EDUCATION—*Edited by Catherine Hughes**

HEALTH AND MEDICAL ECONOMICS—*Edited by Ted J. Ackroyd**

LABOR ECONOMICS—*Edited by Ross E. Azevedo**

ECONOMIC HISTORY OF CANADA—*Edited by Trevor J. O. Dick**

MATHEMATICAL ECONOMICS AND OPERATIONS RESEARCH—*Edited by Joseph Zaremba**

MONEY, BANKING, AND MACROECONOMICS—*Edited by James M. Rock**

INTERNATIONAL TRADE—*Edited by Ahmed M. El-Dersh***

ECONOMIC DEVELOPMENT—*Edited by Thomas A. Bieler***

*in press
**in preparation

The above series is part of the
GALE INFORMATION GUIDE LIBRARY

The Library consists of a number of separate series of guides covering major areas in the social sciences, humanities, and current affairs.

General Editor: Paul Wasserman, Professor and former Dean, School of Library and Information Services, University of Maryland

HISTORY
OF ECONOMIC
ANALYSIS

A GUIDE TO INFORMATION SOURCES

Volume 3 in the Economics Information Guide Series

William K. Hutchinson

Assistant Professor of Economics
Miami University
Oxford, Ohio

Gale Research Company
Book Tower, Detroit, Michigan 48226

Library of Congress Cataloging in Publication Data

Hutchinson, William Kenneth, 1945-
    History of economic analysis.

    (Economics information guide series; v. 3) (Gale information
guide library)
    Includes indexes.
    1. Economics--History--Bibliography.   I. Title.
Z7164.E2H87   [HB75]   016.3309   73-17578
ISBN 0-8103-1295-6

To Pop and Mom
They always kept the guiding light burning.

VITA

William K. Hutchinson is an assistant professor at Miami University in Oxford, Ohio. He received his B.A. from State University of New York at Geneseo and his M.A. and Ph.D. from the University of Iowa.

His current research projects include analysis of U.S. regional exports to foreign countries, social security and private saving, and time and technology. Hutchinson has contributed to the JOURNAL OF ECONOMIC HISTORY. He is a member of the American Economic Association and the Economic History Association.

CONTENTS

Contents

ACKNOWLEDGMENTS

I wish to express my appreciation to my graduate assistant, Charles Fortuna, who labored many hours to make my part of the task much easier. His searching for needed sources in our library saved me many valuable hours. I also want to thank Nancy Roderer, whose expert typing skills increased the speed and efficiency with which this work was completed.

Finally, I would like to thank my wife and son for their patience and understanding during the period in which I was working on this book.

INTRODUCTION

This work is a sourcebook for the neophyte in the history of economic analysis, one whose knowledge of the forerunners of contemporary analysis is very limited. The reader needs no special skills to use this reference book; but, to make efficient use of the material herein, the student is encouraged to complete a basic economics course or to read through a basic text in order to acquire the jargon of the field. But lack of familiarity with the authors of major works and commentaries listed here need not deter the beginning scholar.

The book is concerned with the era of about 1600-1940. During those 300 years, economics changed from a pastime of the wealthy to a field of scientific inquiry occupied by highly trained specialists. The nature of the work produced by the various writers also changed drastically during these years. One engaged in the history of economic analysis may discover that the writer generally given credit for a particular analytical concept may not have been the originator of the concept, but the one who first made significant use of it.

Little if any analytical work was done in economics before the classical period, and none of any consequence was produced before about 1600, the beginning of the mercantilist period. Many writers in the history of economic analysis believe that, among early writers, only those immediately before Adam Smith and the classical school are worthy of study. I have chosen to begin with the mercantilists, not because of the profundity of their analytical writings, but simply because the term "mercantilist behavior" is frequently employed in subsequent writings and in the popular press. The publication of Keynes's THE GENERAL THEORY OF EMPLOYMENT, INTEREST AND MONEY just before 1940 marked the beginning of modern macroeconomic theory (a topic for another volume in this series) and serves to end this sourcebook.

Each of the following chapters is devoted to a particular school of thought. The major contributions of the various writers in each school follow a brief introduction to the school. The user is cautioned that, although the first group of works listed may be the originals in the field, the listings may not appear under the names of the original writers. Translations, revisions, or inclusion in anthologies would account for such discrepancies. References to critical analyses of the major works follow the original works; these are followed by short listings of works of lesser importance in the school. The shorter references to more esoteric works will, hopefully, provide useful clues for researchers wishing to study the school in more detail.

Two appendices follow chapter 6. The first is a listing of the major organizations concerned with the history of economic analysis; the second lists journals that print articles pertaining to that field. Addresses for both the organizations and the periodicals are included. Author, title, and subject indexes conclude the book.

Chapter 1

FORERUNNERS OF CLASSICAL ECONOMICS

Chapter 1

FORERUNNERS OF CLASSICAL ECONOMICS

A. INTRODUCTION

The period from 1600 to about 1760 was dominated primarily by three movements in economics. The mercantilists were identified with policies that produced a favorable balance of trade--that is, the inflow of gold and silver--and stimulated the manufacture of products for export. This school of thought generally tended to measure a country's wealth in terms of the quantity of gold the country possessed, which was the motive force behind the drive for a favorable balance of trade.

Around 1750 there was a reactionary group in France known as the Physiocrats who opposed whatever the mercantilists advocated. These economic thinkers were agriculturally oriented and were unconcerned with production of manufactured goods. The biases of both groups were reflected in their writings and sometimes resulted in the formulation of invalid theories. The Physiocrats, however, were the first group of economists to produce any complete explanation for the workings of the economic system, and so are regarded by many to be the first true school of economic analysis.

The third movement was by far the least organized of the three. Sometimes referred to as the transitionalists, these economists began to write about the functioning of the entire economic system. They used deductive logic to formulate their theories and so initiated scientific economic analysis. These writers, in other words, were economic theorists instead of economic thinkers as most of the mercantilists had been. There had been many bright spots in the evolutionary path of the development of economics; but these transitional writers, especially in England, founded a new science--economics.

B. MAJOR CONTRIBUTIONS

1. Abbott, Leonard Dalton. MASTERWORKS OF ECONOMICS. Vol. 1.
    New York: McGraw-Hill, 1973. 260 p.

    This volume contains, in digest form, ENGLAND'S TREASURE

3

BY FOREIGN TRADE, by Thomas Mun, and REFLECTIONS ON
THE FORMATION AND DISTRIBUTION OF RICHES, by Anne
Robert Jacques Turgot. The first is the work of a mercantilist
writer who regarded as wrong the prohibition of bullion exports.
Although lacking in theoretical rigor it does demonstrate an understanding of the exchange mechanism under the gold standard.
Turgot, in REFLECTIONS, indirectly introduces the concept of
diminishing marginal utility. Both are highly recommended to
the student of this period.

2.   Cantillon, Richard. ESSAI SUR LA NATURE DU COMMERCE EN GEN-
ERAL. Edited and translated by Henry Higgs. New York: Augustus M.
Kelley, 1964. 394 p.

This volume contains both French and English versions of the
ESSAI along with a table of contents from the original and a
discussion of previous editions. There is also an essay by William Stanley Jevons on Cantillon and the origins of economics.
The translator has included an essay on the author's life and
work. There are two appendices: the first deals with the paral-
lels between Malachy Pastlethwayt's UNIVERSAL DICTIONARY
OF TRADE AND COMMERCE and Cantillon's ESSAI; the second
is a bibliography of sources and of contemporary writers who
referred to Cantillon. Cantillon's ESSAI is considered by some
as the first piece of classical economics literature.

3.   Child, Sir Josiah. A NEW DISCOURSE OF TRADE. 4th ed. London:
F. Hodges, On London Bridge, c. 1670. 260 p.

This essay was written to discuss many aspects of commercial
activity. Such topics as the Navigation Acts, the balance
of trade, woolen manufacturing, relief and employment of the
poor, and various aspects of interest on money and usury are
covered. The author also discusses the relationship between
plantations and the home government of the kingdom. Much
history, as well as the economics of the late seventeenth century, may be learned from this book.

4.   du Puys, Jacques. THE RESPONSE OF JEAN BODIN TO THE PARA-
DOXES OF LORD MALESTROIT AND THE PARADOXES. Translated by
George Albert Moore. Washington, D.C.: Country Dollar Press, 1946.
90 p.

Originally published in French by the Bookshop of Jacques du
Puys (Paris, 1578), this book contains the paradoxes of Lord
Malestroit, as presented by him to the King of France in 1566,
and Jean Bodin's responses, presented to the King in 1568.
Bodin's responses are concerned primarily with monetary management, inflation, and international trade policy. Many historians believe that Bodin was the first to articulate the quantity theory of money.

5. Hull, Charles Henry, ed. THE ECONOMIC WRITINGS OF SIR
    WILLIAM PETTY. 2 vols. Cambridge: At the University Press, 1899.
    xci, 700 p.

    This collection of Petty's writings contains "Observations Upon
    the Bills of Mortality," the authorship of which is a topic of
    debate. It was published as the work of Captain John Graunt,
    but many feel that Petty actually wrote the piece. The long
    introduction contains an extended discussion of the attribution
    debate based on the lives of the two men and Petty's other
    writings. The 700 pages in the two volumes contain sixteen
    other writings that were published by Petty, including "Politi-
    cal Arithmetick"; "A Treatise on Taxes and Contributions"; an
    essay on money; and eight essays on "political arithmetick."
    The rest deal with population and city growth problems in
    England and Ireland.

6. Kapp, K. William, and Kapp, Lore L., eds. HISTORY OF ECONOMIC
    THOUGHT: A BOOK OF READINGS. 2nd ed. New York: Barnes &
    Noble, 1963. 444 p.

    This is a collection of original writings by various authors and
    begins with St. Thomas Aquinas. Each school of thought is
    preceded by a brief introduction describing the main tenets of
    its writers. The period's writers whose works are represented
    are Jean Bodin, Phillip W. von Hornick, Sir William Petty,
    David Hume, and Francois Quesnay. Although the included
    works are not complete, they do serve to give the reader an
    idea of what these writers were thinking and writing.

7. Kuczynski, Marguerite, and Meek, Ronald L., eds. QUESNAY'S TAB-
    LEAU ECONOMIQUE. New York: Augustus M. Kelley, 1972.
    160 p.

    This is a rare work produced for the Royal Economic Society
    and the American Economic Association. Meek includes an
    essay on the first three editions of the TABLEAU and Kuczyn-
    ski follows with an essay on the search for the "Third Edition"
    of the TABLEAU. These are followed by the French and the
    English translations of the TABLEAU (third edition) and the ex-
    planatory notes that accompanied it. Appendices and the notes
    to all three editions conclude the book.

8. McCulloch, J.R., ed. EARLY ENGLISH TRACTS ON COMMERCE.
    Cambridge: At the University Press, 1970. 663 p.

    This work was first published in 1856 by the Political Economy
    Club of London and was reprinted in 1952 and reissued in 1954,
    prior to this reprinting. McCulloch wrote a preface in which
    each author and included work is discussed in relation to its
    time. Authors whose work is included are Thomas Mun (two
    works), Lewis Roberts, Samuel Fortrey, Sir Dudley North, and

three anonymous works. The works were taken from their original publications.

9. Meek, Ronald L., ed. PRECURSORS OF ADAM SMITH. Totowa, N.J.: Rowman & Littlefield, 1973. 201 p.

    The book contains an introduction by Professor Meek and a selected bibliography for the authors of the works included in the text. It is a collection of excerpts from eight different works by the following authors: Richard Cantillon, Francis Hutcheson, David Hume, A.R.J. Turgot, Marquis de Mirabeau, Francois Quesnay, Sir James Stuart, and Josiah Tucker. These works were selected according to their relation to Adam Smith's WEALTH OF NATIONS and each is preceded by a note explaining the key ideas and the link to the WEALTH OF NATIONS.

10. Mirabeau, Victor. THE ECONOMIC TABLE. New York: Bergman Publishers, 1968. 216 p.

    This is a reprint of a translation of Francois Quesnay's TABLEAU and the Marquis de Mirabeau's "Explanations." It is an early translation (1766), and is thus written in older style English, but may be read with little difficulty. There is a fold-out with seven different variations of the TABLEAU as originally produced by Quesnay. An excellent source of the original English translation.

11. Monroe, Arthur Eli. EARLY ECONOMIC THOUGHT: SELECTIONS FROM ECONOMIC LITERATURE PRIOR TO ADAM SMITH. Cambridge, Mass.: Harvard University Press, 1930. 399 p.

    The author has produced edited versions of the more important writings of many writers from the period before Smith. Each work is preceded by a brief biographical sketch of the particular writer and a note on the significance of the particular work. The works of primary interest are by the following authors: A. Serra, T. Mun, W. Petty, W. von Homick, R. Cantillon, F. Galiani, D. Hume, F. Quesnay, A.R.J. Turgot, and J. von Justi. This is an excellent source for the student more interested in what was written during this period than in interpretations of the works.

12. Rotwein, Eugene, ed. DAVID HUME: WRITINGS ON ECONOMICS. Madison: University of Wisconsin Press, 1955. cxi, 224 p.

    The book contains a 111-page introduction to Hume and his economic ideas. It is a very enlightening discussion of the various facets of Hume. Nine of Hume's essays on economics are followed by "relevant extracts" from Hume's correspondence from 1749 to 1776. This book contains all of Hume's major writings on economics.

13. Turgot, Anne Robert Jacques. REFLECTIONS ON THE FORMATION AND THE DISTRIBUTION OF RICHES. In ECONOMIC CLASSICS, edited by Sir William J. Ashley, pp. 1-112. London: Macmillan, 1898.

This edition of Turgot's REFLECTIONS contains a thirteen-page introduction by the editor which includes biographical material as well as a complete description of the writings of Turgot. REFLECTIONS first appeared in EPHIMERIDES DU CITOYEN, the organ of the Physiocratic party, and it was heavily edited by Du Pont de Nemours, the editor of that journal. Alterations nearly doubled the length, but the original has been restored, as nearly as possible, for this edition. There is also a brief collection of Turgot's correspondence at the end of the book. One should notice that many of Turgot's ideas concerning, for instance, the concept of diminishing marginal utility, were not unlike those to issue from the classical school and later.

C. COMMENTARIES ON THE MAJOR CONTRIBUTIONS

14. Arkin, Marcus. "The Economic Writings of David Hume--A Reassessment." THE SOUTH AFRICAN JOURNAL OF ECONOMICS 24 (September 1956): 204-20.

This article is actually a book review of Rotwein's DAVID HUME: WRITINGS ON ECONOMICS (see 12). It is a rather extensive review that covers all aspects of the writings of Hume that Rotwein included and their relationship to Adam Smith.

15. Beer, M. EARLY BRITISH ECONOMICS. London: George Allen & Unwin, 1938. Reprint ed., New York: Augustus M. Kelley, 1967. 250 p.

Beer discusses economic thought that prevailed in Great Britain between the thirteenth and the mid-eighteenth centuries, and covers most of the relevant pre-Smithian economics. The first sixty pages are devoted to premercantilist writings, but the remainder of the book is devoted to various aspects of mercantilist thought. Topics covered include money and exchange, balance of trade, and the importance of manufacture both for foreign and domestic buyers. The last major section deals with the transitional writers between British mercantilism and classical economics.

16. Bloomfield, Arthur I. "The Foreign-Trade Doctrines of the Physiocrats." AMERICAN ECONOMIC REVIEW 28 (December 1938): 716-35.

This article examines previously neglected comments on foreign trade by the Physiocrats. Bloomfield finds that, although they discussed many popular topics, they contributed very little new theory. Their contribution was the popularization of the concept of free trade (although their main concern was restricted to free exports of grain). An excellent piece for the student of the Physiocratic system.

17.   Bowley, Marian. STUDIES IN THE HISTORY OF ECONOMIC THEORY BEFORE 1870. London: Macmillan, 1973. 228 p.

An in-depth discussion of economic analysis in the seventeenth century and the problems of money supply, interest, prices, and value it was supposed to solve. A little more than 100 pages is devoted to the precursors of the classical school. Most of the work relates to mercantilist or transitional writers because of their great concern with the topics noted above. A good treatment of the thinking and problems of the preclassical period. (Also cited in Chapter 2, entry 126.)

18.   Burtt, Everett Johnson, Jr. SOCIAL PERSPECTIVES IN THE HISTORY OF ECONOMIC THEORY. New York: St. Martin's Press, 1972. 297 p.

A good discussion of the positive-normative debate as it has evolved over the years. In the first chapter, examples from all periods are provided. The second chapter addresses natural-law economics and concentrates on the writings of Sir William Petty, John Locke, and Francois Quesnay. Other authors are mentioned in passing and some are discussed briefly.

19.   Chalk, Alfred F. "Natural Law and the Rise of Economic Individualism in England." JOURNAL OF POLITICAL ECONOMY 59 (August 1951): 330-47.

The author demonstrates how, through reinterpretation of ancient natural-law doctrine, the transitional economists between mercantilism and classicism in England developed a foundation for the idea that individual freedom to pursue one's own economic interests would best serve the interest of the society.

20.   Cochrane, James L. MACROECONOMICS BEFORE KEYNES. Glenview, Ill.: Scott, Foresman and Co., 1970. 105 p.

The author has attempted to provide a macroeconomic model for each of the major schools of thought beginning with the Physiocrats. In about eleven pages the author discusses the Physiocratic system and develops an input-output system to simulate Quesnay's TABLEAU. This is recommended for the reader who has read other more detailed works on the Physiocrats.

21. Cole, Charles L. THE ECONOMIC FABRIC OF SOCIETY. New York: Harcourt, Brace & World, 1969. 246 p.

This book provides the novice reader with a brief but good first chapter on the scope and basic concepts of economics. The second chapter devotes six pages to "economic thinkers," and the next twenty pages to mercantilism and Physiocracy, giving about equal space to each.

22. Cole, Charles Woolsey. FRENCH MERCANTILIST DOCTRINE BEFORE COLBERT. New York: Richard R. Smith, 1931. 243 p.

Acknowledging that mercantilism and Colbertism were synonymous, the author examines predecessors of Cardinal Richelieu and Colbert to locate the origins of their economic policy. The span of the study was 1453 to 1629--from the end of the Hundred Years War to the time prior to the rise of Richelieu-- which was the period in which France rose to nation-state status. There is an eleven-page bibliography of primary and secondary sources. The book is divided into four sections: the first is concerned with general concepts of mercantilism; the second is addressed to the influence of Barthelemy de Laffemas and Henry the IV; the third section is a study of the work of Antoine de Montchetein, the originator of the term 'political economy'; the fourth section and the conclusion are concerned with mercantilist developments contemporary with Richelieu and Colbert in France.

23. Gould, J.D. "The Trade Crisis of the Early 1620's and English Economic Thought." JOURNAL OF ECONOMIC HISTORY 15 (June 1955): 121-33.

The author examines the arguments of two mercantilists--Thomas Mun (nonbullionist) and G. Malynes (bullionist)--regarding the benefits to be derived from allowing the export of gold bullion. The issue turns on the assumed elasticity of demand by foreign countries for England's goods. More important, however, is the demonstration that Mun only lacked one step in order to have stated the specie-flow adjustment process for international trade. This was 100 years before Hume's final exposition of the self-adjusting process.

24. Grampp, William D. ECONOMIC LIBERALISM. 2 vols. New York: Random House, 1965. Vol. I, 186 p.; vol. II, 153 p.

In volume I, the author examines the ideas expressed by many premercantilist writers as well as the mercantilists of England and the Continent. In volume II, the ideas of the classical economists are examined at considerable length, with emphasis on those of A. Smith and J.S. Mill. It is implied that there is a great deal of carry-over between the two schools.

25. Gray, Alexander. THE DEVELOPMENT OF ECONOMIC DOCTRINE. London: Longmans, Green, 1936. 384 p.

This book was designed for the beginning student of economics and the history of economic analysis. The author concentrates on the major writers from each period. There is a general introduction to mercantilism and the tenets of the school, and a brief discussion of four mercantilist writers (each from a different country). There were, however, better-known mercantilists, especially in England. Gray's chapter on the Physiocrats is devoted primarily to Quesnay and only considers briefly work by Turgot. There is a fold-out of the TABLEAU ECONOMIQUE from the Marquis de Mirabeau's ELEMENS DE LA PHILOSOPHIE RURALE, which was used by the Physiocrats to depict the circular flow of economic activity. (Also cited in Chapter 3, entry 296.)

26. Gregory, T.E. "The Economics of Employment in England, 1600-1713." ECONOMICA 1 & 2, no. 1 (1921): 37-51.

The author attempts to deal with the problem of labor "policy" during this period as it was treated by the basically mercantilist writers Petty and Davenant. He illustrates that no real theory of labor existed but that many had quite strong ideas regarding labor, the poor, and the treatment of the poor by the more prosperous. Some of the ideas advanced were not unlike those put forth today regarding the unskilled poor.

27. Groenewegen, P.D. "A Re-Interpretation of Turgot's Theory of Capital and Interest." THE ECONOMIC JOURNAL 81 (June 1971): 327-40.

The author attempts to analyze Turgot's capital and interest theory on the basis of many of Turgot's more obscure writings in conjunction with the REFLECTIONS. Most critics had previously relied only upon the REFLECTIONS. Turgot's analysis of interest determination is examined as part of the general theory of exchange, and there is a two-part discussion of the underlying forces of the supply of and demand for capital. Turgot's theory is finally compared with those of his contemporaries. This is an important article to the student of capital theory.

28. Heckscher, Eli F. MERCANTILISM. 2 vols. 2nd rev. ed. Edited by E.F. Soderlund. Translated by Mendel Shapiro. London: George Allen & Unwin, 1955. Vol. I, 474 p.; vol. II, 453 p.

This work was first published in Swedish in 1931. The first volume is a treatment of the actual facts which preceded mercantilism and how it developed in various countries. Volume II consists of four parts: "Mercantilism as a System of Power"; "Mercantilism as a System of Protection"; "Mercantilism as a Monetary System"; and "Mercantilism as a Conception of Society." Mercantilism is understood as "a phase in the history of economic policy."

29. Heimann, Eduard. HISTORY OF ECONOMIC DOCTRINES; AN INTRO-
DUCTION TO ECONOMIC THEORY. New York: Oxford University
Press, 1964. 263 p.

The book was first published in 1947. The author spends nearly
twenty pages describing the problems of economics and the
method with which the history of economics should be studied.
The second chapter is devoted to the mercantilists (Petty, Cantillon, North, Locke, and Hume), and the third chapter deals
in part, with the concept of naturalism and its application in
Physiocracy by Quesnay. (Also cited in Chapter 3, entry 298.)

30. Higgs, Henry. THE PHYSIOCRATS. London: Macmillan, 1897. Reprint ed., New York: Augustus M. Kelley, 1968. 158 p.

The book contains six lectures delivered by Higgs to the London School of Economics in 1896. The topics covered are:
the reasons for the rise of the Physiocratic school, the doctrines
of the school (two essays), the national and international relations of the school, the opponents of the school, and the
influence of the school on later economists. It was the first
book in English about the Physiocratic school, considered by
Higgs to have been the first school of economics.

31. Hoselitz, Bert F. "The Early History of Entrepreneurial Theory." EX-
PLORATIONS IN ENTREPRENEURIAL HISTORY 3 (April 1951): 193-220.

The author traces the uses of the word "entrepreneur" from
before Cantillon in France and Smith in England. The uses
of this concept by the Physiocrats are examined, as well as
the links between Say and Cantillon with respect to this concept. For many years Say was thought to have been the first
to employ the word "entrepreneur," and then Cantillon was
found to have used it, as had Quesnay after him.

32. Hoselitz, Bert F., et al. THEORIES OF ECONOMIC GROWTH. New
York: The Free Press, 1961. 344 p. (Paperbound ed., 1965.)

The first essay, written by Joseph J. Spengler, presents an
extensive analysis of the theory of economic growth in mercantilist and Physiocratic terms. He bases his mercantilist
theory upon the writings of British, French, Italian, German,
and Spanish authors, and uses the major French Physiocrats to
develop the theory of growth. The mercantilist section is sup-
plemented by a thirty-six-page appendix that summarizes the
developmental programs of representative mercantilists from the
above countries.

33. Hull, Charles H[enry]. "Petty's Place in the History of Economic Theory."
THE QUARTERLY JOURNAL OF ECONOMICS 14 (May 1900): 307-40.

11

The author concludes that: "If we understand mercantilism to consist. . .in a tendency to force the transition from local to national economic coherence by means of governmental interference with the activities of individuals in business, then Petty was one of the most extreme among English mercantilists." This is inconsistent with theories in which Petty is considered a free trader. This article emphasizes that Petty's contributions to tax theory and policy were greater than his contributions to trade.

34. Johnson, E.A.J. PREDECESSORS OF ADAM SMITH. New York: Prentice-Hall, 1937. 426 p.

The book does not consider all the British predecessors of Smith, but rather only ten of the more important. There is little discussion of monetary economics or the free trade movement. Johnson does not believe that all pre-Smithian economists were either mercantilists or free-traders, and his treatment of the ten writers reflects this particular bias and provides the reader with another view of these writers.

35. Johnson, Jerah. "The Role of Spending in Physiocratic Theory." THE QUARTERLY JOURNAL OF ECONOMICS 80 (November 1966): 616-32.

The author examines the crucial role of money and spending in the Physiocratic scheme. Spending must occur in sufficient amounts and in the correct pattern by sectors, and money is the means by which the system functions--the medium of exchange. He provides a good discussion of production, consumption and spending, money, and agriculture, as well as the pattern of activity.

36. Keynes, John Maynard. THE GENERAL THEORY OF EMPLOYMENT, INTEREST AND MONEY. London: Macmillan, 1936. 403 p. (Paperbound ed., New York: Harcourt, Brace & World, 1950.)

Keynes provides a very strong case for the mercantilists by drawing lines of analogy to his own work on the insufficiency of investment. He credits the mercantilists with having been many years ahead of the mainstream of classical theory with respect to macroeconomic policy and thinking in this area of economics. (Also cited in Chapter 6, entry 937.)

37. Letwin, William. THE ORIGINS OF SCIENTIFIC ECONOMICS. Garden City, N.Y.: Doubleday & Co., 1964. 345 p.

Letwin develops the notion that it is the logical form of a theory which makes it scientific and that theories must be consciously produced. The book is divided between the "Old Style"--Sir Josiah Child and Nicholas Barbon--and the "New

Style"--J. Collins, W. Petty, J. Locke, and D. North. The closing chapter discusses economic theory in general for the 1700s. There are five appendices dealing with various aspects of the works by J. Child, D. North, and J. Locke, and an essay on the recoinage controversy.

38. McCulloch, J.R. TREATISES AND ESSAYS ON SUBJECTS CONNECTED WITH ECONOMICAL POLICY. Edinburgh: Adam and Charles Black, 1853. Reprint ed., New York: Augustus M. Kelley, 1964. 487 p.

One of the essays is a fourteen-page "Sketch of the Life and Writings of Francois Quesnay," which provides a good account of Quesnay's life and career. It must be remembered that Quesnay did not write in economics until he was sixty years old; but he spent the last twenty years of his life working in the field of political economy.

39. Marx, Karl. THEORIES OF SURPLUS VALUE. Translated by G.A. Bonner and Emile Burns. New York: International Publishers, 1952. 432 p.

Pages 15-107 are devoted to an analysis of the Physiocrats and various other preclassical economic writers. Besides Turgot, Quesnay, and the TABLEAU ECONOMIQUE, Marx discusses the work of Petty, Davenant, North, Locke, Hume, Massie, and Sir J. Stuart with respect to their theories of surplus value. The Marx-Engels-Lenin Institute in Moscow recently produced a complete English translation of the full manuscript. This translation contains only selections from books I and II and nothing from book III. That which is contained in this text will not be found in the three volumes of CAPITAL. (Also cited in Chapter 2, entry 101.)

40. Meek, Ronald L. THE ECONOMICS OF PHYSIOCRACY: ESSAYS AND TRANSLATIONS. London: George Allen & Unwin, 1962. 432 p.

Only two books in English about Physiocracy preceded this one by Meek. He begins the book with an attempt to attract the reader to the subject, then presents a section of translations of Physiocratic writings. The last portion of the text consists of five specialized essays addressed to the following topics: the TABLEAU ECONOMIQUE, the concept of profit, underconsumption theories, the connection between Physiocracy and British classicism, and an interpretation of Physiocracy.

41. _____. "Physiocracy and Classicism in Britain." ECONOMIC JOURNAL 26 (March 1951): 26-47.

The author regards the Physiocrats and the eighteenth-century classicists as trying to explain capitalist production. He suggests that Smithian and subsequent theory and Physiocracy are best regarded as two different species of the genus classicism.

The Physiocratic controversies served to force the thinking of
the classical school beyond that of Smith to Ricardo and a
theory of <u>value</u> and a theory of <u>rent</u>.

42. Monroe, Arthur Eli. MONETARY THEORY BEFORE ADAM SMITH. Cambridge, Mass.: Harvard University Press, 1923. 312 p.

The author discusses monetary writings from the ancient world
to the time of A. Smith, dividing this era into five divisions
representing particular variations in political philosophy as
well as economics. The two divisions that deal with the mercantilist and Physiocratic writers are subdivided into nine major
topics. The introductory section briefly names the important
contributors of the time span and their important works. The
other eight subdivisions are given over to presenting various
thought on particular topics in monetary theory: origin and
functions of money; policy questions; coinage system; value of
money; theory of price change; principles of circulation, velocity of circulation; and problems of reform. A six-page bibliography follows the text.

43. Noonan, John T., Jr. THE SCHOLASTIC ANALYSIS OF USURY. Cambridge, Mass.: Harvard University Press, 1957. 432 p.

The author has divided the book into three parts: the first
covers scholastic theory from 1150 to 1450; the second covers
scholastic theory from 1450 to 1750; and the final division
looks at usury theory from three viewpoints. The body of
scholastic writers were Catholic theologians and canonists using
traditional terminology and methods of the medieval schools.
The intent of the study was to suggest the interaction of the
intellectual and the economics of religious demands and business pressures.

44. Roover, Raymond de. "Scholasticism and Mercantilism: A Contrast."
THE QUARTERLY JOURNAL OF ECONOMICS 69 (May 1955): 161-
90.

An attempt is made to depict the fundamental differences between the schoolmen (scholastics) and the proponents of mercantilist theory and to illustrate how these two theories evolved
in comparison with each other. The differing roles desired for
the state by members of each school are discussed, and the
author also shows how the mercantilists' role changed.
Many characteristics attributed to the mercantilists applied
originally to the scholastics.

45. Samuels, Warren J. "The Physiocratic Theory of Property and State."
THE QUARTERLY JOURNAL OF ECONOMICS 75, no. 1 (February 1961):
96-111.

The author considers the relationship between individual property rights and the state's position vis-a-vis the individual. Acknowledging that the state's function was to protect the rights of one individual against another, he questions the Physiocratic view of the individual's rights versus those of public or social interests and concludes that, beyond a doubt, private property rights were always contingent upon the consonance of the use of these rights with public interest as defined by the state, and that there were no established and everlasting property rights.

46. Schumpeter, Joseph Alois. HISTORY OF ECONOMIC ANALYSIS. New York: Oxford University Press, 1954. 1260 p.

Like all of Schumpeter's work, this is an extensive study that considers all aspects of economic analysis. Chapter 7 of part II is devoted entirely to analysis of the mercantilists.

47. Sen, S.R. THE ECONOMICS OF SIR JAMES STUART. London: G. Bell and Sons, 1957. 207 p.

Sen, according to some, saved Stuart from oblivion with this detailed and insightful study. He believed that Stuart was a pioneer in the field of economic planning and that he had a significant influence on Karl Marx. The author has also included four appendices: (A) The Corrected Copy of the 'Principles of Political Oeconomy'...; (B) Typical Definitions of Stuart's; (C) a list of authorities referred to by Stuart; and (D) a table of interesting events between 1648 and 1767. Also includes a selected bibliography.

48. Senior, Nassau [William]. SELECTED WRITINGS ON ECONOMICS. Reprint ed., New York: Augustus M. Kelley, 1966. Var. pag.

Contained in this collection of writings are three "Lectures on the Transmission of the Precious Metals from Country to Country and the Mercantile Theory of Wealth." First published in 1827, the lectures represent the ideas of a classical economist on mercantilism. He, like many classical writers, was a free trade advocate. (Also cited in Chapter 2, entry 111.)

49. Shirras, G. Findlay, and Craig, J.H. "Sir Isaac Newton and the Currency." THE ECONOMIC JOURNAL 55 (June-September 1945): 217-41.

The article examines the contributions of Newton to currency theory during his thirty-one years at the Royal Mint. The authors conclude that Newton contributed little if anything to currency theory and even failed to realize the limitations and implications of Gresham's Law, and that writers on currency such as McCulloch have given Newton as economist more praise than he deserved.

50. Smith, Adam. AN INQUIRY INTO THE NATURE AND CAUSES OF THE WEALTH OF NATIONS. Edited by Edwin Cannan. New York: Random House, 1937. lx, 976 p.

Book IV is devoted to the discussion of alternative systems of political economy. Smith felt there were two such alternatives: the system of commerce (mercantilism) and the system of agriculture (Physiocracy). Since he was an advocate of free trade among nations, Smith was very critical of the mercantilist system. He disagrees with both the mercantilist and the Physiocratic definitions of wealth. This is a good critical essay by a classical economist. (Also cited in Chapter 2, entry 112.)

51. Spengler, Joseph J. "The Physiocrats and Say's Law of Markets." JOURNAL OF POLITICAL ECONOMY 53 (September 1945): 193-211, (December 1945): 314-47.

The author points out that the Physiocratic emphasis on consumption and expenditure, and the associated theory of production, both anticipated and contributed to the Mill-Say "law of markets." The comparison is well done and very complete, showing the possible similarities between the thinking of the Physiocrats and J.B. Say, a classical theorist.

52. _____. "Richard Cantillon: First of the Moderns." JOURNAL OF POLITICAL ECONOMY 62 (August 1959): 281-95, (October 1959): 406-24.

The author describes the various reasons for considering Cantillon, rather than Adam Smith, as the founder of modern economics. This is probably the most detailed study of Cantillon and his ESSAI.

53. Spiegel, Henry William. THE GROWTH OF ECONOMIC THOUGHT. Englewood Cliffs, N.J.: Prentice-Hall, 1971. 816 p.

This is a very extensive work in which three chapters (5-7) are devoted to mercantilism and mercantilist writers. Chapter 8 is devoted to Physiocracy and various physiocratic writings. The ideas of a few of the transitional economists are presented in chapter 9. The author also provides approximately twenty pages of annotated bibliographic notes. A good book for beginners. (Also cited in Chapter 3, entry 314.)

54. Suviranta, B.R. THE THEORY OF THE BALANCE OF TRADE IN ENGLAND: A STUDY IN MERCENTILISM. Helsingfors, Finland: Privately printed, 1923. Reprint ed., New York: Augustus.M. Kelley, 1967. 171 p.

This work provides a brief account of the evolution of the mercantilist concept paralleling the development of the nation state and, in subsequent chapters, asks various questions re-

garding the "mechanism of the balance of trade": How did it
function? What were the limitations? How was it measured?
Two chapters on the functions performed by gold and silver and
one on the importance of a favorable balance are included.
In the closing chapter, the author provides an all-too-brief
summary of his conclusions. He does, however, remind the
reader that the mercantilists were not theorists, but merely
practical men addressing themselves to everyday problems. A
six-page bibliography of English economic literature up to
Adam Smith is included.

55. Taylor, O.H. ECONOMICS AND LIBERALISM: COLLECTED PAPERS.
Cambridge, Mass.: Harvard University Press, 1955. 321 p.

The first three essays deal with the economic and political
philosophy that prevailed in the seventeenth and eighteenth
centuries and produced the classical liberalism of the nineteenth century. The first article was written as a response
to R.H. Tawney's RELIGION AND THE RISE OF CAPITALISM
(Harcourt, Brace, 1926) and the manner in which Tawney described classical liberal philosophy as the "creed" of established
laissez-faire "capitalism." The second two articles should be
read together and deal with the "idea" of "natural laws" in
economics--supposedly analogous to those in physics--and the
"idea" of a body of ethical "natural law" to be embodied in
the legal system of the ideal liberal society. The search for
natural laws was the underlying motive for much of the early
economic enquiry.

56. Taylor, W.L. FRANCIS HUTCHESON AND DAVID HUME AS PREDE-
CESSORS OF ADAM SMITH. Durham, N.C.: Duke University Press,
1965. 180 p.

After showing the heritage common to all three writers, Hutcheson and Hume are compared with Smith. The second part of
the book consists of seven discussions of topics treated by all
three writers, and interpretive statements by the author. A
good source for material concerning the foundations of Smithian economics and the roles played by Hutcheson and Hume in
shaping these foundations.

57. Tucker, G.S.L. PROGRESS AND PROFITS IN BRITISH ECONOMIC
THOUGHT, 1650-1850. Cambridge: At the University Press,
1960. 206 p.

The book deals with "the doctrine that the growth of capital
tends to depress the general rate of return on real investment
throughout an economy." The concept is found in modern
theory under Keynes's diminishing marginal efficiency of capital.
Chapters 2 and 3 are concerned with writers from the period prior
to Adam Smith and their method of confronting the concept of

falling interest and the role of interest in general. (Also
cited in Chapter 2, entry 196.)

58. Vickers, Douglas. STUDIES IN THE THEORY OF MONEY 1690-1776.
Philadelphia: Chilton Co., 1959. 313 p.

This work is an attempt to examine the theory of money that
was both empirically relevant to preclassical times and logically
consistent in itself. The book treats the work of nine theorists
divided into three groups according to the type of contribution
to monetary theory made by each. The work of John Locke,
Nicholas Barbon, and Sir Dudley North is used to derive the
propositions upon which the theory was based. John Law,
George Berkeley, and Jacob Vanderlint are discussed relative
to some overlooked theoretical contributions. Finally, Richard
Cantillon, David Hume, and Sir James Stuart are considered
as representative of the more theoretical work which was the
most complete "movement toward the conception that the theory of money implied, and constituted a part of, a general
theory of the economic process."

59. Viner, Jacob. STUDIES IN THE THEORY OF INTERNATIONAL TRADE.
London: George Allen & Unwin, 1955. 650 p.

The first two parts of the book are a discussion of "English
Theories of Foreign Trade Before Adam Smith." The first part
deals with why mercantilism was desirable and the second deals
with legislative proposals and the fall of mercantilism. In all,
there are 119 pages of well-written discussion regarding nearly
all aspects of mercantilism.

60. Wu, Chi-Yuen. AN OUTLINE OF INTERNATIONAL PRICE THEORIES.
London: Routledge & Kegan Paul, 1939. Reprint ed., Nendeln, Liechtenstein: Kraus-Thomson, 1970. 373 p.

The author devotes the second chapter (sixty-five pages) to the
various stages (there were supposedly four) of mercantilist development. Each state encompasses a significant period in the
development of the capitalist system in England. The beginning
of chapter 3 concerns the international trade theory of David
Hume. The author also discusses Adam Smith and the Physiocrats in the second section of chapter 3. It is a fairly detailed
discussion of the theories associated with each period and the
main proponents of those theories. (Also cited in Chapter 2,
entry 198, and Chapter 4, entry 534.)

D. CONTRIBUTIONS OF LESSER IMPORTANCE

61. Allen, William R. "Modern Defenders of Mercantilist Theory." HISTORY
OF POLITICAL ECONOMY 2 (1970): 381-97.

62. Balogh, T. "Some Theoretical Aspects of the Gold Problem." ECO-NOMICA n.s. 4 (August 1937): 274-94.

63. Bauer, Stephen. "Quesnay's TABLEAU ECONOMIQUE." ECONOMIC JOURNAL 5 (March 1895): 1-21.

64. Cassel, Gustav. "The Restoration of the Gold Standard." ECONOMICA 3, no. 9 (1923): 171-85.

65. Coats, A.W. "The Interpretation of Mercantilist Economics: Some Historiographical Problems; With a Rearguard Response by William R. Allen." HISTORY OF POLITICAL ECONOMY 5 (1973): 485-98.

66. Condliffe, J.B. "The Value of International Trade." ECONOMICA n.s. 5 (May 1938): 123-37.

67. Dempsey, Bernard W. "The Historical Emergence of the Quantity Theory." QUARTERLY JOURNAL OF ECONOMICS 50 (1935-36): 174-92.

68. Eagly, Robert V. "A Physiocratic Model of Dynamic Equilibrium." JOURNAL OF POLITCAL ECONOMY 77 (January/February 1969): 66-84.

69. Evans, G. Heberton, Jr. "The Law of Demand--The Roles of Gregory King and Charles Davenant." QUARTERLY JOURNAL OF ECONOMICS 81 (August 1967): 483-92.

70. Ficek, Karel F. "Benthamism and Protection." ECONOMIC JOURNAL 44 (June 1934): 342-44.

71. Foley, V. "An Origin of the TABLEAU ECONOMIQUE." HISTORY OF POLITICAL ECONOMY 5 (1973): 121-50.

72. Groenewegen, P.D. "A Reappraisal of Turgot's Theory of Value, Exchange, and Price Determination." HISTORY OF POLITICAL ECONOMY 2 (1970): 177-98.

73. Higgs, Henry. "Cantillon's Place in Economics." QUARTERLY JOUR-NAL OF ECONOMICS 6 (1891-92): 436-56.

74. _____. "Richard Cantillon." ECONOMIC JOURNAL 1 (June 1891): 262-91.

75. Hoffman, M.L. "A Note on the Working of the Gold Standard." ECO-NOMICA n.s. 5 (February 1938): 84-89.

76. Hutchison, T.W. "Bentham as an Economist." ECONOMIC JOURNAL 66 (June 1956): 288-306.

77. Jones, J.H. "The Gold Standard." ECONOMIC JOURNAL 43 (December 1933): 551-74.

78. Leigh, Arthur H. "John Locke and the Quantity Theory of Money." HISTORY OF POLITICAL ECONOMY 6 (1974): 200-19.

79. Muchmore, Lynn. "Gerrard de Malynes and Mercantile Economics." HISTORY OF POLITICAL ECONOMY 1 (1969): 336-58.

80. Paish, F.W. "Causes of Changes in Gold Supply." ECONOMICA n.s. 5 (November 1938): 379-409.

81. Patten, Simon N. "Mandeville in the Twentieth Century." AMERICAN ECONOMIC REVIEW 8 (March 1918): 88-98.

82. Samuels, Warren J. "The Physiocratic Theory of Economic Policy." QUARTERLY JOURNAL OF ECONOMICS 76 (February 1962): 145-62.

83. Schwoh, Philippe. "French Monetary Policy and its Critics." ECONOMICA n.s. 2 (August 1935): 277-97.

84. Stark, W. "Jeremy Bentham as an Economist." ECONOMIC JOURNAL 51 (April 1941): 56-79.

85. Stephens, W.W. LIFE AND WRITINGS OF TURGOT. London: Longmans, Green, 1895. 325 p.

86. Viner, Jacob. "Power versus Plenty as Objectives of Foreign Policy in the Seventeenth and Eighteenth Centuries." In his THE LONG VIEW AND THE SHORT, pp. 277-305. Glencoe, Ill.: The Free Press, 1958.

87. Ware, Norman J. "The Physiocrats: A Study in Economic Rationalization." AMERICAN ECONOMIC REVIEW 21 (December 1931): 607-19.

88. Wasserman, Max J., and Beach, Frank H. "Some Neglected Monetary Theories of John Law." AMERICAN ECONOMIC REVIEW 24 (December 1934): 646-57.

Chapter 2

CLASSICAL ECONOMICS

Chapter 2

CLASSICAL ECONOMICS

A. INTRODUCTION

The economists who were writing during the period from 1776 to 1870 are usually classified as classical economists. These writers were the first to develop theories that were internally consistent and, in varying degrees, comprehensive in nature. The use of scientific method in reasoning and deducing the results of various occurences marked the beginning of economics as a science.

The list of works below is in no way exhaustive; it should, however, serve the scholar as a substantial introduction to the classical economists and their writings. Economic liberalism as it is known today began in this school with Adam Smith's publication of the WEALTH OF NATIONS in 1776. The economics of the classical writers is generally macroeconomics, in that it was concerned with the ·effects of particular variables on the economy as a whole.

The work of Karl Marx is included in this chapter because he based his economic theory of capitalism on various classical premises, and because most of his economic theory can be found in the works by Smith (entry 112) and Ricardo (entries 107-8). Only some of Marx's major works are cited because there are many other available sources and because most scholars are more familiar with his work than with that of other writers.

Classical economics scholars, popularizers of the term "laissez faire," were to have a great effect on the early economic policies of the United States. Smith's WEALTH OF NATIONS was available very soon after 1776 and Say's TREATISE ON POLITICAL ECONOMY was translated in 1821. Classical economic theory was developed primarily in England and France; however, it had widespread effects on other countries. For, while men in other countries were using the classical framework, they were not as yet actively seeking to extend the analysis. The next school of thought, the inductivist, marks the beginning of a generalized spread of economic theory outside the French-English areas--not only to the remainder of the Continent, but also to the United States.

B. MAJOR CONTRIBUTIONS

89. Abbott, Leonard Dalton. MASTERWORKS OF ECONOMICS. 3 vols.
New York: McGraw-Hill, 1973. Vol. I, 260 p.; vol. II, 181 p.;
vol. III, 302 p.

These three volumes contain condensations, in digest format,
of original works by A. Smith, T.R. Malthus, D. Ricardo,
J.S. Mill, and K. Marx. Useful as in introduction to the various
classical authors.

90. Caimes, John Elliott. THE CHARACTER AND LOGICAL METHOD OF
POLITICAL ECONOMY. 2nd ed. New York: Harper & Brothers, 1875.
Reprint ed., New York: Augustus M. Kelley, 1965. 235 p.

Caimes argues that mathematics cannot be applied to the development of economic truth and that the only possible use of
mathematics might be to exhibit economic doctrines derived
with other tools. The author is very much concerned in this
work about the theoretical logical consistency of political economy
as others have written it. The book provides a viewpoint for
classical theory and its methodology.

91. _____. ESSAYS IN POLITICAL ECONOMY, THEORETICAL AND AP-
PLIED. London: Macmillan, 1873. Reprint ed., New York: Augustus
M. Kelley, 1965. 371 p.

The first group of essays in this collection is an attempt to
apply extant theory to the problem of gold discoveries in
Australia and California. The remaining essays are theoretical,
treating the subject of laissez faire in an expository fashion
and criticizing the work of Comte and Bastiat. These articles
began to appear in journals in the late 1850s--the last half
of the period of currency and banking controversies in England.

92. _____. SOME LEADING PRINCIPLES OF POLITICAL ECONOMY NEW-
LY EXPOUNDED. New York: Harper & Brothers, 1874. Reprint ed.,
New York: Augustus M. Kelley, 1967. 421 p.

Caimes basically accepted the works of Smith, Ricardo, Malthus, and Mill with respect to their assumptions about human
character and the physical conditions of external nature that
constitute the ultimate premises of economic science. He does
take issue with some of their "axiomata media." As a result,
he has examined trade unions, with respect to the relation of
capital and labor, and the external trade of the United States
and its system of protection, which is in disagreement with all
theory as having any benefit.

93. Coumot, Augustin. RESEARCHES INTO THE MATHEMATICAL PRINCIPLES
OF THE THEORY OF WEALTH. Homewood, III.: Richard D. Irwin,

1963. xix, 174 p.

> This edition reprints the 1927 translation, which included an introduction and bibliography on Cournot and mathematical economics prior to 1897 along with "Notes on Cournot's Mathematics"--all by Irving Fisher. Cournot's book was written in 1838 and was the first noteworthy writing in mathematical economics. Walras and Jevons were the first economists to recognize the value of this work. The reader should be able to use calculus in order to completely comprehend Cournot's argument. He will be able to grasp merely the general content of the book if he does not have a command of calculus.

94. Godwin, William. OF POPULATION: AN ENQUIRY CONCERNING THE POWER OF INCREASE IN THE NUMBERS OF MANKIND. London: Longman, Hurst, Rees, Orme and Brown, 1820. Reprint ed., New York: Augustus M. Kelley, 1964. 626 p.

> This volume answers the attack of T.R. Malthus on Godwin and Condorcet, writers who proffered a population theory based on the goodness of mankind. Malthus reacted against such writings as Godwin's ENQUIRY CONCERNING POLITICAL JUSTICE, and Goodwin in turn responded with this volume in an attempt to dissuade the public from believing the doom forecast by Malthus.

95. McCulloch, J.R. THE WORKS OF DAVID RICARDO. London: John Murray, 1888. xxxiii, 584 p.

> This work contains the PRINCIPLES OF POLITICAL ECONOMY AND TAXATION (third edition), HIGH PRICE OF BULLION ...REPLY TO MR. BOSANQUANT'S PRACTICAL OBSERVATIONS ON THE REPORT OF THE BULLION COMMITTEE, an essay on the price of corn and level of profits, an essay on currency, a plan for establishing a national bank, an ESSAY ON THE FUNDING SYSTEM, and a few political works. There is also a thirty-page sketch of Ricardo's life.

96. Malthus, Thomas Robert. AN ESSAY ON THE PRINCIPLE OF POPULATION AS IT AFFECTS THE FUTURE IMPROVEMENT OF SOCIETY. London: J. Johnson, 1798. Reprint ed., London: Macmillan, 1966. xxvii, 396 p.

> This is the first edition of his ESSAY ON POPULATION--the deductive theoretic essay as opposed to the more inductive approach utilized in the later editions. This reprint contains an essay by James Bonar entitled "Notes on Malthus's First Essay." The essay contains much sharp comment on the writings of Condorcet and Godwin, whose writings precipitated his ESSAY. Later editions are more readily available.

97. _____. PRINCIPLES OF POLITICAL ECONOMY. 2nd ed. New York:

Augustus M. Kelley, 1951. liv, 446 p.

This edition of Malthus's POLITICAL ECONOMY was written thirty-eight years after his ESSAY ON THE PRINCIPLE OF POPULATION (1798) and thirty-three years after the much revised and enlarged second edition of the ESSAY. The second edition of POLITICAL ECONOMY, which was an extensive revision of the first edition, appeared in 1836, by which time Malthus had become an unquestioning believer in the labor theory of value. When the first edition appeared, he had held that value was measured according to some mean between corn and labor. He did not use his population theory, as Ricardo did, to derive the "Iron Law of Wages" to explain wage rate adjustment.

98. Marx, Karl. CAPITAL. 3 vols. Translated by Samuel Moore and Edward Aveling. Edited by Frederick Engels. Moscow: Progress Publishers, 1965-67. Vol. I, 807 p.; vol. II, 554 p.; vol. III, 948 p.

This is probably the most commonly recognized but infrequently read economics text ever published. Due to its extreme length, most scholars rely on interpreters of Marx's writing. Volume I is "A Critical Analysis of Capitalist Production"; volumes II and III address different aspects of "A Critique of Political Economy." The last two volumes cover, respectively, the process of circulation of capital and the process of capitalist production as a whole.

99. _____ . A CONTRIBUTION TO THE CRITIQUE OF POLITICAL ECONOMY. Translated by S.W. Ryazanskaya. Edited by Maurice [H.] Dobb. New York: International Publishers, 1970. 263 p.

Marx examines the system of bourgeois economy according to capital, landed property, wage labor, the state, foreign trade, and world market. This was written before CAPITAL and is prefatory to that work .

100. _____ . THE GUNDRISSE. Translated and edited by David McLellan. New York: Harper & Row, Publishers, 1971. 156 p.

In this edited version, McLellan has attempted to include the most important passages, and to add commentary to enhance the reader's understanding. He feels that this volume is central to Marx's work.

101. _____ . THEORIES OF SURPLUS VALUE. Translated by G.A. Bonner and Emile Burns. New York: International Publishers, 1952. 432 p.

This book contains analyses of surplus value theories of various writers. Approximately 70 pages are devoted to Smith and his concept of productive labor. The more than 225 pages on Ricardo are divided into two categories: surplus value and profit, and accumulation of capital and crises. It must be remembered that this work is not a complete translation of THEORIES OF SURPLUS VALUE, but it does contain much analysis that is of importance. The complete three volumes of this book have also been published in recent years by the Progress Publishers in Moscow under the editorship of S.W. Ryazanskaya. (Also cited in Chapter I, entry 39.)

102. Mill, James. ELEMENTS OF POLITICAL ECONOMY. 3rd ed., rev. and corrected. London: Henry G. Bohn, 1844. Reprint ed., New York: Augustus M. Kelley, 1965. 304 p.

This was one of the more widely used texts during the classical period. The author's son, J.S. Mill, benefited greatly from its careful reading. The author intended the book for school use.

103. Mill, John Stuart. ESSAYS ON SOME UNSETTLED QUESTIONS OF POLITICAL ECONOMY. London: Longmans, Green, Reader & Dyer, 1874. Reprint ed., New York: Augustus M. Kelley, 1968. 164 p.

This is a collection of five essays written between 1829 and 1830 on various topics that were not of foremost interest to the public at the time: the theory of international trade and the gains from trade; the effect of consumption on production; the use of the concepts productive and unproductive; profits and interest; and the definition of political economy and the methods of investigation.

104. _____. PRINCIPLES OF POLITICAL ECONOMY. New ed. by Sir William J. Ashley. London: Longmans, Green, 1909. Reprint ed., Clifton, N.J.: Augustus M. Kelley, 1973. xxxi, 1013 p.

This is one of the classic works in economics from which one may still learn. Mill wrote it in an attempt to incorporate the modern economic theory and philosophy of society into a treatise similar to A. Smith's WEALTH OF NATIONS. Thus, it was the culmination of the advancements that the classical school had made in economic theory integrated with the political and social conditions of mid-nineteenth-century England.

105. Rae, John. STATEMENT OF SOME NEW PRINCIPLES ON THE SUBJECT OF POLITICAL ECONOMY, EXPOSING THE FALLACIES OF THE SYSTEM OF FREE TRADE, AND SOME OTHER DOCTRINES MAINTAINED IN THE "WEALTH OF NATIONS." Boston: Hilliard, Gray, 1834. Reprint ed., New York: Augustus M. Kelley, 1964. 414 p.

This is a critique of A. Smith's WEALTH OF NATIONS which concentrates primarily on Smith's use of the term "wealth." Rae contends that, due to a wrong conception of wealth, Smith arrived at incorrect conclusions regarding, for example, free trade. This misconception resulted from Smith's "notion of the exact identity of the causes giving rise to individual and national wealth." The argument becomes quite involved.

106. Ramsay, George. AN ESSAY ON THE DISTRIBUTION OF WEALTH. Edinburgh: Adam and Charles Black, 1836. Reprint ed., Clifton, N.J.: Augustus M. Kelley, 1974. 506 p.

In this very useful volume, Ramsay examines in great detail the various aspects of the distribution process, both for income components and additions wealth. The labor theory of value is rejected, and scarcity and utility along with production cost--demand and supply--determine value or prices. This is not the work of the traditional classicist, even though Ramsay retains the use of the wages fund concept.

107. Ricardo, David. PRINCIPLES OF POLITICAL ECONOMY AND TAXATION. 3rd. ed. Edited with an introduction by R.M. Hartwell. Baltimore: Penguin Books, 1971. 427 p.

Ricardo had three objectives in mind when he wrote his PRINCIPLES: to determine the laws which regulate the distribution of income; to understand the effect of the progress of wealth on profits and wages; and to trace the influence of taxation on different classes. Ricardo was interested in relative values of goods and how these relative values affected distribution. Ricardo's work is one of the first to carefully examine the distribution of income and wealth.

108. _____. THE WORKS AND CORRESPONDENCE OF DAVID RICARDO. 10 vols. Edited by Piero Sraffa and Maurice H. Dobb. Cambridge: At the University Press, 1951-55.

Volume 1 contains the PRINCIPLES, volume 2 the unpublished "Notes on Malthus." Volumes 3 and 4 contain both published and unpublished pamphlets and papers, and volume 5 contains parliamentary speeches and evidence. Volumes 6 to 9 contain private correspondence, and volume 10 presents biographical materials.

109. Say, Jean-Baptiste. A TREATISE ON POLITICAL ECONOMY. 6th American ed. Translated by C.R. Princep with notes. Philadelphia: Grigg & Elliot, 1834. 403 p.

The alternate title of this book, THE PRODUCTION, DISTRIBUTION, AND CONSUMPTION OF WEALTH, is much more revealing of the content. The work has been classified as an interpreted version of Smith's WEALTH OF NATIONS. It is the source of the infamous Say's Law: "Supply creates its own demand." A worthwhile reading for any student of classical thought, it has been reprinted by Augustus M. Kelley, but the reprint is from the 1880 version of this translation.

110. Senior, Nassau William. AN OUTLINE OF THE SCIENCE OF POLITI-
CAL ECONOMY. London: W. Clower and Sons, 1836. Reprint ed.,
New York: Augustus M. Kelley, 1951. 249 p.

Senior defines political economy as "the Science which treats
of the Nature, the Production, and the Distribution of Wealth,"
a much narrower definition than that used by some of his contemporaries. The book is a discussion of the nature of wealth
and presents the "Four Elementary Propositions of the Science."
He was the first to introduce the abstinence theory of capital
accumulation. He also nearly comes to using demand and supply simultaneously.

111. _____. SELECTED WRITINGS ON ECONOMICS. Reprint ed., New
York: Augustus M. Kelley, 1966. Var. pag.

This volume is a collection of pamphlets written between 1827
and 1852. The contents are an "Introductory Lecture on Political Economy," "Three Lectures on the Transmission of the
Precious Metals," "Two Lectures on Population with a Correspondence between the Author and T.R. Malthus," "Three Lectures
on the Cost of Obtaining Money," "Two Letters on the Factory Acts," "Three Lectures on the Value of Money," and
"Four Introductory Lectures on Political Economy." Senior is
considered to have been one of the more perceptive economists of
the late classical period. (Also cited in Chapter 1, entry 48.)

112. Smith, Adam. AN INQUIRY INTO THE NATURE AND CAUSES OF THE
WEALTH OF NATIONS. Edited by Edwin Cannan. New York: Random House, 1937. lx, 976 p.

This is one of the oldest genuinely analytical works in economics,
and one may benefit from reading many parts of this text. Smith
intended here to reproach the mercantilists and, in some ways,
the Physiocrats. Some consider this book as marking the birth of
economic liberalism. (Also cited in Chapter 1, entry 50.)

113. Torrens, Robert. THE BUDGET ON COMMERCIAL AND COLONIAL
POLICY. London: Smith, Elder, 1844. Reprint ed., New York:
Augustus M. Kelley, 1970. lxxii, 427 p.

In this collection of essays the author has attempted to apply
Ricardo's principles of international exchange to the important
questions of commercial policy. These essays deal with the
relative productivity of labor between countries and its consequences for trade and the effect of imposition of duties.

114. _____. AN ESSAY ON THE EXTERNAL CORN TRADE. New ed.
London: Longman, Rees, Osme, Brown, and Green, 1829. Reprint ed.,
Clifton, N.J.: Augustus M. Kelley, 1972. 477 p.

This is an answer to Thomas Tooke's demonstration that, given

a constant money stock, taxation cannot create inflation. Torrens endeavors to explain how taxation does increase the quantity of money. He has also added to this edition a section on
free trade.

C. COMMENTARIES ON THE MAJOR CONTRIBUTIONS

115. Anderson, B.L. CAPITAL ACCUMULATION IN THE INDUSTRIAL REVO-
LUTION. Totowa, N.J.: Rowman & Littlefield, 1974. xxvii, 212 p.

This volume contains excerpts from many of the leading economic
treatises of the period from 1776 to 1850. The attention
of the reader is focused upon the attitudes of these classical
writers toward capital accumulation and economic development.
The writers whose works are included are A. Smith, W. Ellis,
John Rae, J.S. Mill, A. Hooke, P. Colquhoun, G.R. Porter,
and Sir Robert Giffen. The editor tries to sort out the real
conditions surrounding economic growth in the classical theory.

116. Ashton, T.S., and Sayers, R.S. PAPERS IN ENGLISH MONETARY HIS-
TORY. London: Oxford University Press, 1954. 167 p.

This collection of essays is not concerned directly with any
particular theorist, except for a twenty-page article on Ricardo's views on monetary questions. The remaining ten essays
provide the reader with some of the economic history of England during the eighteenth and nineteenth centuries.

117. Bagehot, Walter. ECONOMIC STUDIES. Edited by Richard Holt Hutton. London: Longmans, Green, 1898. Reprint ed., New York: Augustus M. Kelley, 1973. 280 p.

That Bagehot did most of his writing late in the classical
period is reflected in his discussions of the "cost of production" and "the growth of capital." More than 200 pages of
the book are devoted to the classical writers A. Smith, T.R.
Malthus, and D. Ricardo. The first essay (90 pages) deals
with the underlying postulates of English economic thought--
classical theory.

118. Balassa, Bela A. "John Stuart Mill and the Law of Markets." QUAR-
TERLY JOURNAL OF ECONOMICS 73 (May 1959): 263-74.

The writer proposes to reexamine Mill's work--especially his
concept of money and his treatment of Malthus's theory of
gluts, which he attempts to refute. These two aspects are
usually ignored but are essential to an understanding of Mill's
views on the Law of Markets. A comment on this article may
be found in QUARTERLY JOURNAL OF ECONOMICS
(Volume 74, February 1960, page 158).

119. Barnett, Harold J., and Morse, Chandler. SCARCITY AND GROWTH. Baltimore: The John Hopkins University Press, 1963. 288 p.

This work provides an excellent review of the doctrines of Malthus, Ricardo, and Mill as they related to the population/resource problem. It also contains an untraditional reformulation of the theories of Malthus and his contemporaries along with applications and tests of these theories. It is a work that illustrates how advanced the classical writers really were in many areas.

120. Blaug, Mark. ECONOMIC THEORY IN RETROSPECT. Rev. ed. Homewood, Ill.: Richard D. Irwin, 1968. 710 p.

This is a very rigorous and analytical text concerning the classical school. There are six chapters (260 pages) on various writers and topics of the classical school. Blaug provides reader's guides to the major works of many authors (Smith, Ricardo, Mill, Marx, and others) which are helpful for the scholar interested only in particular aspects of a writer's work.

121. _____. RICARDIAN ECONOMICS. New Haven, Conn.: Yale University Press, 1958. 269 p.

The theme of this study is the "rise and decline of the school of Ricardo in England." More rigorous than St. Clair's A KEY TO RICARDO (see 183), Blaug's book goes further in attempting to solve such problems as the invariable measure of value and the controversy over Say's Law. There are appendices on "Ricardo and Marx," "Malthus and Keynes," and "McCulloch's Critique of the Factory System."

122. Bober, M.M. KARL MARX'S INTERPRETATION OF HISTORY. 2nd ed., rev. New York: W.W. Norton & Co., 1965. 442 p. Paperbound.

The author does not attempt to distinguish which thoughts belong to Marx and which to Engels in the works of Marx that were edited by Engels. An objective and accurate interpretation of Marx's economic and historical concepts is presented within context of actual historical development. This edition is much more extensive than the first.

123. Bohm-Bawerk, Eugen. HISTORY AND CRITIQUE OF INTEREST THEORIES. Vol. I of CAPITAL AND INTEREST, translated by George D. Huncke and Hans F. Sennholz. South Holland, Ill.: Libertarian Press, 1959. 490 p.

This monumental work discusses the various theories of interest from the ancient philosophers to approximately 1900. There is a very extensive treatment of the classical writers and Karl Marx with respect to their various theories of interest.

124. Bonar, James. MALTHUS AND HIS WORK. London: Macmillan, 1885. 432 p.

Bonar discusses each of Malthus's works as it relates to the ESSAY ON POPULATION. The first part deals with the ES-SAY and the second with Malthus's economic theory; the third adds ethics, politics, and philosophy to Malthus's economic thinking. The fourth part consists of criticism of the critics of the ESSAY, and the fifth and final part is a biographical discussion of Malthus.

125. Bowley, Marian. NASSAU SENIOR AND CLASSICAL ECONOMICS. New York: Augustus M. Kelley, 1949. 358 p.

This book is an attempt to bring to the attention of economists and historians of economic thought the merits of N.W. Senior by means of an analysis of his views on the general as well as the controversial issues of his day--value theory, wages, capital and interest, and the poor laws. It contains a bibliography of all of Senior's writings.

126. _____. STUDIES IN THE HISTORY OF ECONOMIC THEORY BEFORE 1870. London: Macmillan, 1973. 228 p.

Bowley examines problems defined by various writers in the context of their own contemporary analytical climates, rather than in terms of modern economic theory. Topics relevant to study of the classical school are the price mechanism, utility theory, market structure and value, and wage and profit theory. Most of the prominent and some lesser classical theorists are discussed. (Also cited in Chapter 1, entry 17.)

127. Breit, William. "The Wages Fund Controversy: A Diagramatic Exposition." CANADIAN JOURNAL OF ECONOMICS 33, (November 1967): 523-28.

This is a geometric demonstration that the wages fund doctrine was perfectly compatible with demand and supply analysis, as J.S. Mill had argued. Mill was the theorist to finally reject this theory of wages. Mill did define the fund somewhat differently in order to arrive at his results and, after having renounced the wages fund doctrine, demand and supply theory prevailed.

128. Cannan, Edwin. A HISTORY OF THE THEORIES OF PRODUCTION AND DISTRIBUTION IN ENGLISH POLITICAL ECONOMY FROM 1776 TO 1848. 3rd ed. London: Percival & Co., 1917. Reprint ed., New York: Augustus M. Kelley, 1967. 336 p.

This is one of the first analytical histories of economics and is, therefore, an excellent source of information regarding the production and distribution theories of the classical school. In the second edition (1903) Cannan added two sections to the last chapter that describe the changes in theories since 1848 and the usefulness of the existing theories. An excellent source for the scholar who has more than a casual interest in the history of economics.

129. _____. A REVIEW OF ECONOMIC THEORY. London: P.S. King and Son, 1930. 448 p.

This book contains much information on the development of various lines of theory. It is arranged according to topics and not chronologically. The reader must, therefore, sort out the discussions of particular theorists, but may easily learn what various writers had to say regarding particular theoretical topics.

130. Cassels, John M. "A Re-Interpretation of Ricardo on Value." QUARTERLY JOURNAL OF ECONOMICS 49 (May 1935): 518-32.

Ricardo's concern with value theory is considered to have been incidental to the problems of distribution. He was not concerned with the determination of value but rather with the way in which ratios of exchange changed over time, and how these changes affected the functional distribution of income. The author concludes that Ricardo did in fact examine and reject a labor theory of value.

131. Corry, B[ernard] A. "Lauderdale and the Public Debt--A Reconsideration." In ESSAYS IN HONOUR OF LORD ROBBINS, edited by Maurice Peston and Bernard [A.] Corry, pp. 153-59. White Plains, N.Y.: International Arts & Sciences Press, 1972.

Whereas the author has argued elsewhere that the underconsumptionist economists were concerned with the rapid switch from consumption to saving, which was automatically invested, the argument here is that the view of Lauderdale--first of the underconsumptionists--was very similar to Keynes's theory of public debt. Their original was a dynamic Harrod-Domar-type problem instead of the Keynesian short-run macroequilibrium problem--no assurance that savings are transformed into real investment.

132. _____. MONEY, SAVING, AND INVESTMENT IN ENGLISH ECONOMICS, 1800-1850. New York: St. Martin's Press, 1962. 188 p.

The book is an attempt to provide better understanding of aggregate economics and deals primarily with the originators of aggregate analysis--the classical school. The basic classical model is produced from the works of Smith and the two Mills, and some variations are discussed with respect to the model. The variables in the title are discussed in general and with respect to particular classical economists, including those who dissented from the traditional classical model.

133. _____. "The Theory of the Economic Effects of Government Expenditure in English Classical Political Economy." ECONOMICA n.s. 25 (February 1958): 34-48.

Corry analyzes the application of classical theoretical principles to the controversy over the alleged economic effects of government spending. The intent is to show why the institutionalist writers failed to breach the gap in the structure of classical economics.

134. Crouch, R.L. "Laissez-Faire in Nineteenth Century Britain: Myth or Reality?" MANCHESTER SCHOOL OF ECONOMIC AND SOCIAL STUDIES 35 (September 1967): 199-215.

Crouch attempts to refute the recent contention of historians that laissez faire was a myth. The author tries to reestablish the notion that the period from about 1825 to 1875 was the era in which "the classical liberal attitude toward state interventionism in the body economic came nearest to realization."

135. Dmitriev, V.K. ECONOMIC ESSAYS ON VALUE: COMPETITION & UTILITY. Translated by D. Fry. Edited with an introduction by D.M. Nuti. Cambridge: At the University Press, 1974. 231 p.

The author was the first Russian mathematical economist and his essays published between 1898 and 1902 are classics. The first essay is "The Theory of Value of David Ricardo"; the second is "The Theory of Competition of Augustine Cournot"; and the third essay deals with marginal utility. The author treats various aspects of the two writers' theories in a very thorough and rigorous fashion. It is not recommended for those who are not mathematically inclined. (Also cited in Chapter 4, entry 344.)

136. Dobb, Maurice H. STUDIES IN THE DEVELOPMENT OF CAPITALISM. New York: International Publishers, 1947. 396 p.

This work does not pertain solely to the classical period, but encompasses the span of time from the feudal period to the period between the world wars. It is not a history of theory but rather an economic history of the growth of capitalism as a viable institution. The author's belief that one cannot separate economics from history was one of his main reasons for writing the book.

137. _____. THEORIES OF VALUE AND DISTRIBUTION SINCE ADAM SMITH. Cambridge: At the University Press, 1973. 295 p.

The text begins with a thirty-seven-page "Introductory: On

Ideology" which treats the perpetual problem of the content of ideology or relativistic influence that may be allowed in a theory before it ceases to be a theory. He then proceeds with a chapter on each of the following: Smith, Ricardo, reaction against Ricardo, J.S. Mill, and Karl Marx. He does consider the works of some marginalists such as Jevons. Dobb is a good scholar who provides an excellent discussion of the theories of these writers. (Also cited in Chapter 4, entry 444.)

138. Edelberg, Victor. "The Ricardian Theory of Profits." ECONOMICA 13 (February 1933): 51–74.

The author purports to show that the theory of profits is not an "extraneous confusion," as was maintained by many writers, but the ultimate synthesis of classical generalizations and one of Ricardo's most profound innovations in analytical economics.

139. Ferguson, John M. LANDMARKS OF ECONOMIC THOUGHT. 2nd ed. New York: Longmans, Green, 1950. 320 p.

This is a general text of economic thought which includes more than 100 pages on the classical school and Marx. Ferguson includes chapters on the transition from, for example, A. Smith to Ricardo, and from Ricardo to J.S. Mill. There is also a chapter concerned with the classical school on the Continent, a topic not always well covered by writers.

140. Fetter, Frank A. "Lauderdale's Oversaving Theory." AMERICAN ECONOMIC REVIEW 35 (June 1945): 263–83.

Relative to more current theories of oversaving, the author examines the work of the initiator of the concept. The examination takes the form of a comparison between the work of Lauderdale and that of Adam Smith since Lauderdale presented his ideas as an attack on various concepts of Smith's theory. Fetter makes many important points regarding the oversaving controversy that was revitalized with the appearance of Keynes's GENERAL THEORY in 1936.

141. Fetter, Frank Whitson. DEVELOPMENT OF BRITISH MONETARY ORTHO-DOXY. Cambridge, Mass.: Harvard University Press, 1964. 296 p.

This is a well-documented account of the monetary controversy that raged in England from about 1797 to 1875. Most of the classical writers were aligned with one side or the other on the banking and currency issues. An excellent account of the economic climate that prevailed during most of the era dominated by classical economics.

142. Glass, D.V., ed. INTRODUCTION TO MALTHUS. New York: John Wiley & Sons, 1953. 205 p.

The editor and various other authors examine particular aspects of Malthus's population theory. They discuss "The Historical Context of the ESSAY on Population," "Malthus and the Limitations on Population Growth," and "Malthus in the Twentieth Century." A list of materials published in Britain between 1798 and 1880 relating to the population question is provided along with reprints of two works by Malthus on the principle of population. This is a useful source for the study of Malthus's population theory.

143. Gordon, Scott. "Why Does Marxian Exploitation Theory Require a Labor Theory of Value?" JOURNAL OF POLITCAL ECONOMY 76 (January/February 1968): 137-40.

Gordon, answering the question put by his title, concludes that, although the product exhaustion problem requires the labor theory, as strict a theory as Marx proposed is unnecessary even though there are certain proportionality requirements.

144. Grampp, William D. "Adam Smith and the Economic Man." JOURNAL OF POLITICAL ECONOMY 56 (August 1948): 315-36.

In contrast to the image of the "economic man" given by the critics of classical theory, Grampp contends that Adam Smith described social behavior on many different levels--national conduct being only one. The author examines the chronological development of the economic aspect of Smith's ideas of social behavior.

145. _____. "Malthus on Money Wages and Welfare." AMERICAN ECONOMIC REVIEW 46 (December 1946): 924-36.

The Corn Law controversy from the point of view of Malthus is discussed with reference to the crucial assumptions made and the results obtained when one uses these assumptions. Indifference curve analysis is used by the author to illustrate the conditions under which Malthus was correct and those under which his argument was invalid. These assumptions are shown as the crux of the argument between Ricardo and Malthus.

146. _____. THE MANCHESTER SCHOOL OF ENGINEERING. Stanford, Calif.: Stanford University Press, 1960. 155 p.

This work reassesses the Manchester School, a group of businessmen who were attempting to have the Corn Laws repealed in England between 1838 and 1846. The author attempts to explain the composition of the school, the position of economics vis-a-vis the school, the Corn Law issue, the method of the campaign against the Corn Laws, the motives for the campaign, and what the school did after 1846.

147. Grubel, Herbert G. "Ricardo and Thornton on the Transfer Mechanism." QUARTERLY JOURNAL OF ECONOMICS 75 (February 1961): 292-301.

This work examines Hume's gold standard model, the extension of this basic model by Ricardo, and the refinements applied by Thornton. The workings of various classical models under the paper standard are then examined. The contradictory results of Ricardo and Thornton focused modern attention on the co-existence of both price and income effects as essential to the theory of the transfer mechanism.

148. Hayek, F.A. von. PROFITS, INTEREST AND INVESTMENT AND OTHER ESSAYS ON THE THEORY OF INDUSTRIAL FLUCTUATIONS. New York: Augustus M. Kelley, 1969. 266 p.

Although there is a short section on the "Ricardo Effect" in the first chapter, it is chapter 7 that is of primary interest to a student of the classical school. This chapter is "A Note on the Development of the Doctrine of Forced Saving." Jeremy Bentham is considered the originator of this concept, which reappears in economic theory from that time.

149. _____. THE PURE THEORY OF CAPITAL. Chicago: University of Chicago Press, 1962. 454 p.

This work is purely analytical, but the author has taken great pains to illustrate why the classical theories of capital were unable to satisfy the needs of those using them. Many of the prominent classical theorists are discussed.

150. Hegeland, Hugo. THE QUANTITY THEORY OF MONEY. Reprint ed. New York: Augustus M. Kelley, 1969. 262 p.

This work attempts to trace the development of the quantity theory of money from Confucius to Keynes. There were many interpretations, correct and incorrect, of this theory and the classical economists were among the most active interpreters. Monetary economics was a topic of major concern during the period from 1776 to 1870. It is an excellent discussion of the various aspects of the quantity theory. (Also cited in Chapter 4, entry 457.)

151. Hicks, J.R. "Ricardo's Theory of Distribution." In ESSAYS IN HONOUR OF LORD ROBBINS, edited by Maurice Peston and Bernard [A.] Corry, pp. 160-67. White Plains, N.Y.: International Arts & Sciences Press, 1972.

The author reexamines an aspect of Ricardo's distribution theory that was assessed as wrong by Cannan and others. The findings are two-fold: the ideas of distribution are analytically correct as were Ricardo's notions of growth and retardation. Hicks draws attention to the dichotomy between the empirical assumptions of Ricardo's theory and the analytical structure.

152. Hollander, Jacob H. "The Development of Ricardo's Theory of Value."
      QUARTERLY JOURNAL OF ECONOMICS 18 (August 1904): 455-91.

      The object of the article is to trace the origin and develop-
      ment of the theory of value in Ricardo's thought and writing.
      This was possible due to the collections of writings that had
      been published by this author along with James Bonar prior to
      1904. It is felt that there were three stages in the develop-
      ment of Ricardo's value theory.

153. Hollander, S. THE ECONOMICS OF ADAM SMITH. Toronto: Univer-
      sity of Toronto Press, 1973. 351 p.

      The analysis concerns both the degree of success Smith had in
      attempting to 'scientifically' explain existing economic condi-
      tions and the quality of his policy program in terms of logical
      consistency with an underlying theoretical structure. Virtually
      every major facet of Smith's WEALTH OF NATIONS is examin-
      ed, and Smith's relationship to predecessors, contemporaries,
      and successors is considered.

154. _____ . "The Role of Fixed Technical Coefficients in the Evolution of
      the Wages-Fund Controversy." OXFORD ECONOMIC PAPERS n.s. 20
      (November 1968): 320-41.

      The author has distinguished an ex ante and an ex post form
      of the wages fund theory, the latter being an equilibrium solu-
      tion to a market system where production coefficients are con-
      stant, that is, where the capital-labor ratio is constant. The
      result is the existence of a supply-demand relation for labor
      instead of the usual wages fund result. It is a somewhat tech-
      nical but very interesting article.

155. Hunter, L.C. "Mill and Cairnes on the Rate of Interest." OXFORD
      ECONOMIC PAPERS n.s. 11 (February 1959): 63-87.

      Cairnes sent Mill extensive notes on a new theory of the rate
      of interest and this article examines the effect these notes had
      on Mill's formulation of his theory of the rate of interest. The
      three stages in the development of Mill's theory of the rate of
      interest are traced up to and including the time of Cairnes's
      letter. It is interesting to note Mill's lack of complete under-
      standing.

156. Keynes, John Maynard. "Lives of Economists: Robert Malthus." In his
      ESSAYS IN BIOGRAPHY, edited by Geoffrey Keynes, pp. 81-124. New
      ed. with 3 additional essays. New York: W.W. Norton & Co., 1963.
      Paperbound.

      This short biographical sketch draws attention to the factors
      which Keynes considered most important. These factors were the
      ones which concerned Malthus's intellect and his ideas that were

similar to concepts advanced by Keynes. There is no doubt
that Keynes felt Malthus's work was more promising than that
of the more dominant Ricardo. An excellent essay for one
desiring to learn about Malthus the man as well as the political economist.

157. Knight, Frank H. "The Ricardian Theory of Production and Distribution."
CANADIAN JOURNAL OF ECONOMICS AND POLITICAL SCIENCE 1
(February 1935): 3-25, (May 1935): 171-96.

A study of the various aberrations in the classical system that
generate difficulties with respect to producing a viable model
of the exchange system. Knight examines the distribution system of Ricardo and, of necessity, the production system. Ricardo was primarily concerned with the process of distribution,
which would account for Knight's emphasis. The logic and
theoretical reasoning are rigorous and, as is all of Knight's
work, very well stated.

158. Laidler, David. "Thomas Tooke on Monetary Reform." In ESSAYS IN
HONOUR OF LORD ROBBINS, edited by Maurice Peston and Bernard [A.]
Corry, pp. 168-85. White Plains, N.Y.: International Arts & Sciences
Press, 1972.

It is argued that the recommendations of Thomas Tooke, member of the banking school, were based on greater insight into
the monetary system than those of his opponents in the currency school. In fact, Tooke's recommendations were very much
what a modern economist might suggest, given the constraints
of nineteenth-century policy goals.

159. Levy, S. Leon. NASSAU W. SENIOR, 1790-1864. New York: Augustus M. Kelley, 1970. 336 p.

In this thorough biography of Senior, Levy presents Senior's
attitudes and arguments on the social, political, and economic
issues of the period. There are fourteen appendices that contain the actual communications of Senior and various corre-
spondents. There is also a portrait of Nassau Senior in the
front of the book.

160. Link, Robert G. ENGLISH THEORIES OF ECONOMIC FLUCTUATIONS,
1815-1848. Columbia Studies in the Social Sciences, no. 598. New
York: Columbia University Press, 1959. 226 p.

To dispel the underestimation of the relevance of economics in
England during this period, the works of six economists are
examined. The use of these writers' works and the resultant
policy recommendations are also examined. The six authors
are: T.R. Malthus, Thomas Tooke, J.S. Mill, Thomas Atwood,
Thomas Joplin, and James Wilson. A twelve-page bibliography
is included.

161. Lowe, Adolph. "The Classical Theory of Economic Growth." SOCIAL RESEARCH, Summer 1954, pp. 127-58.

The intent of the author was to demonstrate that the classical economists had a much more complete conceptualization of the economic system than did those who have followed them in time. They accounted for the social factors that are not purely economic, and that are excluded from some current theories. One must remember that every model has a set of background and initial conditions that account for these factors. The author asks whether these factors change and if changes are acknowledged.

162. Luxemburg, Rosa. THE ACCUMULATION OF CAPITAL. Translated by Agnes Schwarzschild. New Haven, Conn.: Yale University Press, 1951. 473 p.

This is a critical treatment of Marx and Marxian economics. There can be no doubt, especially when the biographical sketch by W. Stark included here is considered, that Rosa Luxembourg is a Marxist. Joan Robinson has provided an extensive introduction to prepare the reader for the difficult task of reading this book. Many of the prominent classical economists are discussed in terms of their relationship to Marx or other socialists.

163. Macdonald, Robert A. "Ricardo's Criticisms of Adam Smith." QUARTERLY JOURNAL OF ECONOMICS 26 (August 1912): 549-92.

The author compares the positions of Smith and Ricardo on eight basic topics, examining each writer's view separately and then attempting to account for conflicts of opinion. These results are then used to formulate the principles that underlie them.

164. Macfie, A.L. "Adam Smith's Moral Sentiments as Foundation for His Wealth of Nations." OXFORD ECONOMIC PAPERS n.s. 11 (October 1959): 209-28.

There are many connecting factors between the THEORY OF MORAL SENTIMENTS and the WEALTH OF NATIONS by Adam Smith. The author asserts that the latter was merely a special case (economic case) of the former. The WEALTH OF NATIONS supposedly works out the economic aspect of the "self-love" concept developed in THEORY OF MORAL SENTIMENTS.

165. Machlup, Fritz. ESSAYS ON ECONOMIC SEMANTICS. Edited by Merton H. Miller. Englewood Cliffs, N.J.: Prentice-Hall, 1963. 304 p.

This work was compiled from earlier publications by Machlup on topics of semantics, i.e., topics of misunderstanding among economists that result basically from different interpretations of the same word or phrase. Many such cases arose in the classical period and are used in these essays.

166. Meek, Ronald L. "Some Notes on the 'Transformation Problem'." ECONOMIC JOURNAL 66 (March 1956): 94-107.

The article attempts to accomplish three things: (1) to examine Marx's discussion of the transformation of "values" into "product prices"; (2) to review two solutions of the "transformation problem"; and (3) to comment on a gap in Marx's argument that remains even after the transformation problem has been solved.

167. _____. STUDIES IN THE LABOUR THEORY OF VALUE. 2nd ed. London: Lawrence & Wishart, 1973. xliv, 332 p.

When first written in 1956 this book was an attempt to show that the labor theory of value was good science not only in Marx's time, but today as well. The present edition contains an extensive introduction that considers each chapter of the first edition with respect to modifications or extensions. The chapters are exactly the same as in the first edition and an appendix on Marx's economic method has been added to this later edition. The labor theories of Ricardo, Smith, and Marx are discussed.

168. _____, ed. MARX AND ENGELS ON MALTHUS. Translated from German by Dorothea L. Meek and Ronald L. Meek. New York: International Publishers, 1954. 190 p.

The editor, with the help of a second translator, has compiled a set of writings by Marx and Engels concerned with various aspects of Malthus's writing. The introduction deals with Malthus yesterday and today and what may be generally said of Marx's and Engels's comments. The second portion is devoted to an examination of their comments on population theory (sixty pages). Part three is concerned with economic theory in general (fifty-seven pages). The fourth and final section discusses "Marx and Engels on Malthus and Darwinism." A useful source for the comments of two of this period's more critical commentators.

169. Mints, Lloyd W. A HISTORY OF BANKING THEORY IN GREAT BRITAIN AND THE UNITED STATES. Chicago: University of Chicago Press, 1945. 319 p.

A history of very early writings is given, but the classical period (1775-1870) is considered in three chapters on England (over seventy pages) and three chapters on the United States (over seventy pages). The author has written the book in an attempt to dispel the notion that if banks follow the "real bills" doctrine, all will be well.

170. Myint, Hla. THEORIES OF WELFARE ECONOMICS. New York: Augustus M. Kelley, 1965. 240 p.

> The first section of this book (eighty-eight pages) is devoted to analysis of the welfare economics of the classical school. Myint discusses the problems that confronted classical economists and the methods they employed to cope with these problems. Classical economics is described as welfare analysis at the physical level, i.e., the quantities of satisfaction of the physical wants of given individuals are used as a measure of economic welfare. (Also cited in Chapter 4, entry 492.)

171. Myrdal, Gunnar. THE POLITICAL ELEMENT IN THE DEVELOPMENT OF ECONOMIC THEORY. Translated from the German by Paul Streeten. Cambridge, Mass.: Harvard University, 1954. 248 p.

> This is a critical analysis of economic theory from the time of the Physiocrats through the classical school and on into the neoclassical marginalist school. Myrdal attempts to sort out the political elements of the theory and to illustrate that the theory is self-supporting. He believes that value judgments may be incorporated into the theory so that the analyst may make a scientific policy decision. The book is nonpolitical although it attempts to find the proper relationship between politics and economics. There is an appendix by the translator concerning recent (since 1929) controversies. (Also cited in Chapter 4, entry 493.)

172. Neisser, Hans. "General Overproduction." JOURNAL OF POLITICAL ECONOMY 42 (August 1934): 433-65.

> This article is a study of Say's Law of Markets in response to the conditions of the time (1934) and the general belief in the validity of this law--that, in other words, general overproduction was impossible. Neisser discusses the monetary basis of Say's Law and the concepts of underconsumption and overcapitalization as possible sources of gluts and, consequently, cycles.

173. Paglin, Morton. MALTHUS & LAUDERDALE: THE ANTI-RICARDIAN TRADITION. New York: Augustus M. Kelley, 1961. 184 p.

> The author has attempted to interpret Malthus's role as both a contributor to and an opponent of the Ricardian tradition, as well as the conflict between Malthus's ESSAY and his PRINCIPLES. Paglin considers Malthus and Lauderdale as participants in a conservative traditionalism stemming from Burke, in contrast with the Mill-Bentham utilitarianism of Ricardo. There is also an appendix analyzing recent contributions to the old controversy regarding Ricardo's theory of value.

174. Patterson, S. Howard. READINGS IN THE HISTORY OF ECONOMIC THOUGHT. New York: McGraw-Hill, 1932. 745 p.

A good collection of excerpts from the various economic writers, beginning with Mandeville. Many of the works represented are not commonly available in this form. The major works for Smith, Ricardo, and J.S. Mill are not included, but some of their lesser known works are here. In total, over 300 pages of classical works are included in this book.

175. Pigou, A.C. "Mill and the Wages Fund." ECONOMIC JOURNAL 57 (1949): 171-80.

This was written on the one-hundredth anniversary of the publication of Mill's PRINCIPLES OF POLITICAL ECONOMY. Mill recanted the wages fund theory in 1869 only to retain the doctrine in the last edition of his PRINCIPLES. Pigou discusses the process of Mill's rejection of the wages fund, and how the "wages flow" remained as the relevant concept for Mill.

176. Polanyi, Karl. THE GREAT TRANSFORMATION. New York: Farrar & Rinehart, 1944. 305 p.

This work traces the birth, rise, and supposed fall of the market economy as a way of conducting everyday national and international activities. All of the economic interrelations in the world cannot produce a lasting world peace, for that may only be had as a result of the discovery of a world society. Even in this world society the institutional fabric must maintain control of economic conditions.

177. Robbins, Lionel. ROBERT TORRENS AND THE EVOLUTION OF CLASSICAL ECONOMICS. London: Macmillan, 1958. 367 p.

Admitting that Torrens was not a great economist, the author proceeds to illustrate the role played by this writer who was in the classical movement from its inception. Every possible aspect of Torren's contributions to theory and the theory of policy is considered.

178. Robertson, H.M., and Taylor, W.L. "Adam Smith's Approach to the Theory of Value." ECONOMIC JOURNAL 67 (June 1957): 181-98.

This article examines the relationship between Smith and his predecessors, as well as his contemporaries, regarding their relative concepts of value. Many others before Smith came very close to marginal utility, but Smith failed to utilize and extend what such writers as Hutcheson had proposed.

179. Robinson, Joan. COLLECTED ECONOMIC PAPERS. Vol. III. Oxford: Basil Blackwell, 1965. 215 p.

This collection contains four essays (about thirty pages in part III) on various topics related to Marxism, capitalism, and the theory of value. The author is one of the better known interpreters of Marx's work and her discussions are informative.

180. _____. AN ESSAY ON MARXIAN ECONOMICS. New York: St. Martin's Press, 1966. 104 p. Paperbound.

The intent of this essay was to "explain what I understand Marx to have been saying in language intelligible to the academic economist." Robinson believes that Marx had a great deal to offer and that Marxists can learn from the academic economist. The primary example is the theory of effective demand.

181. _____. "The Labour Theory of Value." SCIENCE AND SOCIETY 18 (Spring 1954): 141-51.

The author maintains that there are two aspects of the theory of value: ratio of profits to wages (the rate of exploitation) and relative prices of particular commodities. This article is addressed to the latter of these two aspects.

182. Rosenberg, Nathan. "Adam Smith on the Division of Labour: Two Views or One." ECONOMICA 32 (May 1965): 127-40.

Rosenberg notes that Smith's comments on the benefits to be derived from the division of labor, presented in Book I of WEALTH OF NATIONS, apparently conflict with those on the same topic in Book V. He concludes, however, that there is no contradiction but merely a sharp awareness on Smith's part of the social effects of technological change, especially with regard to the working poor.

183. St. Clair, Oswald. A KEY TO RICARDO. New York: Augustus M. Kelley, 1965. 364 p.

The author was a retired businessman who decided that some sort of everyman's source for Ricardo's writings was needed. His KEY is an excellent account of Ricardo's position on economic issues confronting the classical economists. There are also many citations from Malthus's PRINCIPLES OF POLITICAL ECONOMY, with which Ricardo's work is compared.

184. Schoup, Carl S. RICARDO ON TAXATION. Morningside Heights, N.Y.: Columbia University Press, 1960. 285 p.

This work presents Ricardo's general sentiments regarding taxation as well as his comments on many special types of taxes. The author closes with an appraisal of Ricardo's tax analysis. Ricardo was in fervent opposition to almost any form of government intervention, a bias which tended to color his policy prescriptions.

185. Sowell, Thomas. "The General Glut Controversy Reconsidered." OXFORD ECONOMIC PAPERS n.s. 15 (November 1963): 193-203.

It is demonstrated that, due to a lack of understanding between Malthus and Ricardo regarding each other's economic systems, the general glut controversy was not a forerunner of modern economic debates on overproduction. Malthus's problems were impossible in Ricardo's system because the assumptions of the latter precluded their existence.

186. _____. "Marx's 'Increasing Misery' Doctrine." AMERICAN ECONOMIC REVIEW 50 (December 1960): 111-20.

This article is addressed to the question of whether it was the absolute level of labor or the relative position of labor to other classes that would decline with the advance of capitalism. Sowell argues that only increasing misery in an absolute sense is consistent with the crucial role of work in human self-realization that Marx emphasized. The misery results from a decline in the labor content of the wages, not a decline in the monetary value of the wages. It is an excellent analysis.

187. _____. SAY'S LAW. Princeton, N.J.: Princeton University Press, 1972. 247 p.

The author tells of the controversy that has surrounded Say's Law and presents the various dissenting viewpoints. Dissenters include Sismondi, Malthus, Marx, and finally J.M. Keynes. The positions of the neoclassical school and J.S. Mill are also presented. There is an annotated bibliography of the best sources for the study of Say's Law.

188. Spiegel, Henry William, ed. THE DEVELOPMENT OF ECONOMIC THOUGHT: GREAT ECONOMISTS IN PERSPECTIVE. New York: John Wiley & Sons, 1952. 811 p.

The editor has collected the writings of various economists representing different schools of thought. There are ten articles about seven classicists, all written by prominent postclassical economists. These would be useful for learning what later economists thought of the classical authors.

189. Stark, W. THE IDEAL FOUNDATIONS OF ECONOMIC THOUGHT. London: Routledge & Kegan Paul, 1948. 219 p.

This book contains three essays on the philosophy of economics, the first two of which apply to the classical school. The first is the "Philosophical Foundations of Classical Economics"; the

second is "The End of Classical Economics or Liberalism and
Socialism at the Crossroads." These would be excellent for
the scholar interested in methodology.

190. Stigler, George J. "The Ricardian Theory of Value and Distribution."
JOURNAL OF POLITICAL ECONOMY 60 (June 1952): 187-207.

The author shows, by analyzing the theory of population and
the rent theory used by Ricardo, that Ricardo added little to
either of these fields of theory. Ricardo's contribution was
his synthesis of these theories with a general theory of value
and distribution. Stigler views Ricardo as a "master analyst"
who "fashioned what is probably the most impressive of all models in economic analysis." This is reprinted in George J.
Stigler, ESSAYS IN THE HISTORY OF ECONOMICS (University of Chicago Press, 1965).

191. _____. "Ricardo and the 93 Per Cent Labor Theory of Value." AMERI-
CAN ECONOMIC REVIEW 48 (June 1958): 357-67.

The intent of the article is to define exactly Ricardo's theory
of value and to examine the interpretations of the theory by
his leading contemporaries. The author feels that the confusion
on the part of interpreters was primarily the result of their
failure to distinguish between analytical and empirical propositions. According to Stigler, Ricardo's propositions were
empirical, which was the reason for Ricardo's emphasis on the
importance of labor in determining value.

192. Stonier, Alfred W., and Hague, D.C. A TEXTBOOK OF ECO-
NOMIC THEORY. London: Longmans, Green, 1959. 513 p.

This book contains an excellent discussion of Ricardian rent
theory in terms of modern economic theory. There are more
recent editions of this book. The relevant material in all
editions appears in chapter 13.

193. Sweezy, Paul M. THE THEORY OF CAPITALIST DEVELOPMENT. New
York: Monthly Review Press, 1956. 398 p.

This text was written to provide a comprehensive analytical
study of Marxian political economy. Sweezy's primary divisions are: Value and Surplus Value; The Accumulation Process;
Imperialism; and two appendices, both original works by other
authors. Sweezy attempts to examine the works of others as
well as those of Marx, but openly states that his own interpretations will also be presented.

194. Theocharis, Reghinos D. EARLY DEVELOPMENTS IN MATHEMATICAL
ECONOMICS. London: Macmillan, 1961. 142 p.

While much of the work discussed was written before the classical period, this volume will be of great interest to the mathematically inclined. The works covered were all written prior to 1838 and are, for the most part, not the work of British economists. The principal contributors to early mathematical economics were French, Italian, and German.

195. Tucker, G.S.L. "The Origin of Ricardo's Theory of Profits." ECO-NOMICA n.s. 21 (November 1954): 320-33.

This is an attempt to discover whether Ricardo's theory of profits arose from the currency controversy or from the Corn Law controversy in which he was involved with Malthus. The author tends to favor the former but the evidence is not concrete.

196. _____. PROGRESS AND PROFITS IN BRITISH ECONOMIC THOUGHT, 1650-1850. Cambridge: At the University Press, 1960. 206 p.

Although very early work is discussed, most of the volume is devoted to the classical school. Smith is viewed as the transitional figure between the early theorists and those propounding the classical theory of interest and profits. The works of Ricardo and Malthus are treated separately and the uses to which theories of profits were put are also examined. (Also cited in Chapter 1, entry 57.)

197. Viner, Jacob. "Adam Smith and Laissez Faire." JOURNAL OF POLITICAL ECONOMY 35 (April 1927): 198-232.

Viner, after stating that Smith's greatest achievement was the application to the economic world of the concept of a unified natural order, attempts to show that there are irreconcilable conflicts between the THEORY OF MORAL SENTIMENTS and the WEALTH OF NATIONS. He also attempts to show that it is because of Smith's changed position that the WEALTH OF NATIONS has remained a living book. Specifically, Smith abandoned the absolutism, rigidity, and romanticism that characterized the THEORY OF MORAL SENTIMENTS.

198. Wu, Chi-Yuen. AN OUTLINE OF INTERNATIONAL PRICE THEORIES. London: Routledge & Kegan Paul, 1939. Reprint ed., Nendeln, Liechtenstein: Kraus-Thompson, 1970. 373 p.

In his discussion of the works of writers from many schools, Wu devotes approximately eighty pages to the international trade theory espoused by the classical school. Writers covered are A. Smith, D. Ricardo, Torrens, J.S. Mill, and Tooke. Some special debates are discussed as are a few writers of lesser note. (Also cited in Chapter 1, entry 60, and Chapter 4, entry 534.)

199. Zweig, Ferdinand. ECONOMIC IDEAS: A STUDY OF HISTORICAL PERSPECTIVES. New York: Prentice-Hall, 1950. 197 p.

This unique little work offers the reader a different way of

viewing the progression of economics and economic systems.
A good work for those interested in the various philosophical
aspects of economics.

D. CONTRIBUTIONS OF LESSER IMPORTANCE

200. Barrington, Donald. "Edmond Burke as an Economist." ECONOMICA
n.s. 21 (August 1954): 252-58.

201. Berle, Adolf A. "The Impact of the Corporation on Classical Economic
Theory." QUARTERLY JOURNAL OF ECONOMICS 79 (1965): 25-40.

202. Bhaduri, Amit. "On the Significance of Recent Controversies on Capital
Theory: A Marxian View." THE ECONOMIC JOURNAL 79 (September
1969): 532-39.

203. Birck, L.V. "Theories of Over-Production." THE ECONOMIC JOUR-
NAL 37 (March 1927): 19-32.

204. Bitterman, Henry J. "Adam Smith's Empiricism and the Law of Nature,
Parts I & II." JOURNAL OF POLITICAL ECONOMY 48 (August 1940):
487-520, (October 1940): 703-34.

205. Black, R.D. Collison. "The Classical Economists and the Irish Problem."
OXFORD ECONOMIC PAPERS n.s. 5 (March 1953): 26-40.

206. Blaug, Mark. "The Classical Economists and the Factory Acts--A Re-
examination." QUARTERLY JOURNAL OF ECONOMICS 72 (1958): 211-
26.

207. _____. "The Empirical Content of Ricardian Economics." JOURNAL
OF POLITICAL ECONOMY 64 (February 1956): 41-58.

208. Bloom, Solomon F. "Man of His Century: A Reconsideration of the Historical Significance of Karl Marx." JOURNAL OF POLITICAL ECONO-
MY 51 (December 1943): 494-505.

209. Bonar, James. "Adam Smith, 1723 and 1923." ECONOMICA 3 (June
1923): 89-92.

210. _____. "The Economics of John Stuart Mill." JOURNAL OF POLITI-
CAL ECONOMY 19 (November 1911): 717-25.

211. _____. PHILOSOPHY AND POLITICAL ECONOMY IN SOME OF THEIR
HISTORICAL RELATIONS. London: Swan Sonnenschein, 1893. 410 p.

212. _____. "Ricardo's Ingot Plan." THE ECONOMIC JOURNAL 33 (September 1923): 281-304.

213. _____. "The Value of Labor in Relation to Economic Theory." QUARTERLY JOURNAL OF ECONOMICS 5 (1890): 137-64.

214. Bowley, Marian. "Nassau Senior's Contribution to the Methodology of Economics." ECONOMICA n.s. 3 (August 1936): 281-305.

215. Cannan, Edwin. "Adam Smith on Twentieth Century Finance." ECONOMICS 3 (June 1923): 93-97.

216. Checkland, S.G. "The Prescriptions of the Classical Economist." ECONOMICA n.s. 20 (February 1953): 61-72.

217. _____. "The Propagation of Ricardian Economics in England." ECONOMICA n.s. 16 (February 1949): 40-52.

218. Corry, B[ernard] A. "Malthus and Keynes--A Reconsideration." ECONOMIC JOURNAL 69 (December 1959): 717-24.

219. Eagly, Robert V. "A Macro Model of the Endogenous Business Cycle in Marxist Analysis." JOURNAL OF POLITICAL ECONOMY 80 (May/June 1972): 523-39.

220. Ekelund, Robert B., Jr. "Professor Stigler on Dupuit and the Development of Utility Theory: Comment." JOURNAL OF POLITICAL ECONOMY 80 (September/October 1972): 1056-59.

221. Fetter, Frank Whitson. "Robert Torrens: Colonel of Marines and Political Economist." ECONOMICA n.s. 29 (May 1962): 152-65.

222. George, William H. "Proudhon and Economic Federalism." JOURNAL OF POLITICAL ECONOMY 30 (August 1922): 531-42.

223. Gonner, E.C.K. "Ricardo and His Critics." QUARTERLY JOURNAL OF ECONOMICS 4 (1889): 276-90.

224. Grossman, Henryk. "The Evolutionist Revolt against Classical Economics, Parts I & II." JOURNAL OF POLITICAL ECONOMY 51 (October 1943): 381-96, (December 1943): 506-22.

225. Harris, Abram L. "J.S. Mill on Monopoly and Socialism: A Note." JOURNAL OF POLITICAL ECONOMY 67 (December 1959): 604-11.

226. Harris, Donald J. "On Marx's Scheme of Reproduction and Accumulation." JOURNAL OF POLITICAL ECONOMY 80 (May/June 1972): 505-22.

227. Hayek, F.A. von. "The Ricardo Effect." ECONOMICA n.s. 9 (May 1942): 127-52.

228. _____. "Three Elucidations of the Ricardo Effect." JOURNAL OF POLITICAL ECONOMY 77 (March/April 1969): 274-85.

229. Himes, Norman E. "The Place of John Stuart Mill and of Robert Owen in the History of English Neo-Malthusianism." QUARTERLY JOURNAL OF ECONOMICS 42 (1928): 627-40.

230. Hollander, Jacob H. "The Residual Claimant Theory of Distribution." QUARTERLY JOURNAL OF ECONOMICS 17 (1902): 261-79.

231. Hollander, S. "Malthus and Keynes: A Note." THE ECONOMIC JOURNAL 72 (June 1962): 355-59.

232. Hutchison, T.W. "Ricardo's Correspondence." ECONOMICA n.s. 20 (August 1953): 263-73.

233. _____. "Some Questions about Ricardo." ECONOMICA n.s. 19 (November 1952): 415-32.

234. Kemp, Murray C. "The Mill-Bastable Infant-Industry Dogma." JOURNAL OF POLITICAL ECONOMY 68 (February 1960): 65-67.

235. Leontief, Wassily. "The Significance of Marxian Economics for Present-Day Economic Theory." AMERICAN ECONOMIC REVIEW 28, Supplement (March 1938): 1-9.

236. Lindgren, J. Ralph. "Adam Smith's Theory of Inquiry." JOURNAL OF POLITICAL ECONOMY 77 (November/December 1969): 897-915.

237. Marx, Karl. THE ECONOMIC AND PHILOSOPHICAL MANUSCRIPTS OF 1844. Translated by Martin Milligan. Edited by Dick Struick. New York: International Publishers, 1964. 255 p.

238. Mason, E.S. "Saint-Simonism and the Rationalisation of Industry." QUARTERLY JOURNAL OF ECONOMICS 45 (1931): 640-49.

239. Mason, Will E. "Ricardo's Transfer-Mechanism Theory." QUARTERLY JOURNAL OF ECONOMICS 71 (February 1957): 107-15.

240. Meek, Ronald L. "Adam Smith and the Classical Concept of Profit." SCOTTISH JOURNAL OF POLITICAL ECONOMY 1 (June 1954): 138-53.

241. _____. "The Decline of Ricardian Economics in England." ECONOMICA n.s. 17 (February 1950): 43-62.

242. Mill, John Stuart. "John Rae and John Stuart Mill: A Correspondence." ECONOMICA n.s. 10 (August 1943): 253-56.

243. _____. "Notes on N.W. Senior's POLITICAL ECONOMY." ECONOMICA n.s. 12 (August 1945): 134-39.

244. Nicholson, J.S. "Adam Smith on Public Debts." THE ECONOMIC JOURNAL 30 (March 1920): 1-12.

245. O'Leary, James J. "Malthus and Keynes." JOURNAL OF POLITICAL ECONOMY 50 (December 1942): 901-19.

246. _____. "Malthus's General Theory of Employment and the Post-Napoleonic Depressions." JOURNAL OF ECONOMIC HISTORY 3 (November 1943): 185-200.

247. Oncken, August. "The Consistency of Adam Smith." THE ECONOMIC JOURNAL 7 (September 1897): 443-50.

248. Pentose, E.F. "Malthus and the Underdeveloped Areas." THE ECONOMIC JOURNAL 67 (June 1957): 219-39.

249. Rae, John. "Letters of Rae (1796-1872) to Mill on the Malthusian Doctrine of Population." THE ECONOMIC JOURNAL 12 (March 1902): 111-20.

250. Robbins, Lionel. "A Letter from David Ricardo." ECONOMICA n.s. 23 (May 1956): 172-74.

251. Roberts, R.O. "Ricardo's Theory of Public Debts." ECONOMICA n.s. 9 (August 1942): 257-66.

252. Robinson, Joan. "Marx on Unemployment." ECONOMIC JOURNAL 51 (June-September 1941): 234-48.

253. Rosenberg, Nathan. "Adam Smith, Consumer Tastes, and Economic Growth." JOURNAL OF POLITICAL ECONOMY 76 (May/June 1968): 361-74.

254. Samuelson, Paul A. "A Modern Treatment of the Ricardian Economy: Part I, The Pricing of Goods and of Labor and Land Services; Part II, Capital and Interest Aspects of the Pricing Process." QUARTERLY JOURNAL OF ECONOMICS 73 (February 1959): 1-35, 217-31.

255. Smith, Victor E. "The Classicists' Use of 'Demand'." JOURNAL OF POLITICAL ECONOMY 59 (June 1951): 225-42.

256. Sowell, Thomas. "Marxian Value Reconsidered." ECONOMICA n.s. 30 (August 1963): 297-308.

257. Stigler, George J. "Sraffa's Ricardo." AMERICAN ECONOMIC REVIEW 43 (September 1953): 586-99.

258. Thomson, Herbert F. "Adam Smith's Philosophy of Science." QUARTERLY JOURNAL OF ECONOMICS 79 (1958): 212-33.

259. Thornton, Henry. AN INQUIRY INTO THE NATURE AND EFFECTS OF THE PAPER CREDIT OF GREAT BRITAIN, TOGETHER WITH HIS EVIDENCE GIVEN BEFORE THE COMMITTEES OF SECRECY OF THE TWO HOUSES OF PARLIAMENT ON THE BANK OF ENGLAND, SOME MANUSCRIPT NOTES, AND HIS SPEECHES ON THE BULLION REPORT. Edited with an introduction by F.A. von Hayek. Reprint ed., New York: Augustus M. Kelley, 1968. 368 p.

260. Torrens, Robert. ON WAGES AND COMBINATIONS. Reprint ed., New York: Augustus M. Kelley, 1969. 133 p.

261. Tucker, G.S.L. "Ricardo and Marx." ECONOMICA n.s. 28 (August 1961): 252-69.

262. Veblen, Thorstein. "The Socialist Economics of Karl Marx and His Followers. I. The Theories of Karl Marx." QUARTERLY JOURNAL OF ECONOMICS 20 (1906): 575-95.

263. _____. "The Socialist Economics of Karl Marx and His Followers. II. The Later Marxism." QUARTERLY JOURNAL OF ECONOMICS 21 (1906): 299-322.

264. West, E.G. "The Political Economy of Alienation: Karl Marx and Adam Smith." OXFORD ECONOMIC PAPERS 21 (March 1969): 1-23.

265. Whitaker, A.C. "The Ricardian Theory of Gold Movements and Professor Laughlin's Views of Money." QUARTERLY JOURNAL OF ECONOMICS 18 (1904): 220-54.

266. Winch, D.N. "Classical Economics and the Case for Colonization." ECONOMICA n.s. 30 (November 1963): 387-99.

Chapter 3

THE INDUCTIVISTS

Chapter 3

THE INDUCTIVISTS

A. INTRODUCTION

This group of economists, relative to the actual number of historicists writing, had a significant impact on the profession. The school arose in opposition to the classical school and its abstract theories, which included the use of the deductive method of reasoning. This group, most of whom were from Germany, felt that classical theories were not based on sufficient information and that it was not possible to generalize "laws" in all circumstances.

This opposition group of scholars, then, set about the task of gathering great quantities of data about all aspects of economic life. They submitted that only by this procedure--induction--could one prepare to formulate any kind of general law. Although laws were not considered completely general--that is, true in all instances--they were viewed as being based on much stronger evidence.

In addition to their methodological argument, the German contingent, unlike many of the English, felt that the "laissez faire" dictum of classical economics was not justifiable on grounds that took into account the society as a whole. The state, therefore, was a far more important variable in the German historical schema than in either the classical doctrines or those of many other historicists.

The works annotated below are mainly those of the historicist authors, since there has been little critical consideration of their work. This is especially true for the English historicists. Their methodology, the collection and presentation of large amounts of data, is apparent, to some extent even today, in the field of economic history. The work of the early economic historians, W. Mitchell, A. Bums, J.R. Commons, and others, is representative of inductivist methods and will be discussed under the American school called institutionalists. Many of these economists studied in Germany during the reign of historicism.

H. von Thunen is included here with the historicists even though his work was not as inductive as that of Roscher and others. His methodology did, however, tend to be more closely aligned with the historical approach and his theory was advanced beyond even the classical school. His work in location theory is still a classic in the field.

Although the deductive method of analysis has prevailed over the inductive method as the preferred approach to economic theorizing, the historicists performed a great service to the profession by emphasizing the empirical side of the science. This has not been forgotten and has served to further the understanding of economic systems and economic activity in general.

B. MAJOR CONTRIBUTIONS

267.   Ashley, Sir William J. "The Early History of the English Woolen Industry." In PUBLICATIONS OF THE AMERICAN ECONOMIC ASSOCIATION, pp. 302-80. Boston: American Economic Association, 1888.

> The author has provided an excellent preface on the comparative advantages of the deductive versus the historical or statistical method. He defines the attributes of both and calls for recognition of each by the other. The essay accounts for the growth of the woolen industry and all of the institutional ramifications of that growth--guilds, immigration, changes in class structure, and others.

268.   _____. AN INTRODUCTION TO ENGLISH ECONOMIC HISTORY AND THEORY, PARTS I & II. New York: Augustus M. Kelley, 1966. 728 p.

> This is a one-volume edition of the work originally published in two volumes six years apart. Part I (227 pages) covers the "Middle Ages" and part II (501 pages) covers the "End of the Middle Ages." It is an account of the development of the economic system from the manors and village communities to towns and nations. There is a discussion of the woolen industry, the agrarian revolution, the relief of the poor, and, finally, a discussion of the German works on the history of canon law and commercial law.

269.   _____. SURVEYS: HISTORIC AND ECONOMIC. New York: Augustus M. Kelley, 1966. 476 p.

> This is an excellent collection of essays and notes covering many topics. There is an introductory section on why one should study economic history. Sections on medieval agrarian and urban structures serve as the background for the discussion of more recent developments in the economic systems. There are sections on economic opinion and on the economic relations between England and America, as well as on industrial organization of various industries. There are also biographical sketches and notes.

270. _____. THE TARIFF PROBLEM. 4th ed. London: P.S. King & Son, 1920. Reprint ed., New York: Augustus M. Kelley, 1968. 269 p.

The author treats the problem of state intervention in international trade in general and the arguments for free imports as stated by the original advocates. He then turns to assessment of the effects of, and future prospects for, existing policy, including considerations of world politics and colonial policies.

271. _____, ed. BRITISH INDUSTRIES: A SERIES OF GENERAL REVIEWS FOR BUSINESSMEN AND STUDENTS. 2nd ed. London: Longmans, Green, 1907. 232 p.

A good book for the reader interested in British industrial organization in the first decade of the twentieth century, the volume consists of ten lectures, each given by a noted authority in a particular field of business. Industries covered are: iron and steel, cotton, woolen, linen, railroads, shipping, and the trust movement in Great Britain.

272. Brentano, Lujo. ON THE HISTORY AND DEVELOPMENT OF GILDS AND THE ORIGIN OF TRADE-UNIONS. New York: Burt Franklin, 1969. cxcix, 232 p.

This work was originally published in 1870. The author discusses the origin of guilds in general and then the formation of religious or social guilds, town guilds, craft guilds, and finally trade unions. Studies of specific types of gild support every aspect of the discussion. It is another work very much in the German historical tradition.

273. Cunningham, W. THE INDUSTRIAL REVOLUTION. Cambridge: At the University Press, 1908. 482 p.

This is a reprint of the sections entitled "Parliamentary Colbertism" and "Laissez Faire" which originally appeared in THE GROWTH OF ENGLISH INDUSTRY AND COMMERCE IN MODERN TIMES (1907). The pagination and the original divisions have been maintained. This work deals with the revolution that occurred in England during the eighteenth and first half of the nineteenth century in an attempt to outline the background of the existing situation in 1908.

274. Cunningham, W., and McArthur, Ellen A. OUTLINES OF ENGLISH INDUSTRIAL HISTORY. New York: Macmillan, 1908. 274 p.

This is a very detailed history of the economic development of England from the defeat of the Romans in about 449 A.D. to around the end of the nineteenth century. The authors define each step in the cultural development of political groups and their interaction. After national life was established, the analysis shifts to the economic problems of nations--both internal and external.

275. Ingram, John Kells. A HISTORY OF POLITICAL ECONOMY. New ed.,
enl. London: Adam and Charles Black, 1915. 315 p.

This edition includes an introduction by Richard T. Ely and a
chapter on the Austrian school by William A. Scott. The portions written by Ingram commence with ancient times and progress through the historical school. He spends a disproportion-
ate amount of space developing the system of natural liberty
(a philosophy of the classical school), but then defines the
historical school, with Comte's PHILOSOPHIE POSITIVE as its
basis, as the only viable successor to the previous stage of
development.

276. List, Frederick. NATIONAL SYSTEM OF POLITICAL ECONOMY. Translated from the German by G.A. Matile. Note on the French translation
by Henri Richelot. Preliminary essay by Stephen Colwell. Philadelphia:
J.B. Lippincott, 1856. lxxxiv, 497 p.

Although List favored freedom of exchange among people and
countries, he realized that exchange could be beneficial only
if all trading partners followed the same policy. In his application of theory to practice, the state was the overriding concern for him, and in 1821 he proposed the concept of a German Customs Union to promote the development of Germany.
Theorists usually thought of individuals, but rarely of separate
nations.

277. Roscher, Wilhelm. "Preface and Selections from the Introduction to Grun-
driss." Translated by Sir William J. Ashley. QUARTERLY JOURNAL
OF ECONOMICS 8 (October 1894): 99-105.

This preface was the first clear statement of the new movement
in academic circles and is regarded by many as the program
not only for Roscher's work but for the work of the entire school.
The portion of the "Introduction" given here distinguishes the
role of political economy in the method of the political sciences in general. A good source for the essence of the historical school.

278. _____. PRINCIPLES OF POLITICAL ECONOMY. 2 vols. Translated
from the 13th German edition by John J. Labor. New York: Henry
Holt, 1878. Vol. I, 464 p.; vol. II, 465 p.

To the PRINCIPLES have been added chapters on paper money,
international trade, and the protective system, along with an
"Essay on the Historical Method in Political Economy" by L.
Wolowski. The two volumes treat every possible facet of economic thinking, both analytic and otherwise, as would be expected from the founder of the historical school.

279. _____. THE SPANISH COLONIAL SYSTEM. Translated by Edward Gay-

lord Bourne. Reprint ed., Cambridge, Mass.: G.E. Stechert, 1944. 48 p.

This is a typical historicist study of the institution of colonization as it was practiced by the Spanish. Roscher examines
closely the effects of Spanish social, political, and economic
policies on the development of colonial economic systems.

280. Schmoller, Gustav. THE MERCANTILE SYSTEM AND ITS HISTORICAL
SIGNIFICANCE. New York: Macmillan, 1897. 95 p.

Originally published as a chapter in Schmoller's STUDIEN
UBER DIE WIRTLISCHAFTLICHE POLITIK FRIEDRICHS DES
GROSSEN, this work is a historical description of how an economic system evolves from the village to a "community of nations."
There is an appendix on the Prussian silk industry in the
eighteenth century. It is an excellent example of the work of
one of the historical school's most dogmatic writers.

281. _____. "Schmoller on Roscher." In THE DEVELOPMENT OF ECO-
NOMIC THOUGHT: GREAT ECONOMISTS IN PERSPECTIVE,
edited by Henry William Spiegel, pp. 363-77. New York:
John Wiley & Sons, 1952.

This is a translation and slight abridgment of work which originally appeared in Schmoller's ZUR LITTERATUREGESCHICHTE
DER STAATS-UND SOCIALWISSENSCHAFTEN (Leipzig: Dunker
und Humbolt, 1888). The author includes a biographical sketch
of Wilhelm Roscher and the historical school, explaining why
Roscher is considered the father of the school. Much space is
devoted to Roscher's world view and Schmoller's argument for
its superiority.

282. Sombart, Werner. SOCIALISM AND THE SOCIAL MOVEMENT. Translated from the 6th German edition with an introduction and notes by M.
Epstein. London: J.M. Dent, 1909. Reprint ed., New York: Augustus M. Kelley, 1968. 319 p.

Sombart offers a definition of socialism and explains what constitutes a social movement before he presents a discussion of
the many variants of socialism, particularly as practiced in
different countries, and a critical evaluation of Marx's work.
His analysis and approach to socialism are historical.

283. Tawney, R.H. THE ACQUISITIVE SOCIETY. London: G. Bell and Sons,
1948. 242 p.

Here, as in other work, Tawney employs a religious context for
his discussion of the problem of acquiring wealth. Although
not bad in itself, acquisition of wealth becomes an evil when
it is the result of shortsighted planning and decision making.
Thus, the author argues, the industrial problem lies not so much
with those suffering material misery but with those whose material misery is slight.

284. _____. THE BRITISH LABOR MOVEMENT. New York: Greenwood Press, 1968. 189 p.

This is a collection of six lectures given by the author at the Williamstown Institute of Politics in 1924. It traces the roots of the labor movement from 1815 to 1914 and then considers the Labor Party's constitution, the nationalization of coal, education, foreign affairs, and socialism. It is the work of a fine economic historian.

285. _____. EQUALITY. London: George Allen & Unwin, 1951. 285 p.

This work considers not one but many different types or concepts of equality--economic, political, religious, and social. Tawney discusses various distributions of income and collective provisions and equality with respect to liberty. As in all of his work, there is a very strong historical perspective.

286. Toynbee, Arnold. LECTURES ON THE INDUSTRIAL REVOLUTION OF THE 18TH CENTURY IN ENGLAND, POPULAR ADDRESSES, NOTES AND OTHER FRAGMENTS. New York: Humboldt Publishing Co., 1884. 263 p.

This edition contains a "Memoir" by B. Jowett that identifies Toynbee both personally and professionally. He was a historicist of less extreme English tradition. This edition contains five essays and some collected jottings which were deleted when the work was reprinted as THE INDUSTRIAL REVOLUTION (Boston: Beacon Press, 1956). The notes and fragments were compiled from his notes and the notes of his students after his death at the age of thirty.

287. Weber, Max. GENERAL ECONOMIC HISTORY. Translated by Frank H. Knight. London: George Allen & Unwin, 1939. 401 p.

The highly technical "Definitions and Concepts" prepared by the original German editors were omitted in this edition by Knight. This work was published posthumously and therefore lacks the refinements that Weber would have made. The significance of the work is Weber's application of a historicist model of economic life to the explanation of the evolution of modern capitalism.

288. _____. THE METHODOLOGY OF THE SOCIAL SCIENCES. Translated and edited by Edward A. Shils and Henry A. Finch. New York: The Free Press, 1949. 188 p.

These three essays on methodology, written by Weber between 1903 and 1917, are: "The Meaning of 'Ethical Neutrality' in Sociology and Economics"; "Objectivity in Social Science and Social Policy"; and "Critical Studies in the Logic of the Cultural Sciences." Each essay was born of a particular situation in Weber's career.

289. _____. THE THEORY OF SOCIAL AND ECONOMIC ORGANIZATION. Translated by A.M. Henderson and Talcott Parsons. Edited by Talcott Parsons. New York: The Free Press, 1964. 436 p.

This work was chosen for translation because it "contains the nearest approach to a comprehensive statement" of the system of scientific theory that may be found in all of Weber's published works. His intention here was to analyze his conviction that both German historical economics and jurisprudence and Marxism were inadequate for the solution of social problems.

C. COMMENTARIES ON THE MAJOR CONTRIBUTIONS

290. Bonar, James. "Knapp's Theory of Money." ECONOMIC JOURNAL 32 (March 1922): 39-47.

This is a review of Knapp's THE STATE THEORY OF MONEY which considers the various concepts of money in the world at that time--primarily before World War I. To Knapp, money was whatever the sovereign decreed to be legal tender. Bonar outlines Knapp's theory of money with respect to the major world economies of the period.

291. Dorfman, Joseph. "The Role of the German Historical School in American Economic Thought." AMERICAN ECONOMIC REVIEW 45 (May 1955): 17-28.

Beginning with the contention that Americans followed German leadership, Dorfman qualifies by noting that the Americans distinguished between German methods and political philosophy. The article provides an excellent survey of the economists who integrated historical methods with American practices. Ten pages of discussion by noted authors follow this paper.

292. Dunbar, C.F. "Wagner on the Present States of the Economy." QUARTERLY JOURNAL OF ECONOMICS 1 (October 1886): 113-33.

This translation by Dunbar of an article by Adolf Wagner allows one to see the problems that resulted from the appeal to morality made by some of the historicists. In this case the article portrays an ever increasing state bureaucracy with the military ruling all.

293. Eldridge, J.E.T., ed. MAX WEBER: THE INTERPRETATION OF SOCIAL REALITY. London: Michael Joseph, 1971. 302 p.

This book contains excerpts from many of Weber's works, some of which were translated for this volume. Each chapter is preceded by an introductory note that facilitates understanding of the chapter. The complexity of his work makes Weber a difficult author to read. Most of this text is devoted to sociologi-

cal work, but there are specific works on economics. The editor
has attempted to follow Weber's divisions--sociology of economic
life, law, religion, and others--in organizing his chapters so
that Weber's analytical method is more readily apparent.

294. Giddens, Anthony. CAPITALISM AND MODERN SOCIAL THEORY: AN
ANALYSIS OF THE WRITINGS OF MARX, DURKHEIM, AND MAX WEB-
ER. Cambridge: At the University Press, 1971. 261 p.

Although this work is concerned primarily with sociological
aspects of work by the writers named, some discussion of economics is included. The sociological ideas of each writer are
presented and then the ideas of Durkheim and Weber are compared with those of Marx.

295. Gide, Charles, and Rist, Charles. A HISTORY OF ECONOMIC DOC-
TRINES FROM THE TIME OF THE PHYSIOCRATS TO THE PRESENT. Translated by R. Richards. 2nd ed. New York: D.C. Heath, 1949.
800 p.

This work contains a chapter on "The Historical School and
the Conflict of Methods" which treats the origin and development, the critical ideas, and the positive ideas of the historical school. The school is given a fair and complete analysis.

296. Gray, Alexander. THE DEVELOPMENT OF ECONOMIC DOCTRINE.
London: Longmans, Green, 1936. 384 p.

Gray presents a thirty-page discussion of Adam Muller, Fried-
rick List, and Johann H. von Thunen, three of the earlier historicists, showing how they made quite different contributions to economics as a result of their differing backgrounds and philosophical
beliefs. The fact that von Thunen was more theoretical than other
historicists is discussed in relation to his development of central
place theory. (Also cited in Chapter 1, entry 25.)

297. Grossman, Henryk. "The Evolutionist Revolt against Classical Economics."
JOURNAL OF POLITICAL ECONOMY 51 (October 1943): 381-96,
(December 1943): 506-22.

The author attempts to show that the French and the English
played a decisive role in establishing the basis for modern
evolutionary theories of economics and especially for the work
of Karl Marx. Richard Jones was the leading English representative of evolutionary ideas and much of the author's discussion is related to Jones's work.

298. Heimann, Eduard. HISTORY OF ECONOMIC DOCTRINES; AN INTRO-
DUCTION TO ECONOMIC THEORY. New York: Oxford University
Press, 1964. 263 p. Paperbound.

This general text includes a short section on the historicists

and their methodological counterparts in the United States. It is
a good introduction to the tenets of the school and the members
who followed that tradition. (Also cited in Chapter 1, entry 29.)

299. Hoselitz, Bert F. "Theories of Stages of Economic Growth." In THEORIES
OF ECONOMIC GROWTH, by Bert F. Hoselitz et al., pp. 193-238.
New York: The Free Press, 1961. (Paperbound ed., 1965.)

The article deals with theories that employ a series of stages
in the evolution of economic systems. The German historicists
were outstanding in this area; hence, consideration of these
scholars constitutes a substantial portion of the paper.

300. Kapp, K. William, and Kapp, Lore L., eds. HISTORY OF ECONOMIC
THOUGHT; A BOOK OF READINGS. 2nd ed. New York: Barnes &
Noble, 1963. 444 p.

The collection of original writings contains a section on "Economic Historicism" which includes the works of three authors:
Auguste Comte, the philosophical founder of the school,
Richard Jones, an outstanding spokesman for the English followers, and Gustav Schmoller, principal exponent of the German historicists.

301. Keynes, John Neville. THE SCOPE AND METHOD OF POLITICAL
ECONOMY. London: Macmillan, 1930. 382 p.

This well-written work on methodology presents the views of
both the British and the German historicists. It is demonstrated
that extremists exist in both schools, but that the German contingent was by far the more vehement about their conviction
that abstract deductive theory was a waste of time. This is
an excellent source for the study of the historical school. A
reprint edition was brought out by Augustus M. Kelley.

302. Lekachman, Robert, ed. THE VARIETIES OF ECONOMICS. Vol. II.
New York: World Publishing Co., 1962. 317 p.

This work contains an excerpt from Weber's introduction to THE
PROTESTANT ETHIC AND THE SPIRIT OF CAPITALISM here
entitled "Capitalist Rationality." There is also an excerpt from
Werner Sombart's THE JEWS AND MODERN CAPITALISM entitled "Jewish Influence." These two excerpts facilitate the
study of one of the conflicts--origin of capitalism--that existed
in the German historical school.

303. Mitchell, Wesley C. TYPES OF ECONOMIC THEORY FROM MERCAN-
TILISM TO INSTITUTIONALISM. Vol. II. Edited by Joseph Dorfman.
New York: Augustus M. Kelley, 1969. 875 p.

Mitchell devoted a sixty-four-page chapter to the German historical school and Gustav Schmoller, one of the more extremist

members of the school with respect to correct methodology. Schmoller was exemplary of the involvement that historical school ideology presupposed as the role of a political economist. The author discusses the German historical school in comparison with the British classical school in terms of the uses of theory and the institutions in which theory was taught and used.

304. Montague, F.C. "Arnold Toynbee." In JOHNS HOPKINS UNIVERSITY STUDIES IN HISTORICAL AND POLITICAL SCIENCE, vol. VII, edited by Herbert B. Adams, pp. 5-70. Baltimore: Johns Hopkins University, 1889.

This is a biographical essay on Toynbee, his life and work. There are also a couple of accompanying essays on topics of interest to Toynbee and a letter (21 January 1880) from Toynbee to Thomas Illingworth concerning an account of the credit system.

305. Newman, Philip C., et al., eds. SOURCE READINGS IN ECONOMIC THOUGHT. New York: W.W. Norton & Co., 1954. 762 p.

This book of excerpts from original works contains two pieces representative of the German historical school. The work by Sombart was a summary, written for the ENCYCLOPAEDIA OF THE SOCIAL SCIENCES, of his MODERN CAPITALISM. The second piece is by Max Weber (translated by Talcott Parsons) and was taken from the introduction to his THE PROTESTANT ETHIC AND THE SPIRIT OF CAPITALISM. Both writers refer to the then current form of capitalism as only one of many types, viewing it as a very flexible system. (Also cited in Chapter 4, entry 495.)

306. Nussbaum, Frederick L. A HISTORY OF THE ECONOMIC INSTITUTIONS OF MODERN EUROPE. New York: F.S. Crofts, 1933. 448 p.

This book is also listed as AN INTRODUCTION TO "DER MODERNE KAPITALISMUS" OF WERNER SOMBART. The author has attempted to fashion a plausible history of Europe along the same lines as those used by Sombart in his work. It is a good economic history of Europe, which is what many members of the historical school were writing, and provides much information about institutional change and resultant effects on economic policy.

307. Oser, Jacob. THE EVOLUTION OF ECONOMIC THOUGHT. 2nd ed. New York: Harcourt, Brace & World, 1970. 458 p.

This somewhat unusual approach to the analysis of schools of thought contains a nineteen-page chapter on the German historical school in which Oser first analyzes the school in his particular way, and then proceeds to discuss the following

writers: List, Roscher, Schmoller, Weber, and Sombart. There
is a short bibliography at the end of the chapter.

308. Popper, Karl R. THE POVERTY OF HISTORICISM. London: Routledge
& Kegan Paul, 1960. 193 p.

This is an excellent critique of historicism based on articles
originally published in ECONOMICA in 1944 and 1945. In
this work Popper defines the crucial fallacy of historicism as
a method of scientific analysis. Also available in a Harper
Torchbook edition.

309. Rheinstein, Max, ed. MAX WEBER ON LAW IN ECONOMY AND SO-
CIETY. Translated from the 2nd edition of WIRTSCHAFT AND GESELL-
SCHAFT by Edward Shils. Cambridge, Mass.: Harvard University Press,
1954. lxxii, 363 p.

This is an informative work for the scholar interested in the
development of economic systems considered with respect to
legal systems. Weber was an acknowledged authority in this
area which has, in the past twenty years, attracted the renewed
interest of economists.

310. Roll, Eric. A HISTORY OF ECONOMIC THOUGHT. Rev. ed., enl.
London: Faber and Faber, 1938. 540 p.

This work is a general history of economic thought that treats
many schools and authors. Substantial space is devoted to the
development and growth of the historical school. In a section
on the German Romantics, Roll discusses the works of some forerunners. The chapter on "Transition" deals with both German
and English scholars.

311. Schumpeter, Joseph Alois. HISTORY OF ECONOMIC ANALYSIS.
Edited from manuscript by Elizabeth Boody Schumpeter. New York:
Oxford University Press, 1954. 1260 p.

As in his other work, Schumpeter is concerned with the effects
of the philosophy and ideology of the school on their analytical work. In this case he states that ". . . economists of the
period . . . deviated from the stony path that leads to scientific conquest," although he does acknowledge the benefit gained
from their data-gathering. It is an excellent treatment of the
school and the benefits derived from it by modern economists.

312. Seligman, Ben B. MAIN CURRENTS IN MODERN ECONOMICS: ECO-
NOMIC THOUGHT SINCE 1870. New York: The Free Press, 1963.
887 p.

This text is a general history of thought text in which a gener-
ous amount of space is given to a discussion of the historical

school, both in England and Germany. Writers are grouped according to similarities of views and/or topics of analysis. (Also cited in Chapter 5, entry 779.)

313. Sheehan, James J. THE CAREER OF LUJO BRENTANO. Chicago: University of Chicago Press, 1966. 223 p.

The author attempts to analyze Brentano's career from three major vantage points: his activities as a liberal social reformer, his credentials as a German academician (of greatest relevance here), his relationship to the German state. Bretano was a close friend and colleague of G. Schmoller, who praised his work highly.

314. Spiegel, Henry William. THE GROWTH OF ECONOMIC THOUGHT. Englewood Cliffs, N.J.: Prentice-Hall, 1971. 816 p.

This extensive work contains two chapters on historical economics. The first, "Interludes of Historical Economics: Baconian and Related Variants," covers most of the English portion of the historical school. The second, "The Hegelian Variant of Historical Economics," is devoted to a discussion of the various German historicists. Together they fill approximately thirty-eight pages. (Also cited in Chapter 1, entry 53.)

D. CONTRIBUTIONS OF LESSER IMPORTANCE

315. Ashley, Sir William J. "The Argument for Preference." THE ECONOMIC JOURNAL 14 (March 1904): 1-10.

316. _____. "Aristotle's Doctrine of Barter." QUARTERLY JOURNAL OF ECONOMICS 9 (April 1895): 333-41.

317. _____. "The Rehabilitation of Ricardo." THE ECONOMIC JOURNAL 7 (September 1891): 474-89.

318. _____. "The Statistical Measurement of Profit." THE ECONOMIC JOURNAL 20 (December 1910): 530-50.

319. Clark, Colin. "Von Thunen's Isolated State." OXFORD ECONOMIC PAPERS n.s. 19 (November 1967): 370-77.

320. Cunningham, W. "The Localisation of Industry." THE ECONOMIC JOURNAL 12 (December 1902): 501-6.

321. _____. "On the Value of Money." QUARTERLY JOURNAL OF ECONOMICS 13 (July 1899): 379-85.

322. _____. "The Progress of Economic Doctrine in England in the Eighteenth Century." THE ECONOMIC JOURNAL 1 (March 1891): 73-94.

323. _____. "The Relativity of Economic Doctrine." THE ECONOMIC JOURNAL 2 (March 1892): 1-16.

324. Diehl, Carl. "The Life and Work of Max Weber." QUARTERLY JOURNAL OF ECONOMICS 38 (November 1923): 87-107.

325. Harris, Abram L. "Sombart and German (National) Socialism." JOURNAL OF POLITICAL ECONOMY 50 (December 1942): 805-35.

326. Kiker, B.F. "Von Thunen on Human Capital." OXFORD ECONOMIC PAPERS n.s. 21 (November 1969): 339-48.

327. Leigh, Arthur H. "Von Thunen's Theory of Distribution and the Advent of Marginal Analysis." JOURNAL OF POLITICAL ECONOMY 54 (December 1946): 481-502.

328. Leslie, Thomas Edward Cliffe. ESSAYS IN POLITICAL ECONOMY. 2nd ed. London: Longmans, Green, 1888. Reprint ed., New York: Augustus M. Kelley, 1969. 437 p.

329. _____. ON THE PHILOSOPHICAL METHOD OF POLITICAL ECONOMY. Dublin: Hodges, Foster, & Figgs, 1876. 226 p.

330. Moore, H.L. "Von Thunen's Theory of Natural Wages." Pts. I-II. QUARTERLY JOURNAL OF ECONOMICS 9 (April 1895): 291-304, (July 1895): 388-408.

331. Parsons, Talcott. "'Capitalism' in Recent German Literature: Sombart and Weber." Pts. I-II. JOURNAL OF POLITICAL ECONOMY 36 (December 1928): 641-61; 37 (February 1929): 31-51.

332. Rogin, Leo. "Werner Sombart and the Uses of Transcendentalism." AMERICAN ECONOMIC REVIEW 31 (September 1941): 493-511.

333. Smart, William. "The New Theory of Interest." THE ECONOMIC JOURNAL 1 (December 1891): 675-87.

334. Spiethoff, Arthur. "The 'Historical' Character of Economic Theories." JOURNAL OF ECONOMIC HISTORY 12 (Spring 1952): 131-39.

335. Taussig, F.W. "Schmoller on Protection and Free Trade." QUARTERLY JOURNAL OF ECONOMICS 19 (May 1905): 501-11.

336. _____. "The Wages-Fund Doctrine at the Hands of German Economists." QUARTERLY JOURNAL OF ECONOMICS 9 (October 1894): 1-25.

Chapter 4

THE MARGINALISTS

Chapter 4

THE MARGINALISTS

A. INTRODUCTION

The bibliography of major contributions to this school has been subdivided into two subsections to represent the two major schools of marginalist theory: the Austrian and the neoclassical. The two representatives of the Lausanne School, Walras and Pareto, are included in the Austrian school as are the representatives from the Swedish school (the Swedish and Austrian schools were closely linked, especially in the work of Wicksell).

The concept of marginalism was common to both schools, but their extensions of the theory differed in many respects. The search for a means of determining value was finally ended by the adoption of the concept of subjective value and marginal utility analysis. Such problems as A. Smith's "water-diamond paradox" were solved; that is, the apparent discrepancies between "use" and "exchange" values of various commodities were resolved.

The concept of marginal productivity theory grew out of these schools and, as a result, distribution theory was modernized greatly. The neoclassical school did more in this area than did the Austrians. As for capital theory, the Austrians advanced a theory that had a long-term effect on economic theory. Their approach to capital is currently enjoying a revival in economic literature.

The early Austrian economists were very much nonmathematical, whereas the Lausanne representatives were very concerned with mathematics. The neoclassical economists were somewhere in the middle, some of their representatives being much more mathematically oriented than others. The use of calculus in economics began with the introduction of marginalism. Changes at the margin could be easily expressed in terms of infinitesimal changes.

The logical consistency of the perfectly competitive mode, which grew out of marginalist work, has served as a strong foundation for basic theory in economics. Most of economic theory since the turn of the century has been little more than further refinement of the economic theory advanced by these two schools of thought.

Some of the works annotated below were born of contemporary events; but, as is especially true for works of pure theory, some writers were responding only to the existing body of theory. The theoretical writings, in other words, were very often modifications or extensions of earlier theories.

B. MAJOR CONTRIBUTIONS

1. Austrian School

337. Bohm-Bawerk, Eugen. "The Austrian Economists." ANNALS OF THE AMERICAN ACADEMY OF POLITICAL AND SOCIAL SCIENCE 1 (1891): 361-84.

> The author describes the Austrian school of economics and what it stood for at the time. He touches upon the methodology controversy in which the German historical school and the Austrians, especially Menger, were engaged. The remainder is devoted to explanation of the basic theoretical tenets of the Austrian theory.

338. _____. "Capital and Interest Once More: I. Capital vs. Capital Goods and II. A Relapse to Productivity Theory." QUARTERLY JOURNAL OF ECONOMICS 21 (November 1906): 1-21, (February 1907): 247-82.

> The first part discusses in detail J.B. Clark's writings on capital and capital goods and the distinction that Clark drew between the two. In the second part Bohm-Bawerk examines the apparent use of productivity theory which "finds the effective and adequate explanation of interest in a productive power belonging to capital as such," a position with which the author did not agree.

339. _____. "The Nature of Capital: A Rejoinder." QUARTERLY JOURNAL OF ECONOMICS 22 (November 1907): 28-47.

> This is Bohm-Bawerk's response to J.B. Clark's rebuttal of the former's criticism of capital theory. He asks first whether Clark admits the identity between capital and capital goods and then discusses the difference between knowing the existence of and explaining the return on capital. He further discusses some methodological issues with respect to distribution and, finally, looks at the synchronizing effect of capital.

340. _____. "The Positive Theory of Capital and Its Critics, Parts I, II, and III." QUARTERLY JOURNAL OF ECONOMICS 9 (January 1895): 113-31, (April 1895): 235-56; 10 (January 1896): 121-55.

> In this three-part article the author replies to the criticism of

his theory of capital. The first part is a reply to John B. Clark's "The Genesis of Capital" (YALE REVIEW, 1893, pp. 302-15). The second part is an answer to the attack by F.A. Walker (QUARTERLY JOURNAL OF ECONOMICS, July 1892, p. 399) and the four main points upon which Walker concentrated his attack. The third part is a reply to White, Bilgram, Macvane, and Hawley, each of whom had attacked a different aspect of Bohm-Bawerk's work. This article, therefore, serves as an excellent review of his capital theory from all angles.

341. Cassel, Gustav. "The Depreciation of Gold." ECONOMIC JOURNAL 17 (September 1917): 346-54.

The article pertains to the changing value of gold as a result of price changes for commodities. In various cases these price changes were the result of excess supplies of gold; in the Netherlands the excess was so great that the inflow of gold was restricted. The excess supply of gold need not be the result of an increase in the available gold stock.

342. _____. "The Rate of Interest, the Bank Rate and the Stabilization of Prices." QUARTERLY JOURNAL OF ECONOMICS 42 (August 1928): 511-29.

In the introduction, Cassel draws a distinction between the determination of relative prices and the determination of the level of absolute prices. The latter serves to launch him into the discussion of the means of achieving and maintaining price stability. Emphasis is also placed on the role of interest as a price.

343. _____. "The Theory of Progressive Taxation." ECONOMIC JOURNAL 11 (December 1901): 481-91.

Assuming that the income tax is the keystone of a tax system which should cover the general expenses of the state, the question is: "Which is the proper scale of an income-tax which is intended to cause an equal sacrifice to all citizens?" Cassel finds that for the complete determination of the progressive tax one must only fix three elements.

344. Dmitriev, V.K. ECONOMIC ESSAYS ON VALUE: COMPETITION & UTILITY. Translated by D. Fry. Edited by D.M. Nuti. Cambridge: At the University Press, 1974. 231 p.

This collection of essays by Russia's first mathematical economist covers a broad spectrum of theoretical development. His final essay, "The Theory of Marginal Utility," covers the entire history of the evolution of marginal utility theory. In addition to the works of the traditional economic theorists (Dupuit, Austrian School, Jevons, Walras, and others), Dmitriev discusses the psychological foundations of marginal utility theory. (Also cited in Chapter 2, entry 135.)

345. Lindahl, Erik. STUDIES IN THE THEORY OF MONEY AND CAPITAL. New York: Rinehart, 1950. 391 p.

Part III of this work is of primary importance here. It begins with an attempt to "fuse together the pricing theories of Walras and Cassel on the one hand and the capital theories of Bohm-Bawerk and Wicksell on the other." The last two chapters are devoted to an attempt to render the theory dynamic.

346. Menger, Carl. "On the Origin of Money." Translated by Caroline A. Foley. ECONOMIC JOURNAL 2 (June 1892): 239-55.

Menger's discussion of what money is and why some things serve as money and others do not follows the modern definition of money as whatever is generally acceptable in exchange. General acceptability, therefore, is the reason for the original use of precious metals. An unusual essay for the days of the metalists.

347. _____. PRINCIPLES OF ECONOMICS. Translated and edited by James Pingwall and Bert F. Hoselitz. Glencoe, Ill.: The Free Press, 1950. 328 p.

This is the most representative book of the Austrian school, written by its founder. As his part of the development of marginal utility theory, Menger produced this lucid and very comprehensive analysis of value and distribution. It is a non-mathematical text that could be read even by those with little background in economics.

348. _____. PROBLEMS OF ECONOMICS AND SOCIOLOGY. Translated by Francis J. Nock. Edited by Louis Schneider. Urbana: University of Illinois Press, 1963. 237 p.

This is an account of the polemic between the German historical school and the Austrians from Menger's point of view. He does not believe that German theory was entirely useless, but contends that it did not have sole claim to the treatment of economic problems. A good book for one interested in the German-Austrian debate and Menger's methodological views.

349. Pareto, Vilfredo. MANUAL OF POLITICAL ECONOMY. Translated by Ann S. Schwier. Edited by Ann S. Schwier and Alfred N. Page. New York: Augustus M. Kelley, 1971. 504 p.

This was Pareto's major contribution to economics and has only recently become available in English. As the successor to Walras at Lausanne, Pareto was naturally one who used general equilibrium theory, but this work contains much more than general equilibrium theory. His chapter on population is excellent.

350. _____. "Mathematical Economics." Translated by J.I. Griffen. INTERNATIONAL ECONOMIC PAPERS 5 (1955): 58-102.

Two basic problems involved in applying mathematics are stated and most of the discussion is concerned with the first, with, that is, an exclusively mathematical problem which derives the consequences of certain assumptions. Given the mathematical laws of behavior, Pareto demonstrates the determination of the consequences of these laws. Most of the discussion is concerned with a static state but the dynamic state is also considered. This article is not recommended for those unfamiliar with calculus.

351. Von Mises, Ludwig. HUMAN ACTION: A TREATISE ON ECONOMICS. New Haven, Conn.: Yale University Press, 1949. 889 p.

An unusual treatise on economics, this volume deals with the place of economics in society and how the market place serves to modify the society, as well as the reverse.

352. _____. THEORY AND HISTORY: AN INTERPRETATION OF SOCIAL AND ECONOMIC EVOLUTION. New Haven, Conn.: Yale University Press, 1957. 384 p.

Much more recent than most of von Mises's other work, this volume is not as completely in the marginalist vein. It is a good work on the interaction of society and economics and the role of historicism.

353. _____. THE THEORY OF MONEY AND CREDIT. Translated by H.E. Botson. New Haven, Conn.: Yale University Press, 1953. 493 p.

First published in 1912 in German, von Mises's book deals with the problems of the period (1910) and especially with inflation and the absurd argument being proffered as rationale for difficulties that were traceable to bad monetary policy. The war economies were good examples of those that used inflation but failed to acknowledge the reasons for its existence.

354. Walras, Leon. CORRESPONDENCE OF LEON WALRAS AND RELATED PAPERS, 1857-1909. 3 vols. Edited by William Jaffe. Amsterdam: North-Holland Publishing Co., 1965. Vol. I, 799 p.; vol. II, 763 p.; vol. III, 538 p.

Reprints of most of Walras's correspondence are included but few if any are in English. The scholar who desires to use them must speak French or have them translated. It is, nevertheless, a tremendous source of information on one of the greatest economists.

355. _____. ELEMENTS OF PURE ECONOMICS. Translated by William Jaffe. London: George Allen & Unwin, 1965. 620 p.

This is a classic text in the history of economics, still considered an important book for many courses. The fields of analysis that were engendered by this work are still expanding. The general equilibrium theory advanced in this volume was the first true system of its kind. Although fairly mathematical, any serious student of economics should read at least parts of this book.

356. _____. "Geometrical Theory of the Determination of Prices." ANNALS OF THE AMERICAN ACADEMY OF POLITICAL AND SOCIAL SCIENCE 3 (1892): 45-64.

This was the first piece of Walras's work to appear in English. It is an extremely intricate exposition in which the notation as well as the geometry become almost incomprehensible. If one enjoys such exercises and has time, however, it is a worthwile article to study.

357. Wicksell, Knut. "Gold after the War in Relation to Inflation and the Foreign Exchanges." ECONOMIC JOURNAL 28 (December 1918): 409-12.

This is a reply to a comment by O.T. Falk on Cassel's theory that the "movements of the exchanges are simply determined in the main by the quotient between the inflation of the different countries." In the postwar period when countries suffer large imbalances of trade, the theory may not hold; but Wicksell argues that it is generally valid. He believes that gold will maintain its value by itself if only it is in general use as a standard of value, a situation he favors.

358. _____. "The Influence of the Rate of Interest on Prices." ECONOMIC JOURNAL 17 (June 1907): 212.

Wicksell is concerned here with the relationship between the money rate and the natural rate of interest with respect to price changes. It is not at once an intuitively obvious theory, but many a modern policy maker could learn from the economic analysis involved. This is one of the earliest appearances of Wicksell's work in English.

359. _____. INTEREST AND PRICES. Translated by R.F. Kahn with an introduction by Bertil Ohlin. New York: Augustus M. Kelley, 1962. 219 p.

The article "The Enigma of Business Cycles," translated by

Carl G. Uhr, is also included. In this book a theory of interest is developed so that questions relating to the quantity theory of money and interest rates and prices may be manipulated. Wicksell develops the concept of a bank rate and a natural rate and relates the latter to the real rate of return on physical capital.

360. _____. LECTURES ON POLITICAL ECONOMY. 2 vols. Translated by E. Classen. Edited by Lionel Robbins. London: Routledge & Kegan Paul, 1967. Vol. I, 299 p.; vol. II, 238 p.

This is the general work of the major economist of the Swedish school. Much of his work predated that of Keynes and his value and production theories were of exceptional quality. Volume I contains value theory, production theory, and the theory of capital accumulation. Volume II is completely devoted to the study of various aspects of money and monetary theory.

361. _____. SELECTED PAPERS ON ECONOMIC THEORY. Edited with an introduction by Erik Lindahl. London: George Allen & Unwin, 1958. 292 p.

This work collects four sets of articles, each concerned with a different aspect of Wicksell's theoretical writings. The first set includes an article explaining his attitudes on economics in general and one summarizing his monetary theory. The second set consists of three papers on production and distribution theory. The third group is made up of articles on the works of his contemporaries. The last set contains articles written after World War I about foreign trade problems.

362. _____. VALUE, CAPITAL, AND RENT. Foreword by G.L.S. Shackle. Translated by S.H. Frowein. London: George Allen & Unwin, 1954. 180 p.

In this work the author has attempted to improve and/or clarify the marginalist works in this area. Wicksell begins by reviewing earlier theories of value and then presents and develops the "new" theory of value. The closing chapter relates the new theory of capital to the theory of wages, ground rent, and values of goods.

363. Wieser, Friedrich von. NATURAL VALUE. Translated by Christian A. Malloch. Edited with a preface by William Smart. New York: Kelley & Millman, 1956. xlv, 243 p.

This work is a detailed study of the "entire sphere of the phenomena of value." It is an attempt to supplement work already available, but Wieser here spends little time discussing the assumptions of value theory as he had done in his earlier

works. He also makes an effort to illustrate the usefulness of
the concept and its neutrality, demonstrating that it is biased
for or against any mode of thought.

364. _____. "The Theory of Value." ANNALS OF THE AMERICAN ACAD-
EMY OF POLITICAL AND SOCIAL SCIENCE 2 (1891-92): 600-628.

This article is a reply to an attack by Macvane on the work
of Bohm-Bawerk and Wieser. The reply is restricted to the
relation between marginal utility and cost as viewed by the
Austrian economists. Macvane's attack was based upon the
Ricardian concept of value.

2. Neoclassical School

365. Bagehot, Walter. "A New Standard of Value." ECONOMIC JOURNAL
2 (September 1892): 472-77.

This is a comment on Jevons's MONEY AND THE MECHAN-
ISM OF EXCHANGE and illustrates the difficulty sometimes
encountered with the concept of value, which incorporated
too many chances for variation. This is especially true for
the abstract subjective value of Jevons. In this useful discussion, Bagehot calls for an unvarying standard of value.

366. Bastable, C.F. "The Rule of Taxation for Revenue as a Canon of Public
Finance." ECONOMIC JOURNAL 13 (December 1903): 505-10.

This is a protestation against the suggestion of using taxation
to affect commercial activity--especially international trade.
The author does not feel this to be either an efficient method
or a justifiable use of taxation. He contends that taxation
is solely for raising revenue. It is an interesting argument
for free trade.

367. _____. "Taxation through Monopoly." ECONOMIC JOURNAL 1 (June
1891): 307-25.

Bastable draws the distinction between taxation by levy and
taxation through the exercise of governmental control of the
ownership of, for example, public utilities. Acknowledging
that, when the utility buys its right to operate, both methods
serve to produce revenue for the state, he then defines the
criteria for deciding which type of taxation is the more desirable and efficient.

368. Bonar, James. "The Positive Theory of Capital." QUARTERLY JOUR-
NAL OF ECONOMICS 3 (April 1889): 336-51.

Although not technically a review, this is an extensive examination of Bohm-Bawerk's book, THE POSITIVE THEORY OF CAPITAL. Bonar examines each of the cases of interest payments and discusses these from the Austrian viewpoint with respect to those of earlier economists from other countries.

369. Bowley, A.L. THE MATHEMATICAL GROUNDWORK OF ECONOMICS. Oxford: At the University Press, 1924. 98 p.

This work is an attempt to fill a gap in the literature regarding the mathematical treatment of political economy. The use of uniform notation and the presentation of a synthesis of mathematical methods used by Cournot, Jevons, Pareto, Edgeworth, Marshall, Pigou, and Johnson are the objectives of this work. The portion related to these authors' treatment of the fundamental equation of exchange and elementary taxation is especially well done.

370. Cannan, Edwin. "The Application of the Theoretical Apparatus of Supply and Demand to Units of Currency." ECONOMIC JOURNAL 31 (December 1921): 453-61.

Cannan examines the situation in which the stock of money supply is quite large relative to annual increments, and states that demand depends upon the amount each individual wishes to hold and the number of individuals. Rapid and prolonged changes in either demand or supply render money vulnerable to Gresham's Law. It is an interesting article that explains many aspects of money demand and supply variations.

371. _____. "Capital and the Heritage of Improvement." ECONOMICA n.s. 1 (August 1934): 381-92.

"Heritage of improvement" means the net economic advantage that we possess as a consequence of past enterprise. Cannan's article was addressed to those who were worried about the consumption of capital. He maintains that one must show that the loss of capital is damaging, not simply that it is lost, explaining that new methods may require less capital for the same or greater output.

372. _____. "Professor Cassel on Money and Foreign Exchange." ECONOMIC JOURNAL 32 (December 1922): 506-13.

The author discusses in some detail the relationship laid out by Cassel for movements in money supply and prices. Some controversy exists regarding the effects of inflowing foreign exchange with respect to domestic money creation and domestic price changes.

373. _____. "'Total Utility' and 'Consumer's Surplus'." ECONOMICA 4 (February 1924): 21-26.

The author examines the approaches of Jevons and Marshall
with respect to the concepts named and goes through Marshall's
five hypotheses regarding consumer's surplus. It would be
helpful if one had Marshall's PRINCIPLES handy when reading
this article.

374. _____. "What is Capital?" ECONOMIC JOURNAL 7 (June 1897):
278-84.

This is a response to Irving Fisher's announcement of the true
relation between capital and income and Fisher's contention
that Cannan had made the original discovery. The note is an
explanation of how the author came to view capital and income as being distinguished by their different relation to time.
Cannan alleges that it was not through any great insight that
he formed this opinion.

375. Edgeworth, F.Y. MATHEMATICAL PHYSICS: AN ESSAY ON THE AP-
PLICATION OF MATHEMATICS TO THE MORAL SCIENCES. London:
C. Kegan Paul, 1881. Reprint ed., New York: Augustus M. Kelley,
1961. 150 p.

This work is divided into two parts, theoretical and applied.
The first attempts to apply mathematics to economics by sug-
gesting an analogy between the "principles of greatest happi-
ness" and the "principles of maximum energy, which are among
the highest generalizations of physics." The second part, the
"calculus of pleasure," is handled in two parts, economical
and utilitarian. These latter two are further broken down.
The book may be read by students without a great amount of
mathematical training.

376. _____. "Mr. Pierson on Scarcity of Gold." ECONOMIC JOURNAL
5 (March 1895): 109-12.

In this brief discussion of bimetallism, Edgeworth defines the
criteria which a nation would do well to adopt in this particular monetary system. His comments are generally favorable to
Pierson's work.

377. _____. "Mr. Walsh on the Measurement of General Exchange Value."
ECONOMIC JOURNAL 2 (September 1901). 404-16.

This is a note on the methodology and theoretical applicability
of C.M. Walsh's THE MEASUREMENT OF GENERAL EXCHANGE-
VALUE. Walsh is commended on his search of the literature,
but Edgeworth finds his treatment of the problem of index numbers inadequate.

378. _____. "On a Point in the Theory of International Trade." ECO-
NOMIC JOURNAL 9 (March 1899): 125-28.

This comment takes issue with a statement by J.S. Nicholson regarding the benefits to a nation whose export price falls due to a technological innovation. The argument turns on a statement of Mills's paradox that increased productivity decreases the nation's terms of trade.

379. _____. PAPERS RELATING TO POLITICAL ECONOMY. Vol. I. Reprint ed., New York: Burt Franklin, 1964. 442 p.

This is a collection of papers which appeared during the first thirty years of the ECONOMIC JOURNAL (1891-1921) or were written by Edgeworth. This volume contains articles on value and distribution, monopoly, and money. (See also 380, 381.)

380. _____. PAPERS RELATING TO POLITICAL ECONOMY. Vol. II. Reprint ed., New York: Burt Franklin, 1964. 491 p.

This second volume contains articles on international trade, taxation, and mathematical economics. (See also 379, 381.)

381. _____. PAPERS RELATING TO POLITICAL ECONOMY. Vol. III. Reprint ed., New York: Burt Franklin, 1964. 288 p.

This third volume is composed completely of review articles on books of all topics. There is a twelve-page index at the end of this volume which refers to the complete set of three volumes. (See also 379, 380.)

382. _____. "Professor Bohm-Bawerk on the Ultimate Standard of Value." ECONOMIC JOURNAL 4 (September 1894): 518-21.

Edgeworth insists that there are two standards of value: disutility and utility. Bohm-Bawerk had argued that utility was the only standard of value. A comment on and a reply to this article appeared in the JOURNAL later in 1894 (see pages 719-25).

383. _____. "Professor Graziani on the Mathematical Theory of Monopoly." ECONOMIC JOURNAL 8 (June 1898): 234-39.

This comment by Edgeworth is a defense of the use of the mathematical method to deal with taxation and a monopoly. Graziani maintains that there is nothing of value that cannot be shown without mathematical symbols. Edgeworth illustrates that indeed there are certain situations in which mathematics is most useful.

384. _____. "Professor J.S. Nicholson on 'Consumers' Rent'." ECONOMIC JOURNAL 4 (March 1894): 151-58.

This comment refers to a section of Nicholson's text in which

Nicholson criticizes Marshall's treatment of consumers' rent.
Edgeworth deals with the argument about whether gain or loss
to the consumer can be measured in dollars.

385. _____. "Professor Seligman on the Mathematical Method in Political
Economy." ECONOMIC JOURNAL 9 (June 1899): 286-315.

This is a response to criticism from Seligman on Edgeworth's
use of mathematics in the theory of taxation. Seligman said
that mathematical economists were able to "illumine many a
dark corner of pure theory, not because of their mathematics
but by their power of economic analysis." Edgeworth counters
that, on the contrary, certain failures in Seligman's work must
be attributed not to any deficiency of economic power but to
the "use of unaided reason where the mathematical organon
was required."

386. _____. "The Pure Theory of Taxation, I-III." ECONOMIC JOURNAL
7 (March 1897): 46-70, (June 1897): 226-38, (December 1897): 550-
71.

The first two parts of this article are concerned with what the
author calls the two subjects of the pure theory of taxation--
the laws of incidence and the principle of equal sacrifice.
Edgeworth defines four different combinations of situations that
may exist to which he then opposes four contradictory situations,
making a total of eight different characteristics that may be
compared in combination. The third part discusses the distribution of the fiscal burden among the taxpayers.

387. _____. "The Theory of International Values." ECONOMIC JOURNAL
4 (March 1894): 35-50, (September 1894): 424-43, (December 1894):
606-38.

Edgeworth has attempted to express in simple language propositions of the theory of international trade that have some bearing on practice and a high degree of generality. Topics include the effects of taxes, communication, and scarcity. The
second essay is a mathematical treatment of these propositions,
and the third essay is a critical review of the principal writers
on international trade.

388. _____. "Thoughts on Monetary Reform." ECONOMIC JOURNAL 5
(September 1895): 434-51.

The author treats a few of the many reform proposals offered
at the time. He discusses four different problems that arise
from the proposals and concludes that, if a double standard is
desirable, there may well be one superior to bimetallism. It
is a very detailed and thorough analysis of the related problems
of monetary reform.

389. Giffen, Robert. "The Gresham Law." ECONOMIC JOURNAL 1 (June 1891): 304-6.

This treatment of Gresham's Law extends the application beyond what Giffen believed were the limits of its previous application. Today we take this extension for granted because it does not necessarily mean that the "good" money leaves the country when one says that "bad" money drives out the "good" money. It is an interesting discussion of a topic which is still of major importance today.

390. Hobson, J.A. "The Law of the Three Rents." QUARTERLY JOURNAL OF ECONOMICS 5 (April 1891): 263-88.

This is a discussion of the concept of rent as a residual applied to both labor and capital, in which case rent is treated as a marginal concept. The zero-rent margin for labor and capital is somewhat different than that for land. The author's conclusions are nearly the same as those of a marginal productivity theorist even though the method used to derive these conclusions was much different.

391. Jevons, W. Stanley. "Brief Account of a General Mathematical Theory of Political Economy." JOURNAL OF THE ROYAL STATISTICAL SOCIETY OF LONDON 29 (June 1866): 282-87.

Since economics is concerned with quantities, it has always been mathematical in nature. According to Jevons, the benefit to be derived from mathematical expression had not been realized. In this short essay, he outlines the ways in which economics should adopt mathematical methods, being careful to point to pitfalls inherent in these methods.

392. _____. THE COAL QUESTION. Edited by A.W. Flux. New York: Augustus M. Kelley, 1965. 467 p.

This is an assessment of the British position regarding the supply of coal for future energy in which Jevons proffers projections for various stages of usage rate. Misunderstanding on the part of readers engendered much criticism of Jevons for this work.

393. _____. INVESTIGATIONS IN CURRENCY AND FINANCE. Edited with an introduction by H.S. Foxwell. London: Macmillan, 1909. 347 p.

This collection of essays was completed by Jevons's wife and Foxwell after Jevons's death in 1882, at the request of H. Stanley Jevons. Topics covered are commercial fluctuations (including his sun-spot theory), price fluctuations and the value of gold, and bimetallism.

394. _____. MONEY AND THE MECHANISM OF EXCHANGE. New York:

D. Appleton, 1921. 342 p.

This was an attempt to describe past and present monetary systems of the world and includes all of the inherent issues involved in establishing and maintaining a monetary system, asking, for example, what money is and what "natural" laws govern its circulation. It is an excellent accounting of the various kinds of money and monetary systems, both domestic and international.

395.　　　　. PAPERS AND CORRESPONDENCE. 2 vols. Edited by R.D. Collison Black and Rosamond Konekamp. London: Macmillan, 1972. Vol. I, 243 p.; vol. II, 462 p.

The first of these two volumes contains a biographical introduction by Konekamp and Jevons's journal. A diary of a trip to a gold digging site and the Jevons family trees are also in the first volume. The second volume contains Jevons's correspondence, mostly to or from members of his family, before 1862. Publication of two or more volumes is projected. The third will contain letters from 1863 to 1882 and the fourth will contain the complete set of notes from his lectures at Owens College, Manchester, along with all of the papers not previously collected.

396.　　　　. THE STATE IN RELATION TO LABOUR. 3rd ed. Edited with an introduction by Michael Cababe. London: Macmillan, 1894. 171 p.

This book is an attempt to illustrate the principles of legislation which emerge as one attempts to analyze the actions of the legislature and the state of public opinion with reference to the conflict of labor and capital and the regulation of industry. A major point is expressed by the question: Why is laissez faire generally upheld when in large classes of cases interferences of local or central authorities is invoked?

397.　　　　. THE THEORY OF POLITICAL ECONOMY. 2nd ed. Edited by R.D. Collison Black. Reprint ed., Baltimore, Md.: Penguin Books, 1970. 272 p. Paperbound.

This is one of several available editions of this work and includes an informative introduction by Black. The work is concerned primarily with the development and explication of a theory of subjective value. Jevons does not develop a marginal productivity theory of distribution. The author was also an advocate of the use of mathematics in economics, although this work may be understood with a minimal knowledge of mathematics.

398. Marshall, Alfred. "Distribution and Exchange." ECONOMIC JOURNAL

8 (March 1898): 37-59.

Marshall states that the account of distribution and exchange given in the first volume of his PRINCIPLES (he intended to write two or more) holds for the general system of economics. He explicates his views on the nature and limitations of the so-called "statistical" method. His theory is much like that of Irving Fisher (discussed in the next chapter).

399. _____. INDUSTRY AND TRADE. 3rd ed. London: Macmillan, 1932. 874 p.

This work is intended to study the "technical evolution of industry, and its influences on the conditions of man's life and work." MONEY, CREDIT & COMMERCE (see 400) was considered by the author as a companion to this work. The material here does shed light on many of Marshall's concepts that are but superficially covered in his PRINCIPLES (see 404).

400. _____. MONEY, CREDIT & COMMERCE. London: Macmillan, 1923. 369 p.

This constitutes the third volume in a group of works examining the direction of man's efforts for the attainment of material ends. The PRINCIPLES (see 404) emphasized the continuity of the main work of economic studies and INDUSTRY AND TRADE (see 399) was a study of industrial technique and business organization and their influences on various classes and nations. This volume, published one year before Marshall's death, is a study of the influences on the conditions of man's life and work exerted by the resources available for employment--by money and credit and by international trade and social endeavor.

401. _____. OFFICIAL PAPERS. Edited by J[ohn] M[aynard] Keynes. London: Macmillan, 1926. 428 p.

The volume contains all of Marshall's contributions to official enquiries on economic questions, except his work on the Labour Commission. (His work for the Commission could not be identified from that of other contributors.) This is an excellent source of information on Marshall's thinking on many topics.

402. _____. "The Old Generation of Economists and the New." QUARTERLY JOURNAL OF ECONOMICS 2 (January 1897): 115-35.

This article was the author's address to the first meeting of the Cambridge Economic Club. Marshall traces the development of the current economic scene from the first incipient protests against the classical school's methods. The conclusion on methodology indicates that both the inductive and the analytic methods must be used to produce viable economic theory.

403. _____. "On Rent." ECONOMIC JOURNAL 3 (March 1893): 74-90.

This article is an answer to a book by the Duke of Argyll on the topic of rent and value. Although the Duke had criticized both new and old theories, Marshall contends that the Duke's ideas were not substantially different from the "modem" theory of rent. Marshall believed the differences existed in the areas of marginal production, and its relation to the price of the whole output, and the cloudy concept that rent is not a cost of production. The author presents his own views and then relates them to the Duke's.

404. _____. PRINCIPLES OF ECONOMICS. 2 vols. 9th variorum ed. with annotations by C.W. Guillebaud. London: Macmillan, 1961. Vol. I, 858 p.; vol. II, 886 p.

This is the most recent edition of the PRINCIPLES and the first to be edited by someone other than Marshall, who had produced the eighth edition in 1920. Volume I is a reprint of the eighth edition with the exact pagination; volume II contains the editor's notes on the variations in the text from the first to the eighth editions. The PRINCIPLES is the masterwork of a great economist and is viewed by many as the culmination of a line of theoretical development that had begun with A. Smith, was continued by D. Ricardo, and concluded by Marshall. It is a book worth reading for the serious student of economics just as much today as it was in 1920.

405. _____. PURE THEORY OF FOREIGN TRADE AND PURE THEORY OF DOMESTIC VALUES. London: London School of Economics and Political Science, 1930. 64 p.

These two essays, written in 1879, deduce definite conclusions from definite hypothetical premises which should approximate as closely as possible the facts which are to be analyzed by the theory. Marshall believes that the theory of value has two parts: the theory of domestic values and the theory of foreign values. The first article is the development of Marshall's reciprocal demand curve.

406. Pigou, A.C. THE ECONOMICS OF WELFARE. London: Macmillan, 1920. 976 p.

Pigou was a disciple of A. Marshall and the theoretical context of his work is definitely neoclassical. This book was published in at least three more editions in 1924, 1929, and 1932. In the later editions some chapters were deleted and others were added--usually to accomodate other writings of the author. In the first part of this volume, Pigou defines the conditions for greater economic welfare. Parts II through IV are devoted to the analysis of particular ways in which the national dividend is affected, and part V examines the circumstances under which the poor are made better off at the expense of the total dividend. Part VI is concerned with the causes of variability in the national dividend. Parts IV and VI were deleted in the second and subsequent editions.

407. _____. "Equilibrium under Bilateral Monopoly." ECONOMIC JOURNAL 18 (June 1908): 205-20.

The author poses the questions that must be answered for equilibrium to exist. The answers, moreover, allow one to determine the position of the equilibrium, or at least the path along which it could occur. All of the specifications for equilibrium are designated because, without some restriction, bilateral monopoly does not produce a stable equilibrium solution.

408. _____. "The Incidence of Import Duties." ECONOMIC JOURNAL 17 (June 1907): 289-94.

This is a response to Bickerdike's review of Pigou's PROTECTIVE AND PREFERENTIAL TARIFFS in which the reviewer had suggested that Pigou had neglected important indirect effects of a tariff. The author presents a very complete answer to these accusations. The review article appears in this volume on pages 98-102 and Bickerdike's rejoinder to this reply appears on pages 583-85. The dialogue would be of special interest to one interested in the concept of consumers' surplus.

409. _____. "Monopoly and Consumers' Surplus." ECONOMIC JOURNAL 14 (September 1904): 388-94.

This is an excellent article on the effects of discriminating monopoly pricing as it is known today. The conditions necessary for one firm to exercise its monopoly power to control the entire market are also discussed in the second section.

410. _____. "Pure Theory and the Fiscal Controversy." ECONOMIC JOURNAL 14 (March 1904): 29-33.

The author examines six abstract problems which bear indirectly on the practical issue before the country regarding fiscal measures such as the various types of taxes imposed on domestic goods or foreign imports. He hopes to provide some positive implications for these policy decisions.

411. _____. "Some Remarks on Utility." ECONOMIC JOURNAL 13 (March 1903): 58-68.

The dispute over whether utility is a measure of pleasure or desire is the basic point of this essay. The author illustrates that, "for practical purposes . . ., no difficulty is introduced by the change of opinion . . . with reference to pleasure and desire." He analyzes these concepts with respect to the concept of consumers' rent.

412. Ramsey, F.P. "A Contribution to the Theory of Taxation." ECONOMIC JOURNAL 37 (March 1927): 47-61.

Assuming that a given revenue is to be raised by proportionate taxes on some or all uses of income, Ramsey asks how the various rates should be adjusted in order to obtain a minimum decrement of utility. He first uses a perfectly general utility function, then shifts to a quadratic function, and finally treats various special cases. The fourth part contains applications of the theoretical results obtained in the first three parts.

413. _____. "A Mathematical Theory of Saving." ECONOMIC JOURNAL 38 (December 1928): 543-59.

One of the classic articles on saving and, in economics as a whole, this work offers a very rigorous treatment of saving and consumption. A set of criteria are defined for the determination of the saving rate and the amount. Some of Ramsey's concepts, such as the notion of two classes of savers, were incorporated into the growth theory work of post-World War II economists. To fully understand Ramsay's essay, one must be familiar with calculus, although the article is useful for the astute nonmathematical reader as well.

414. Sidgwick, Henry. "The Economic Lessons of Socialism." ECONOMIC JOURNAL 5 (September 1895): 336-46.

The author defines socialism as "the practical doctrine that it is desirable to abolish private property completely or to a great extent, . . . [thereby] increasing the ordinary remuneration of labour . . . [and] producing a greater equality of incomes," and political economy as the theory of the natural and right mode(s) of arranging production, distribution, and exchange of wealth in political or governed societies of humans. This paper concerns the relations between the two and traces the development of socialism from before Quesnay to 1895.

415. _____. THE PRINCIPLES OF POLITICAL ECONOMY. 3rd ed. London: Macmillan, 1901. 599 p.

Sidgwick's intent here was to restate economic doctrines to include newer criticism and suggestions along with traditional theory in an attempt to end unnecessary controversy. He feared that the controversy would obscure sound and valuable aspects of established work. He treats not only theoretical but methodological issues as well in an attempt to demonstrate the need for inductive reasoning to maintain "realism" in the treatment of, for example, policy decisions.

416. Smart, William. AN INTRODUCTION TO THE THEORY OF VALUE. Reprint ed., New York: Augustus M. Kelley, 1966. 104 p.

This is a reprint of the 1910 edition of the 1901 work which builds on the works of Menger, Wieser, and Bohm-Bawerk. Smart defines value as subjective value which depends entirely upon utility, as Jevons had said. His work defines the role of value, especially subjective value, in economic theory, explaining how subjective values are transmitted through objective values to production.

417. Webb, Sidney. "The Rate of Interest and the Laws of Distribution." QUARTERLY JOURNAL OF ECONOMICS 2 (January 1888): 188-208.

This article expresses a viewpoint on the use of the term "rent" and the application of this term to factors other than land, such as labor and capital. He assigns the concept of "economic rent" to the rent discussion for labor and capital. An important aspect of this essay is that the concept of diminishing marginal returns is brought to bear on all three.

418. Wicksteed, Philip H. THE ALPHABET OF ECONOMIC SCIENCE. New York: Kelley & Millman, 1955. 142 p.

This book was an attempt to illustrate and reinforce Jevons's principle of marginal utility. The principles of value are presented in a mathematical structure and the theory of value is divided into two sections--individual and social.

419. _____. THE COMMON SENSE OF POLITICAL ECONOMY AND SELECTED PAPERS AND REVIEWS ON ECONOMIC THEORY. 2 vols. Edited with an introduction by Lionel Robbins. London: Routledge & Kegan Paul, 1957. Reprint ed., New York: Augustus M. Kelley, 1966. 871 p.

A classic in economic theory, this work contains one of the most definitive discussions of marginal productivity theory ever written. Wicksteed also elaborates the methodological implications of the subjective theory of value. Included in these two volumes are six excellent articles and five review articles, along with some other papers of lesser importance.

420. _____. "On Certain Passages in Jevons' 'Theory of Political Economy'." QUARTERLY JOURNAL OF ECONOMICS 3 (April 1889): 293-314.

The author takes as his task the refinement of work of Jevons. He attempts to carry his results "further inward" rather than extending them "further outward." The author does not feel that the theory of Jevons is sufficiently specific to prevent error, especially when used by those lacking expertise in the field of political economy.

421. _____. "The Scope and Method of Political Economy in the Light of the 'Marginal' Theory of Value and Distribution." ECONOMIC JOURNAL 24 (March 1914): 1-23.

This is a brief but well done explication of the concept of subjective value and the exchange and distribution process. The use of the word "marginal" is eschewed until the last few pages, when its connection and meaning are introduced into the concepts previously discussed. The essay is a snapshot view of Wicksteed's distribution theory.

C. COMMENTARIES ON THE MAJOR CONTRIBUTIONS

422. Bailey, Martin J. "The Interpretation and Application of the Compensation Principle." ECONOMIC JOURNAL 64 (March 1954): 39-52.

In response to a statement made by N. Kaldor in this journal in 1939, Bailey here considers the compensation principle in terms of problems deriving from work by Pareto, Marshall, Pigou, and others. This is a good essay in which geometry constitutes the only nonverbal treatment.

423. _____. "The Marshallian Demand Curve." JOURNAL OF POLITICAL ECONOMY 62 (June 1954): 255-61.

The author criticizes Milton Friedman's choice of demand curves for the Marshallian situation. Bailey favors a revised definition of the demand curve to prevent the misunderstanding that Friedman's definition might precipitate. His conclusion is that the choice of demand curves should depend on the problem under analysis.

424. Barucci, Piero. "The Spread of Marginalism in Italy, 1871-1890." HISTORY OF POLITICAL ECONOMY 4 (1972): 232-51.

Barucci maintained that marginalism in Italy had reached maturity by 1890 and was exhibited in the works of the better known Italian writers who followed. The Austrian school was the most widely known and accepted. Jevons's work was translated in 1875 and some of Walras's papers were also translated, but their overall effect was minimal. Maffeo Pantaleoni, the best known marginalist by 1890, put this theory into perspective for the Italian economy.

425. Baur, P.T. "Interest and Quasi-Rent." ECONOMIC JOURNAL 49 (March 1939): 154-57.

This is a comment on recent discussions of interest and the functional distribution of income. The author makes several good points regarding interpretation of interest with respect to capital theory and income distribution.

426. Bernardelli, H. "The End of Marginal Utility Theory?" ECONOMICA n.s. 5 (May 1938): 192-212.

Building on concepts developed in a 1934 article by J.R. Hicks and R.G.D. Allen in the same journal, the author attempts to show that utility theory in the strict sense of neoclassical and Austrian thinking was useless. Comparison of marginal utilities, as practiced by neoclassical and Austrian economists, was not possible without excessively restricting assumptions concerning utility function. He also discusses the problem arising from comparison of intensities of marginal utility.

427. Bharadwaj, Krishna. "Marshall on Pigou's Wealth and Welfare." ECONOMICA n.s. 39 (February 1972): 32-46.

This is the first appearance of the comments that Marshall had written on Pigou's WEALTH AND WELFARE. Marshall had not disclosed them to Pigou, Pigou's wife kept them closed until after her husband's death. The author presents sixteen numbered comments and then discusses these comments and how Pigou and Marshall differed.

428. Black, R.D. Collison. "Jevons, Bentham, and DeMorgan." ECONOMICS n.s. 39 (May 1972): 119-34.

Originally delivered as a lecture at University College, this is an attempt to demonstrate how and when Jevons acquired his utilitarianism and his mathematical rigor. Black concludes that Jevons's utilitarianism derived from his introduction to the works of Bentham by James Martineau and that his mathematical rigor was acquired first hand from attending the lectures of Augustus DeMorgan.

429. _____. "W.S. Jevons and the Foundation of Modern Economics." HISTORY OF POLITICAL ECONOMY 4 (1972): 364-78.

The author examines Jevons's work in terms of the "special qualities" he possessed and how they may have affected his approach to economics. Black also compares Jevons's expectations with the actual course of development in economics.

430. Blaug, Mark. "Was There a Marginal Revolution?" HISTORY OF POLITICAL ECONOMY 4 (1972): 269-80.

Blaug draws a very interesting picture of the emergence of marginalism in the nineteenth century. He believes that, rather than a single event, revolution was merely an evolving process that owed its success to the professionalization of economics. He further contends that there was no multiple discovery of marginalism. Blaug's arguments are persuasive.

431. Bloch, Henri-Simon. "Carl Menger: The Founder of the Austrian School."

JOURNAL OF POLITICAL ECONOMY 48 (June 1940): 428-33.

Written in commemoration of the hundredth anniversary of Menger's birth, this article deals with Menger's methodological writings and the dispute with the German historical school.

432. Bonar, James. "The Austrian Economists and Their View of Value." QUARTERLY JOURNAL OF ECONOMICS 3 (October 1888): 1-31.

This is an excellent survey of the writers and basic theories of the Austrian school. Together with his later discussion of Bohm-Bawerk's "Positive Theory of Capital" (QUARTERLY JOURNAL OF ECONOMICS, vol. 3, April 1889, pp. 336-51), this essay offers an excellent survey of the Austrian school's economics.

433. Boulding, Kenneth. "The Concept of Economic Surplus." AMERICAN ECONOMIC REVIEW 35 (December 1945): 851-69.

This is an analysis of the historical development of the theory of economic surplus. Boulding points out the many pitfalls that are common to this theory. The attributes of the theory and some uses for it are discussed at the close of the article.

434. Breit, William, and Ramson, Roger L. THE ACADEMIC SCRIBBLERS. New York: Holt, Rinehart and Winston, 1971. 275 p. Paperbound.

Chapters 2 and 3 are devoted to the neoclassicists, who are considered the founders of the economic theory that prevailed for the first forty years of the twentieth century. Chapter 2 discusses the founders of the school; chapter 3 is concerned with Alfred Marshall as the exemplar of neoclassicism.

435. Brown, Harry. "Opportunity Cost: Marshall's Criticism of Jevons." AMERICAN ECONOMIC REVIEW 21 (September 1931): 498-500.

This is a rather unorthodox article defending Jevons's position on rent. Brown's approach to the argument, however suspect, does provide an excellent exercise for the student on the concept of opportunity cost and rent theory.

436. Checkland, S.G. "Marshall and the Wages-Wealth Paradox." ECONOMIC JOURNAL 67 (June 1957): 330-33.

The paradox results from Marshall's conclusion that the only way labor could continually increase its well-being was for capital stock to grow at an increasing rate, that is, the principle of diminishing marginal returns was the rationale for rising wages in the aggregate. Checkland questions the possibility of excess saving as described by Keynes.

437. Chipman, John S. "The Nature and Meaning of Equilibrium in Economic Theory." In FUNCTIONALISM IN THE SOCIAL SCIENCES: THE STRENGTH AND LIMITS OF FUNCTIONALISM IN ANTHROPOLOGY, ECONOMICS, POLITICAL SCIENCE, AND SOCIOLOGY, edited by Don Martindale, pp. 35-64. Philadelphia: American Academy of Political and Social Science, 1965.

Between the law of convexity of preferences and the law of economies of production there exists another principle that is necessary to form the connection that allows the process to find an equilibrium. Chipman approaches this third principle in terms of work by three economists: Walras, Edgeworth, and Keynes. The first two are of interest in this section.

438. _____. "A Survey of the Theory of International Trade; Part I: The Classical Theory, and Part II: The Neoclassical Theory." ECONOMETRICA 33 (July 1965): 477-519, (October 1965): 685-760.

In this two-part survey, Chipman covers nearly every marginalist writer who ever said anything noteworthy about international trade. It is an excellent survey that explains very well the interconnections between theorists and theories. There are extensive bibliographies at the end of each part.

439. Coats, A.W. "Alfred Marshall and the Early Development of the London School of Economics: Some Unpublished Letters." ECONOMICA n.s. 34 (November 1967): 408-17.

Letters to W.A.S. Hewins, the first director of the London School of Economics, exhibit Marshall's belief that the new school (in 1895) had tried to underrate the achievements of Cambridge economics. It provides insight on methodology for those interested in academic politics.

440. _____. "The Economic and Social Context of the Marginal Revolution of the 1870's." HISTORY OF POLITICAL ECONOMY 4 (1972): 303-42.

A new hypothesis regarding the development of economics is here offered by Coats. It is one that deals with logic, methodology, personality, and environmental factors--all in combination with one another. The discussion is conducted with an eye toward the "correct" method of studying the growth of a science.

441. _____. "Retrospect and Prospect." HISTORY OF POLITICAL ECONOMY 4 (1972): 603-31.

This article is a postscript summary of the papers presented to the Villa Serbelloni conference on marginalism in 1971. Most of the significant issues that were discussed are commented on by the author. Nearly all of the papers presented at that conference may also be found in this volume of HISTORY OF POLITICAL ECONOMY.

442. deMarchi, N.B. "Mill and Caimes and the Emergence of Marginalism in England." HISTORY OF POLITICAL ECONOMY 4 (1972): 344-78.

The article attempts to answer the question of why Mill and Caimes failed to develop their theoretical structure in the same direction taken by Jevons. Many "partial explanations" exist, but the basis for their failure is their denial, stemming from their Ricardian conception of land and labor, of the application of mathematics to value and distribution theory. Adherence to "appropriate" points of inquiry was also a limiting factor to the two authors.

443. Divine, Thomas F. "The Derivation of the Marshallian Curve from the Paretian Indifference Curves." AMERICAN ECONOMIC REVIEW 33 (March 1943): 125-29.

This note is a geometric and verbal explanation of how a Marshallian "offer" curve may be derived from a set of Paretian indifference curves. Marshallian curves are used in international trade theory to discuss the effects of changes in tariffs, prices, preferences, and income.

444. Dobb, Maurice [H.] THEORIES OF VALUE AND DISTRIBUTION SINCE ADAM SMITH. Cambridge: At the University Press, 1973. 295 p.

A lengthy chapter (forty-five pages) is devoted to the so-called "Jevonian Revolution" in which the author considers Jevons's contributions in the context of work by the other early marginalists as well as work by such classicists as Ricardo and Marx. All aspects of the topic are discussed including the subjective value theory and the lack of a marginal productivity theory distribution. (Also cited in Chapter 2, entry 137.)

445. Dorfman, Robert. "Waiting and the Period of Production." QUARTERLY JOURNAL OF ECONOMICS 73 (August 1959): 351-72.

The paper is concerned with two basic problems of capital theory. The first problem is to refine the intuitive notion of the "quantity of capital," which must be as measurable as labor and land to be useful in economics. The second problem is the question of why capital always gets a positive return even in equilibrium. It is a fairly mathematical article but may be read by one who possesses intermediate theory background.

446. Encarnacion, Jose, Jr. "Consistency between Say's Identity and the Cambridge Equation." ECONOMIC JOURNAL 68 (December 1958): 827-30.

This is a rigorous mathematical proof of the invalidity of proofs by O. Lange and Don Patinkin, which are purported to show that Say's Law and the Cambridge Equation are inconsistent.

Lange's proof may be found in STUDIES IN MATHEMATICAL
ECONOMICS AND ECONOMETRICS, edited by Oscar Lange
et al., pp. 49-68 (University of Chicago Press, 1942);
Patinkin's work appears in his MONEY, INTEREST AND
PRICES (Harper & Row, 1957).

447. Fellner, William. EMERGENCE AND CONTENT OF MODERN ECO-
NOMIC ANALYSIS. New York: McGraw-Hill, 1960. 459 p.

Part 3 contains seven chapters on neoclassical economics and
marginalism in general. It is an excellent treatment of
various aspects of this theory, especially those which differed
most from previous work. None of Fellner's treatment is mathematical.

448. Fraser, L.M. ECONOMIC THOUGHT AND LANGUAGE. London:
Adam and Charles Black, 1937. 411 p.

The book is an attempt to define economic concepts in a logically consistent manner. Fraser's complaint is that existing
theory is logically ambiguous and, consequently, the manner
of presentation rather than substantive economic problems is
the source of most controversy. Fraser's emphasis is on theory
developed by the Austrians and the neoclassicists.

449. Friedman, Milton. "Leon Walras and His Economic System." AMERICAN
ECONOMIC REVIEW 45 (December 1955): 900-909.

In this review of Jaffe's translation of Walras's ELEMENTS OF
PURE ECONOMICS, Friedman places Walras in perspective by
calling his work a "framework for organizing our ideas." The
substantive content of Walras's framework was to come from
the work of economists such as Marshall. But Walras is credited
with providing a context for discussion of the interdependent-
ness of consumer and factor markets.

450. _____. "The Marshallian Demand Curve." JOURNAL OF POLITICAL
ECONOMY 57 (December 1949): 463-74.

The author maintains that, although Marshall did not give an
explicit definition of the demand curve, the current (1949)
definition is not logically consistent with the remaining analysis. The alternative interpretation, to be had from a literal
reading of Marshall, leaves his theory of demand free from in-
consistency and more useful for analysis. He advocates a con-
stant-real-income demand curve instead of the customary con-
stant-other-prices-and-money-incomes demand curve.

451. Georgesu-Roegen, Nicholas St. "Revisiting Marshall's Constancy of Marginal Utility of Money." SOUTHERN ECONOMIC JOURNAL 35 (October
1968): 176-81.

This article considers Marshall's proposition that the marginal utility of money is constant. The author discusses criticism of the proposition and defines the conditions necessary for the proposition to be true. It is a particular circumstance, but may have had special appeal for Marshall. It is a fairly rigorous article but can be read with some effort by the non-mathematically inclined.

452. Goodwin, Craufurd D. "Marginalism Moves to the New World." HISTORY OF POLITICAL ECONOMY 4 (1972): 551-70.

The transfer of the marginalist theory--the emphasis on the place of the individual utility function in the theory of price and the use of precise incremental analysis for studying human behavior and markets--is discussed for economic situations in the United States, Canada, and Australia. Goodwin also devotes a section to the work of other great revolutions in economic thought to determine if there are any similarities from which generalized hypotheses may be made.

453. Grampp, William D. "Giffen's Paradox and the Marshallian Demand Curve." MANCHESTER SCHOOL OF ECONOMIC AND SOCIAL STUDIES 38 (March 1970): 65-71.

In reassessing the meaning of Giffen's paradox in Marshallian demand analysis, Grampp has shown that the paradox is compatible with Friedman's "constant real-income" interpretation of the Marshallian demand curve. This is achieved by viewing the paradox in a methodological and textual context.

454. Gregory, T.E. "Edwin Cannan: A Personal Impression." ECONOMICA n.s. 2 (November 1935): 365-79.

This is an excellent essay on the evangelical critic of both new and old economic theory. Cannan was a contemporary of the neoclassicists, but much of his work was a commentary of their theory, rather than an extension of it. Cannan's service in this area was great and should be appreciated by those who study economics today.

455. Hanson, Bent. A SURVEY OF GENERAL EQUILIBRIUM SYSTEMS. New York: McGraw-Hill, 1970. 238 p.

This survey of systems attempts to show that nearly all general equilibrium systems are of the same family of theory. The works of Walras and Marshall, as well as many variants of neoclassical theory, are discussed with respect to many different topics. This is intermediate level theory but the mathematics is restricted to simple calculus.

456. Hayek, F.A. von. "Carl Menger." ECONOMICA n.s. 1 (November

1934): 393-420.

This biographical study of Menger was written as an introduction to the reprint of Menger's PRINCIPLES. It is an excellent and detailed examination of the man, his work, and the
influence he had on those who came to know him.

457. Hegeland, Hugo. THE QUANTITY THEORY OF MONEY. Reprint ed.,
New York: Augustus M. Kelley, 1969. 262 p.

The book treats in a critical fashion the historical development and interpretations of the quantity theory. Sections deal
with the Cambridge School, and with French and Italian economists. The second part of the book is an attempt to reconcile the
concept of money in the quantity theory (medium of exchange)
with its role in Keynes's GENERAL THEORY (medium of exchange
and a store of value). (Also cited in Chapter 2, entry 150.)

458. Hicks, J.R. "Edgeworth, Marshall, and the Indeterminateness of Wages."
ECONOMIC JOURNAL 40 (June 1930): 215-31.

This work pertains to the possibility, alluded to by Marshall
and Edgeworth, that wages were indeterminant or arbitrary
even in the absence of combinations. The author treats this
situation while ignoring the generally accepted case in which
combination exists and indeterminateness is generally accepted.
A comment on this article, and a reply from J.R. Hicks, appear in the March 1931 issue of this JOURNAL on pages
142-45.

459. _____. "Marginal Productivity and the Principle of Variation." ECO-
NOMICA 12 (February 1932): 79-88.

Hicks reviews the major theories of marginal productivity,
stating what are, for him, the deficiencies in each. He then
constructs his own theory which avoids the problem incurred
by the others. For a comment on this article, see pages 285-
96 and the article by Henry Schultz, both in the same issue.

460. Hicks, J.R., and Weber, W., eds. CARL MENGER AND THE AUSTRI-
AN SCHOOL OF ECONOMICS. Oxford: At the University Press, 1973.
235 p.

All but one of these papers were presented at a symposium in
Vienna in 1971 honoring the hundredth anniversary of Menger's
PRINCIPLES. Nearly every possible topic is covered, and the
list of contributors exhibits a very assorted group of economists.
Some had been students of Menger or of Menger's students,
but most were economists who realized the debt owed to the
Austrian tradition that descends from Carl Menger.

461. Higgs, Henry. "Friedrich von Wieser, 1851-1926." ECONOMICA 7

(June 1927): 150-54.

> This essay was written in memory of von Wieser approximately one year after his death. The author attempts to outline reasons for the recognition due von Wieser for his works in economics. It is a good biographical sketch of the man and his work.

462. Hollander, Jacob H. "The Concept of Marginal Rent." QUARTERLY JOURNAL OF ECONOMICS 9 (January 1895): 175-87.

> This is a treatment of the concept of rent as determined at the margin. Some of the problem stems from an imprecise usage of words such as "rent." The transfer cost of a factor is definitely part of the marginal cost of production, but the price paid for a unit of land will be determined as a residual --a differential between the price of the commodity and the cost of the other factors. It can in fact be viewed from both sides, as a residual or as a marginal.

463. Homan, Paul T. CONTEMPORARY ECONOMIC THOUGHT. New York: Harper & Brothers, 1928. 475 p.

> The book contains detailed essays on both Alfred Marshall and John A. Hobson (180 pages), both of whom were writing around the turn of the century. These essays attempt to analyze the thought of these writers in order to disentangle the confusing uncertainty in economics and to discern whatever constructive leads may exist.

464. Howey, Richard S. "The Origins of Marginalism." HISTORY OF POLITICAL ECONOMY 4 (1972): 281-302.

> This article traces the origin of the word "marginalism" and the origin of the concept. Marginalism first appeared in order to consider value and later was used with respect to productivity. The author develops the concept for each of the founding triumvirate and then more generally accounts for its acceptance by the profession.

465. Hutchison, T.W. "The 'Marginal Revolution' and the Decline and Fall of English Classical Political Economy." HISTORY OF POLITICAL ECONOMY 4 (1972): 442-48.

> Here Hutchison argues that the marginal revolution, if indeed there were such an event, took place only in England, that is, there was really no orthodoxy against which to revolt on the Continent. Furthermore, it was not a unified movement, but rather a group of separate national occurrences.

466. _____. A REVIEW OF ECONOMIC DOCTRINES, 1870-1929. London: Oxford University Press, 1953. 456 p.

Although out of print, this book remains one of the classic works in the history of economic analysis. Part I deals with particular writers and/or schools of thought. Part II, on the other hand, analyzes the theoretical framework of various areas of economic analysis. Most of the second part is concerned with development after World War I, whereas part I examines writers whose works were dated before this war. The analysis is not restricted to any country or school, but is quite diversified.

467. Jaffe, William. "Leon Walras's Role in the 'Marginal Revolution' of the 1870's." HISTORY OF POLITICAL ECONOMY 4 (1972): 379-405.

The author analyzes the role played by Walras in the marginal utility innovation in order that he might later appraise his performance in terms of economic situations that existed during his lifetime. Jaffe concludes that Walras's great contribution was a demonstration of the need for marginal utility analysis in a general equilibrium framework.

468. _____. "Walras' Theory of Tatonnement: A Critique of Recent Interpretations." JOURNAL OF POLITICAL ECONOMY 75 (February 1967): 1-19.

In an effort to correct what the author and Don Patinkin describe as a failure on the part of modern day economists to understand Walras's tatonnement process, Jaffe here explains the process with respect to exchange and production. He does not discuss the application of this process to capital formation and money. According to Jaffe, Walras was criticized for the treatment of issues he never examined.

469. Johnson, Harry G. "Money in a Neo-Classical One-Sector Growth Model." In his ESSAYS IN MONETARY ECONOMICS, pp. 143-78. Cambridge, Mass.: Harvard University Press, 1967.

The author presents a geometrical exposition of the one-sector growth model and uses it to analyze the role of money in such a model. The remaining sections of the article develop various alternatives that arise from relaxation of particular assumptions.

470. Kauder, Emil. A HISTORY OF MARGINAL UTILITY THEORY. Princeton, N.J.: Princeton University Press, 1965. 248 p.

This is a very scholarly work in which all but fifty pages concern marginalist formulations of marginal utility. Kauder is extremely impressed by the work done by the Austrian school. One is also treated to a discussion of the first discoverers of marginal utility such as Bernoulli and Bentham. Every possible aspect of marginal utility, whether justification or application, is considered.

471.   _____. "The Retarded Acceptance of the Marginal Utility Theory."
QUARTERLY JOURNAL OF ECONOMICS 67 (November 1953): 564-75.

The Continental economists were known to have subjective or
utility-oriented value theories before the English. Kauder here
offers one explanation for that chronology, contending that differing religious and philosophical convictions of the thinkers
were the significant factors. It is an interesting hypothesis.

472. Keynes, John Maynard. "Alfred Marshall, 1842-1924." In his ESSAYS IN
BIOGRAPHY, edited by Geoffrey Keynes, pp. 125-217. New ed. with 3
additional essays. New York: W.W. Norton & Co., 1963.

This is an excellent and detailed biographical essay by one of
Marshall's more famous students. Keynes was not only a student but a close friend of the Marshalls due to his father's
position at Cambridge.

473.   _____. "F.P. Ramsey." In his ESSAYS IN BIOGRAPHY, edited by
Geoffrey Keynes, pp. 239-54. New ed. with 3 additional essays. New
York: W.W. Norton & Co., 1963. Paperbound.

Frank Ramsey's economic thought has only been fully understood
in the last decade due to the great rigor of his theoretical
structure. Keynes was a close friend and provides in this essay an excellent account of Ramsey's academic contributions,
both in philosophy and economics.

474.   _____. "F.Y. Edgeworth." In his ESSAYS IN BIOGRAPHY, edited by
Geoffry Keynes, pp. 218-38. New ed. with 3 additional essays. New
York: W.W. Norton & Co., 1963. Paperbound.

This is one of Keynes's well-written essays about a prominent
economist in which he describes much of Edgeworth's family
background as well as his education and character development.
A full accounting of his academic contributions is also presented
along with the comments and opinions of many of his contemporaries.

475. Knight, Frank H. "Marginal Utility Economics." In ENCYCLOPAEDIA
OF THE SOCIAL SCIENCES, vol. 5, edited by E.R.A. Seligman,
pp. 357-63. New York: Macmillan, 1935.

This is an extensive treatment of marginal utility and its effect on economic theory, especially for the various schools.
Relationships between the new theory of value and pricing are
discussed in detail. The reactions against utility theory by
various groups are also discussed. It is an excellent survey
of the topic.

476. Krupp, Sherman Roy, ed. THE STRUCTURE OF ECONOMIC SCIENCE,
ESSAYS ON METHODOLOGY. Englewood Cliffs, N.J.: Prentice-Hall,
1966. 282 p.

This book is relevant here because most current assumptions and logical constructs of economic theory had their origins in marginalism. The discussion of methodology in the book allows the reader to understand the nature of the controversies over theory construction, the inclusion of mathematics, the limitations of the discipline, and the nature of values in economics.

477. Kuenne, Robert E. EUGEN VON BOHM-BAWERK. Columbia Essays on the Great Economists, no. 2. New York: Columbia University Press, 1971. 76 p.

The book is divided into four parts: (1) discussion of Bohm-Bawerk's work in terms of classical and neoclassical theory; (2) discussion of his views on time, capital, and interest; (3) the three extra-economic grounds which are the source of the superiority of present over future goods and the integration of value theory; and (4) the periods of production investment and enjoyment. Parts of this work are presented mathematically, but the reader should be able to grasp most of the content without difficulty.

478. _____. THE THEORY OF GENERAL ECONOMIC EQUILIBRIUM. Princeton, N.J.: Princeton University Press, 1963. 590 p.

Part II of this book (over 300 pages) is devoted to a logical and historical development of the body of neoclassical general equilibrium analysis. It is a very extensive development that requires a fairly strong mathematical background. The author covers both Austrian and neoclassical theorists.

479. Kuhn, W.E. THE EVOLUTION OF ECONOMIC THOUGHT. Cincinnati: South-Western Publishing Co., 1970. 500 p.

This is a general survey text of the field, but the author includes an extensive study of the various marginalists. They are first discussed individually, then in terms of their contributions to particular areas of economic theory. The volume is a useful introduction to the study of either marginalism or the history of economics in general.

480. Lutz, Friedrich A. THE THEORY OF INTEREST. Chicago: Aldine Publishing Co., 1968. 336 p.

In part 1, Lutz discusses Bohm-Bawerk's capital and interest theory as a model for a "stationary economy," considering and criticizing the theory of Leon Walras. There is also a short chapter on the interrelationship between money and interest rates in various theories, including Bohm-Bawerk's and Marshall's. (Also cited in Chapter 6, entry 1010).

481. Lutz, Friedrich A., and Lutz, Vera. THE THEORY OF INVESTMENT OF THE FIRM. Princeton, N.J.: Princeton University Press, 1951. 253 p.

The first four chapters develop definitions and the various tools and relationships necessary for analysis of investment behavior on the part of the firm. The remainder of the book is constructed around the categories of the balance sheet of the firm, although the order of the categories is altered. The discussion usually deals with single valued expectations, but the work does contain a chapter on uncertainty.

482. Macvane, S.M. "Bohm-Bawerk on Value and Wages." QUARTERLY JOURNAL OF ECONOMICS 5 (October 1890): 24-43.

The author is more disturbed by the definition of value and the source of value proffered by Bohm-Bawerk than he is by the discussion of wages and the demise of the wages fund concept. He does not understand how all of these divergent definitions may be combined in a formula to equate the giving and receiving sides of market exchange.

483. _____. "Capital and Interest." QUARTERLY JOURNAL OF ECONOMICS 6 (January 1892): 129-50.

Macvane here attempts to redefine capital so as to exclude wage goods and include only physical capital. He credits Bohm-Bawerk for having called attention to this problem, which Marshall and others had failed to recognize.

484. Majumdar, Tapas. THE MEASUREMENT OF UTILITY. London: Macmillan, 1958. 149 p.

In this treatment of a complex and poorly defined concept in the measurability of utility, Majumdar sets out his definitions of measurability and presents a group of questions that must be resolved. The second part, wherein the author addresses the propositions, or arguments, regarding the nature and significance of utility, is thus made manageable. The framework for his analysis, in other words, renders the analysis itself much clearer and more meaningful.

485. Marget, Arthur W. "Leon Walras and the 'Cash-Balance Approach' to the Problem of the Value of Money." JOURNAL OF POLITICAL ECONOMY 39 (October 1931): 569-600.

Marget attempted to show that there were others along with Marshall who were of equal stature and who were using a sophisticated form of the cash-balance theory, naming Carl Menger and Leon Walras. Marget chose to discuss the latter because of the transition in his thinking and the mathematical clarity of his exposition.

486. Matsuura, Tamotsu. "Marginalism in Japan." HISTORY OF POLITICAL ECONOMY 4 (1972): 533-50.

An attempt is made to demonstrate marginalism by examining
the work of Japanese writers. In fact, there was no revolution in Japan, but a continual evolution of economic doctrines.
Most of their theory was adopted from Western economics.

487. Maxwell, James A. "An Examination of Some Marshallian Concepts."
AMERICAN ECONOMIC REVIEW 19 (December 1929): 626-37.

The author attempts to clear up some conflicting and erroneous
interpretations of Marshall by drawing rigid lines between such
concepts as "normal" and "abnormal" and "long-period" and
"short-period." He concentrates his analysis on the determination of value and market prices.

488. Meek, Ronald L. "Marginalism and Marxism." HISTORY OF POLITICAL
ECONOMY 4 (1972): 449-68.

Although this comparison was made by many earlier writers,
Meek believes that, due to alterations in Marxist theory, new
aspects of comparison may be recognized. Most importantly,
marginalism was based on the general principle of rationality,
which, with associated techniques employed by marginalists,
was the only principle available when the need for an economics of control arose in practice.

489. Mishan, E.J. "Say's Law and Walras' Law Once More." QUARTERLY
JOURNAL OF ECONOMICS 77 (November 1963): 617-25.

The author accomplishes three objectives in this study: (1) he
demonstrates how an ambiguous use of the term "identity" ham-
pers the process of logical deduction; (2) he shows how the
traditional employment of these laws supports the thesis that
identities are superfluous in economic models; and (3) he provides an opportunity for reexamining the original intentions of
Say and Walras in terms of the propositions attributed to them.

490. Mitchell, Wesley C. TYPES OF ECONOMIC THEORY. Vol. II. Edited by Joseph Dorfman. New York: Augustus M. Kelley, 1969. 875 p.

Written by one of the United States' best known institutionalists, this is an extensive account of the entire marginalist movement, both in England and Austria. The author discusses the
three founders of marginalism and then treats separately Alfred
Marshall and F. von Wieser. There is also a chapter on Gustav Cassel, one of the Swedish economists.

491. Moss, Laurence S. "Isaac Butt and the Early Development of the Marginal Utility Theory of Imputation." HISTORY OF POLITICAL ECONOMY
5 (Fall 1973): 317-38.

Butt combined the technical apparatus of Longfield with the
general utility orientation of Say to form an early version of

what would later become the marginal utility theory of imputation. His work was not noticed by later theorists in their
searches for earlier versions of their theories of imputation.

492. Myint, Hla. THEORIES OF WELFARE ECONOMICS. New York: Augustus M. Kelley, 1965. 240 p.

In approximately 110 pages and five chapters, Myint discusses
the various aspects of marginalism and subjective value. Studies
of the concept of general optimum neoclassical welfare economics, Marshall's surplus analysis, and Pigou's ECONOMICS
OF WELFARE are included. These discussions are focused on the
English neoclassicists, but the Lausanne school as represented
by Pareto, one of the foremost theorists in welfare economics,
is considered. (Also cited in Chapter 2, entry 170.)

493. Myrdal, Gunnar. THE POLITICAL ELEMENT IN THE DEVELOPMENT OF
ECONOMIC THEORY. Translated from the German by Paul Streeten.
Cambridge, Mass.: Harvard University Press, 1954. 248 p.

The author attempts to provide the reader with an account of
the role of political speculation in the development of economic theory. In particular, he discusses the neoclassical theory
of value, economic liberalism, and social value concepts in a
political context. (Also cited in Chapter 2, entry 171.)

494. Nell, Edward J. "Wicksell's Theory of Circulation." JOURNAL OF
POLITICAL ECONOMY 75 (August 1967): 386-94.

This article describes Wicksell's "cumulative process" which
was based on the idea that the price level will be constant
if the natural rate of interest equals the money rate. The
model is described and found unacceptable in terms of its usefulness for growth theory.

495. Newman, Philip C., et al., eds. SOURCE READINGS IN ECONOMIC
THOUGHT. New York: W.W. Norton & Co., 1954. 762 p.

This is a collection of excerpts from the works of various major
writers. Included from the neoclassical and Austrian groups are
works by Carl Menger, Friedrich von Wieser, W.S. Jevons,
Alfred Marshall, A. Cournot, Leon Walras, Vilfredo Pareto,
and Knut Wicksell. Some of the excerpts are from their better
known writings, but many are from more obscure works.
(Also cited in Chapter 3, entry 305.)

496. Noller, Carl W. "Jevons on Cost." SOUTHERN ECONOMIC JOUR-
NAL 39 (July 1972): 113-15.

This note examines the concept of the "alternative product
theory" of cost in Jevons's writings. The author argues that
Frank Knight has misrepresented Jevons's second theory of cost,

the first theory being his objective theory of cost.

497. Ohlin, Bertil. "Some Notes on the Stockholm Theory of Savings and Investment, Parts I & II." ECONOMIC JOURNAL 47 (March 1937): 53-69, (June 1937): 221-40.

Part I outlines the framework of the Stockholm school and compares it with Keynes's GENERAL THEORY. Part II contains critiques of Keynes's theory from the viewpoint of the Swedish school. The Swedish school was primarily neoclassical, as was much of Keynes's theory.

498. Pantaleoni, M. "An Attempt to Analyze the Concepts of 'Strong and Weak' in Their Economic Connection." ECONOMIC JOURNAL 8 (June 1898): 183-205.

Pantaleoni's discussion of the sociological concepts of "strong" and "weak" in terms of their effect on actual economic occurrences centers around the problem of unequal economic power in the market place and the effects this may have on the efficient functioning of the system.

499. Petridis, Anastasios. "Alfred Marshall's Attitudes to the Economic Analysis of Trade Unions: A Case of Anomalies in a Competitive System." HISTORY OF POLITICAL ECONOMY 5 (Spring 1973): 165-98.

Marshall, an acknowledged sympathizer with the laborers, was aware of the uneven power balance between employer and employee. His attitude toward labor unions, originally favorable, became disapproving. Petridis charges that Marshall never considered any other theoretical construct to fill the gap between the competitive and monopoly models.

500. Pigou, A.C. ALFRED MARSHALL AND CURRENT ECONOMIC THOUGHT. London: Macmillan, 1953. 85 p.

The first section contains six lectures that Marshall delivered in 1952. Topics are: mathematical methods, statistics, elasticities, the rate of interest, utilities, and developments toward socialism. The second part of Pigou's volume is devoted to an examination of the application of the principles of the national balancing accounts as they are drawn up for a particular year and compared with other years.

501. Robbins, Lionel. "The Place of Jevons in the History of Economic Thought." MANCHESTER SCHOOL OF ECONOMIC AND SOCIAL STUDIES 7 (1936): 1-17.

In this centenary biographical sketch of Jevons as an economist and an intellectual, Robbins states that, although most scholars are concerned primarily with Jevons's theory, his major contribution was to applied economics and economic policy. Examples offered are THE COAL QUESTION and THE SERIOUS FALL IN THE VALUE OF GOLD.

502. Robertson, D.H. "Utility and All That." In his UTILITY AND ALL THAT, AND OTHER ESSAYS, pp. 13-41. London: George Allen & Unwin, 1952. Reprint ed., New York: August M. Kelley, 1966.

This article surveys the extant utility theory of the post-World War II years and compares it with the theories of Pigou, Marshall, Pareto, and others. Robertson's work is basically a reappraisal of the measurability controversy in utility theory.

503. Robinson, Joan. ECONOMIC PHILOSOPHY. Chicago: Aldine Publishing Co., 1963. 150 p.

Robinson includes a chapter on "The Classics: Value" and "The Neo-Classics: Utility" in which she covers most of the English neoclassicists as well as Walras, and includes a brief mention of Wicksell. Her discussion of the development of the theory is quite critical.

504. _____. "Euler's Theorem and the Problem of Distribution." ECONOMIC JOURNAL 44 (September 1934): 398-414. Reprinted in her COLLECTED ECONOMIC PAPERS, vol. I, pp. 1-19. Oxford: Basil Blackwell, 1966.

This article is a discussion of the so-called "adding-up problem" that troubled theorists throughout the neoclassical period. Euler was a mathematician who stated the conditions under which payments to productive factors would exhaust the output. The author recounts the positions taken in this dispute by the neoclassical and Austrian economists. She then discusses possible variations and generalizations that may be introduced. It is a satirical comment on those who believe that a proposition can be 'mathematically correct' and yet not true.

505. Rolph, Earl. "The Discounted Marginal Productivity Doctrine." JOURNAL OF POLITICAL ECONOMY 47 (August 1949): 542-56.

Although this discussion deals with a revision of an Austrian marginalist school controversy, it is conducted generally in terms of more recent writers. It would be a useful reading for one who had read the ideas of Bohm-Bawerk and Wicksell on this concept, which is a product of the belief that labor and/or land are the productive factors.

506. Schultz, Henry. "Marginal Productivity and the Lausanne School." ECONOMICA 12 (August 1932): 285-96.

In this response to an article by J.R. Hicks, which appeared in

ECONOMICA earlier in the year (see pages 79-88), Schultz states forcefully that Hicks has committed various errors in interpreting Walras and Pareto. In a "Reply," (pages 297-300), Hicks intimates that Schultz has in fact misunderstood what he had written in the original article. The three items constitute an excellent discussion of some problems involved in marginal productivity theory.

507. Schumpeter, Joseph Aloiso. "Alfred Marshall's Principles: A Semi-Centennial Appraisal." AMERICAN ECONOMIC REVIEW 31 (June 1941): 236-48.

The author points out that, although Marshall's analytical apparatus is obsolete, his methodology and the tools he developed to cope with various problems are still useful today. Marshall's establishment of the use of statistical methods and data to manipulate his theories was and is one of his greatest legacies to modern economists. The article gives specific accounts of these and other attributes of Marshall and his work.

508. _____. TEN GREAT ECONOMISTS, FROM MARX TO KEYNES. New York: Oxford University Press, 1965. 305 p.

In five chapters (pages 74-220), Schumpeter presents detailed analyses of the lives and work of five major economists from the marginalist movement: Walras, Menger, Marshall, Pareto, and Bohm-Bawerk. Schumpeter was either a contemporary or a student of each of the five. (Also cited in Chapter 6, entry 1012.)

509. Shackle, G.L.S. "Marginalism: The Harvest." HISTORY OF POLITICAL ECONOMY 4 (1972): 587-602.

The nature of marginalist thought is discussed at some length and the presuppositions of marginalism are examined. The last section of the essay is concerned with marginalism and measurement, especially measurement of value.

510. Shirras, G. Findlay. "The Pareto Law and the Distribution of Income." ECONOMIC JOURNAL 45 (December 1935): 663-81.

Shirras applies Pareto's Law to tax and income data for India in an effort to determine whether Pareto's Law is an analytical law, an empirical law, or not a law at all. In a response to Shirras's essay ("The Pareto Law and the Distribution of Income in India," ECONOMIC JOURNAL, vol. 46, March 1936, pp. 168-71), B.P. Adarkar and S.N. Sen Gupta contend that, although Shirras's data does not disprove the Law, many data sets do and the Law must be considered empirical.

511. Shove, G.F. "The Place of Marshall's Principles in the Development of Economic Theory." ECONOMIC JOURNAL 52 (December 1942): 284-329.

In this essay written on the centenary of Marshall's birth, Shove draws many new--or at least unusual--conclusions from his reading of Marshall's PRINCIPLES. He traces a line of theoretical progression going back through Ricardo to Smith and shows that Marshall filled in missing parts in Ricardo's value and distribution theory. Shove's thesis is more common-ly accepted today than it was in 1942.

512. Smithies, Arthur S. "The Austrian Theory of Capital in Relation to Par-tial Equilibrium Theory." QUARTERLY JOURNAL OF ECONOMICS 50 (November 1935): 117-50.

This paper is a supplement to the Austrian theory of capital. First, it attempts to define precisely the role of durable goods in the roundabout process of production. Second, Smithies analyzes the concept of time in the production process from the viewpoint of the entrepreneur and his production function. He also examines the effect on employment and prices of small changes in the rate of interest.

513. Spengler, Joseph J. "Exogenous and Endogenous Influences in the For-mation of Post-1870 Economic Thought: A Sociology of Knowledge Ap-proach." In EVENTS, IDEOLOGY AND ECONOMIC THEORY, edited by Robert V. Eagly, pp. 159-205. Detroit: Wayne State University Press, 1968.

The essay is concerned more with "how economists do what they do," or how they behave as economic scientists and anal-ysts, than it is with what economists do or to what purposes they apply economics. Spengler asks whether economic thought moves from one theoretical structure to another or is developed in response to external occurrences in the environment.

514. _____. "The Marginal Revolution and Concern with Economic Growth." HISTORY OF POLITICAL ECONOMY 4 (1972): 469-511.

This is an essay concerning post-1860 marginalist thought about economic growth and development in which Spengler contends that theirs was not a formal theory of growth. Both the pre-marginalist and marginalist writers are discussed in terms of factors bearing upon growth at the aggregate or individual level, sources of physical constraint upon development, and institutional factors. After discussing the premarginalists (classi-cal, early marginalists, historicists, and Marxists), Spengler con-siders Jevons, Wicksteed, the Austrians, and Walras, and, in an "Aftermath," relates these writers to Marshall, J.B. Clark, Hayek, Wicksell, and others.

515. Stigler, George J. "The Adoption of the Marginal Utility Theory." HIS-TORY OF POLITICAL ECONOMY 4 (1972): 571-86.

The first section discusses early utility theories developed before the end of the Napoleonic Wars. Although the theory of utility was successfully utilized in economics by Menger, Jevons, and Walras, the effective adoption of the theory comes much later. This essay provides an explanation for the retarded development and adoption of utility theory in economics.

516. _____. "The Development of Utility Theory." JOURNAL OF POLITICAL ECONOMY 58 (August 1950): 307-27, (October 1950): 373-96.

Stigler traces the development of utility theory from Adam Smith to the most recent discoveries in economic analysis--including the abandonment of utility. It is a rigorous essay, requiring basic mathematical skills. The article has been reprinted in many sources, including Stigler's ESSAYS IN THE HISTORY OF ECONOMICS (University of Chicago Press, 1965) and LANDMARKS IN POLITICAL ECONOMY, edited by Earl J. Hamilton et al. (University of Chicago Press, 1962).

517. _____. "The Economics of Carl Menger." JOURNAL OF POLITICAL ECONOMY 45 (April 1937): 229-50.

Acknowledging that Menger's writings fall into three major categories, Stigler elects to deal only with economic theory, ignoring methodology and currency. All of the major theoretical areas--production, imputation, distribution, and value theory--are discussed in a critical manner.

518. _____. "Perfect Competition, Historically Contemplated." JOURNAL OF POLITICAL ECONOMY 65 (February 1957): 1-16.

The evolution of the term "competition" and its usage in modern theory are examined. Although many early economists discussed competition, it was not until about 1871 that the concept was given systematic attention. This article discusses the mathematical economists, Marshall, and the more modern formulators, Clark and Knight.

519. _____. PRODUCTION AND DISTRIBUTION THEORIES. New York: Agathon Press, 1968. 392 p.

This is a critical analysis of the development of the modern theory of productivity and distribution. Although subjective value theory was developed in the 1870s, the marginal productivity theory did not arrive until the 1890s. This study treats all of the prominent theorists of both the Austrian and neoclassical schools who wrote on the concept of marginal productivity and distribution. It is an extremely rigorous work, although there is a minimal amount of mathematics. The works covered include those of Walras and Wicksell.

520. Streissler, Erich. "To What Extent Was the Austrian School Marginalist?" HISTORY OF POLITICAL ECONOMY 4 (1972): 426-41.

Streissler contends that marginalism was not the essence of the Austrians endeavors. Unlike marginalists or neoclassicists, according to Streissler, the Austrians, and especially Menger, were developing an "information theory" or economic theory under uncertainty. Whereas the marginalists did not focus on the restraints of maximization, but merely on objective functions and choice variables, the Austrians were very much concerned with restraints or changes in restraints. Marginalism is labeled as "decision theory."

521. Sweezy, Paul M. "Fabian Political Economy." JOURNAL OF POLITICAL ECONOMY 57 (June 1949): 242-48.

Sweezy analyzes the FABIAN ESSAYS IN SOCIALISM and finds the economic theory therein not Marxian, but a mixture of Ricardian and Jevonian theory, utilizing Jevons's value theory. The economic essays in FABIAN ESSAYS were written by Sidney Webb and G.B. Shaw, the latter having been converted to the utility school by Philip Wicksteed. Sweezy's essay is primarily a lament over the lack of a coherent general theory, such as the one inherent in Marxism, in Fabian socialism.

522. Tarascio, Vincent J. "Paretian Welfare Theory: Some Neglected Aspects." JOURNAL OF POLITICAL ECONOMY 77 (January/February 1969): 1-20.

The major purpose of the study is to "analyze the distinction between Pareto's 'ophelimity' and 'utility' theories." Essentially the distinction is made at the methodological level, with respect to Pareto's views on scope. "Ophelimity" was satisfaction derived from an economic source, whereas "utility" was satisfaction derived from any source. The concept of scope concerns the nature and delimiting characteristics of the source.

523. _____. PARETO'S METHODOLOGICAL APPROACH TO ECONOMICS. Chapel Hill: University of North Carolina Press, 1968. 153 p.

Beginning with the premise that "failure to understand an author's views on scope and method often results in a failure to understand the economic doctrines themselves," Tarascio examines the method and scope of Pareto. All approaches to the study of the history of economics are considers as complements, rather than as an aggregate of opposing doctrines. This study attempts to evaluate Pareto's position on the methodological issues of his time. His views may be expressed in the context of the polemic that took place between the German historical economists and the advocates of traditional economic theory.

524. _____. "Vilfredo Pareto and Marginalism." HISTORY OF POLITICAL ECONOMY 4 (1972): 406-25.

This article attempts to examine those parts of Pareto's methodology relevant to marginalism and to relate his methodology to his economic theories. Tarascio concludes that Pareto generalized economic theory to the extent that he may be regarded as the bridge between the marginal utility theorists and modern economists. Pareto even extended marginalism into sociology. Pareto supposedly felt, as does the author, that through marginalism economics gained rigor but lost scope.

525. Taussig, F.W. WAGES AND CAPITAL. London and New York: Macmillan, 1896. 329 p.

Taussig developed his own theory of wages and capital (considered in the next chapter), and then criticized relevant contemporary work by both American and European economists. The Europeans included Jevons, Menger, Bohm-Bawerk, and Gossen. Although Taussig's work is one of the key books in capital theory, it does not rank among the most highly recommended for discussions of neoclassicist and Austrian economists. (Also cited in Chapter 5, entry 752.)

526. Uhr, Carl G. ECONOMIC DOCTRINES OF KNUT WICKSELL. Berkeley: University of California Press, 1962. 356 p.

This study, intended to be a systematic account and evaluation of Wicksell's scientific contributions as a whole, is a very thorough examination of the Swedish master's works in all major areas. A twelve-page bibliography of Wicksell's works is included.

527. _____. "Knut Wicksell--A Centennial Evaluation." AMERICAN ECONOMIC REVIEW 41 (December 1951): 829-60.

Wicksell, trained as a mathematician, is described as having brought to economics a methodology which, he was convinced, would supersede the sterile empiricism of the German historical school. Wicksell also believed that his method exposed the doctrinaire extravagances of the harmony economists and their Manchester followers, as well as their bitter opponents, the Marxist socialists. Uhr builds on the methodology and social reform characteristics of Wicksell's work in describing his approach to economics.

528. Valk, Wilhelm L. THE PRINCIPLES OF WAGES. London: P.S. King & Son, 1928. 139 p.

This work examines the theories of wages advanced by the Austrian school, von Wieser, Walras, and those who used the marginal productivity theory of distribution. The treatment is critical and the conclusion is that "the theory of wages of the future must find its basis in the synthesis of the theories of Prof. Clark and those of the School of Walras and Prof. Cassel...."

529. Veblen, Thorstein. "Bohm-Bawerk's Definition of Capital, and the Source of Wages." QUARTERLY JOURNAL OF ECONOMICS 6 (January 1892): 247-50.

The author does not in essence attack Bohm-Bawerk's theory and definition of capital but merely supplements it, stating that, from the production side, wages are capital. Veblen draws a further distinction between "wages" and the "laborers' share of consummable goods"--earnings.

530. Viner, Jacob. "Marshall's Economics, in Relation to the Man and to His Times." AMERICAN ECONOMIC REVIEW 31 (June 1941): 223-35.

The article attempts to discuss the effect of ethics on Marshall's economic thought and his methods of approach to various topics. Marshall's attitudes concerning the use of mathematics in economics are also discussed.

531. Walker, Francis A. "Dr. Bohm-Bawerk's Theory of Interest." QUARTERLY JOURNAL OF ECONOMICS 6 (July 1892): 399-416.

Walker criticizes Bohm-Bawerk on four main points: (1) the way in which he treated the myriad of writers and their different interest theories; (2) Bohm-Bawerk's "removal" of capital from its traditional role in production and as a source of interest; (3) the use of "undervaluation of the future" as the source of interest; and (4) Bohm-Bawerk's contention that value comes only from the consumption side and not from production.

532. Winch, Donald. "Marginalism and the Boundaries of Economic Science." In THE MARGINAL REVOLUTION IN ECONOMICS, edited by R.D. Collison Black, A.W. Coats, and Craufurd D. Goodwin, pp. 59-77. Durham, N.C.: Duke University Press, 1973.

Winch examines the statements of the earlier marginalists and ascertains that these writers narrowed the scope of economics. The movement from classical to neoclassical economics did not entail any abrupt shifts in thinking, but merely variations in emphasis. Winch is one who believes there was no revolution, but rather an evolution of economic theory.

533. Wolfe, J.N. "Marshall and the Trade Cycle." OXFORD ECONOMIC PAPERS 8 (February 1956): 90-101.

Many have argued that Marshall neglected the crisis and trade cycle problem; on the contrary, Wolfe writes, Marshall emphasized the effects of price changes whereas Keynes and other later writers did not.

534. Wu, Chi-Yuen. AN OUTLINE OF INTERNATIONAL PRICE THEORIES.
London: Routledge & Kegan Paul, 1939. Reprint ed., Nendeln, Liechtenstein: Kraus-Thompson, 1970. 373 p.

Wu does not devote individual sections to various schools, but
addresses particular questions and, in so doing, discusses the work
of several neoclassicists as well as some members of the Swedish
or American schools. The book covers most of the major controversies in international trade theory that were precipitated by
the transition to the neoclassical way of thinking. (Also cited
in Chapter 1, entry 60, and Chapter 2, entry 198.)

535. Young, Allyn A. "Marshall on Consumer's Surplus in International Trade."
QUARTERLY JOURNAL OF ECONOMICS 39 (November 1924): 144-50.

Young attempts to demonstrate that Marshall made an error in
his analysis of a numerical example in his MONEY, CREDIT
& COMMERCE and considers some of the more general aspects
of the problem. Young claims that Marshall lost sight of some
of his self-imposed limitations for analysis, an error that might
have been avoided if Marshall had employed more mathematics.
The discussion also considers the problem of interpreting consumers' surplus.

536. Zimmerman, Carle C. "Ernst Engel's Law of Expenditures for Food."
QUARTERLY JOURNAL OF ECONOMICS 47 (November 1932): 78-101.

Zimmerman contends that most uses of Engel's Law are incorrect
and, consequently, lead to erroneous policy prescriptions. He
provides an accurate statement of the Law and assesses the
theoretical implications that result from a correct definition.
As an analytic tool, the Law is limited, since the same quantitative changes produce different percentages at different income scales.

D. CONTRIBUTIONS OF LESSER IMPORTANCE

537. Amano, Akihivo. "Stability Conditions in the Pure Theory of International Trade: A Rehabilitation of the Marshallian Approach." QUARTERLY
JOURNAL OF ECONOMICS 82 (May 1968): 326-39.

538. Aoki, Masahiko. "A Note on Marshallian Process under Increasing Returns." QUARTERLY JOURNAL OF ECONOMICS 84 (February 1970):
100-112.

539. Black, J. "Optimum Savings Reconsidered, or Ramsey without Tears."
THE ECONOMIC JOURNAL 72 (June 1962): 360-66.

540. Bowley, A.L. "Does Mathematical Analysis Explain? A Note on Consumer's Surplus." ECONOMICA 4 (June 1924): 135-39.

541. Cannan, Edwin. "Alfred Marshall 1842-1924." ECONOMICA 4 (November 1924): 257-61.

542. _____. "The Demand for Labour." THE ECONOMIC JOURNAL 42 (September 1932): 357-70.

543. _____. "The Division of Income." QUARTERLY JOURNAL OF ECONOMICS 19 (May 1905): 341-69.

544. _____. "The Future of Gold in Relation to Demand." THE ECONOMIC JOURNAL 44 (June 1934): 177-87.

545. _____. "Limitation of Currency or Limitation of Credit?" THE ECONOMIC JOURNAL 34 (March 1924): 52-64.

546. Cassel, Gustav. "Further Observation on the World's Monetary Problem." THE ECONOMIC JOURNAL 30 (March 1920): 39-45.

547. _____. "The Treatment of Price Problems." THE ECONOMIC JOURNAL 38 (December 1923): 589-92.

548. Clay, Henry. "Dr. Cannan's Views on Unemployment." THE ECONOMIC JOURNAL 40 (June 1930): 331-35.

549. Crew, Michael, and Kleindorfer, Paul. "Marshall and Turvey on Peak Load or Joint Product Pricing." JOURNAL OF POLITICAL ECONOMY 79 (November/December 1971): 1369-77.

550. Dobb, Maurice H. "The Entrepreneur Myth." ECONOMICA 4 (February 1924): 66-81.

551. Downey, E.H. "The Futility of Marginal Utility." JOURNAL OF POLITICAL ECONOMY 18 (April 1910): 253-68.

552. Edgeworth, F.Y. "Applications of Probabilities to Economics, Parts I & II." ECONOMIC JOURNAL 20 (June 1910): 284-304, (September 1910): 441-65.

553. _____. "Appreciation of Gold." QUARTERLY JOURNAL OF ECONOMICS 3 (January 1889): 153-69.

554. _____. "Appreciations of Mathematical Theories, Parts I-IV." THE ECONOMIC JOURNAL 17 (June 1907): 221-31, (December 1907): 524-31; 18 (September 1908): 392-403, (December 1908): 541-56.

555. _____. "Contributions to the Theory of Railway Rates, Parts I-IV."
THE ECONOMIC JOURNAL 21 (September 1911): 347-70, (December
1911): 551-71; 22 (June 1912): 198-218; 23 (June 1913): 206-26.

556. _____. "Recent Contributions to Mathematical Economics, Parts I & II."
THE ECONOMIC JOURNAL 25 (March 1915): 36-63, (June 1915): 189-
203.

557. _____. "The Revised Doctrine of Marginal Social Product." THE ECO-
NOMIC JOURNAL 35 (March 1925): 30-39.

558. _____. "The Subjective Element in the First Principles of Taxation."
QUARTERLY JOURNAL OF ECONOMICS 24 (May 1910): 459-70.

559. _____. "The Theory of Distribution." QUARTERLY JOURNAL OF ECO-
NOMICS 18 (February 1904): 159-219.

560. Ekelund, Robert B., Jr. "Jules Dupuit and the Early Theory of Marginal
Cost Pricing." JOURNAL OF POLITICAL ECONOMY 76 (May/June
1968): 462-71.

561. Englund, Eric. "Gustav Cassel's Autobiography." QUARTERLY JOUR-
NAL OF ECONOMICS 57 (May 1943): 466-93.

562. Fowaker, Lawrence E. "The Cambridge Didactic Style." JOURNAL OF
POLITICAL ECONOMY 66 (February 1958): 65-73.

563. Georgesu-Roegen, Nicholas St. "Note on a Proposition of Pareto." QUAR-
TERLY JOURNAL OF ECONOMICS 49 (August 1935): 706-14.

564. Gifford, C.H.P. "The Concept of the Length of the Period of Production." THE ECONOMIC JOURNAL 43 (December 1933): 611-18.

565. Gregory, T.E. "Recent Theories of Currency Reform." ECONOMICS 4
(June 1924): 163-75.

566. Guillebaud, C.W. "The Evolution of Marshall's PRINCIPLES OF ECO-
NOMICS." THE ECONOMIC JOURNAL 52 (December 1942): 330-49.

567. Hague, D.C. "Alfred Marshall and the Competitive Firm." THE ECO-
NOMIC JOURNAL 68 (December 1950): 673-90.

568. Harrison, R. "Two Early Articles by Alfred Marshall." THE ECONOMIC
JOURNAL 73 (September 1963): 422-30.

569. Harrod, R.F. "Walras: A Re-Appraisal." THE ECONOMIC JOURNAL 66 (June 1956): 307-16.

570. Hicks, J.R. "Marshall's Third Rule: A Further Comment." OXFORD ECONOMIC PAPERS n.s. 13 (October 1961): 262-65.

571. Hirshleifer, J.A. "A Note on the Bohm-Wicksell Theory of Interest." REVIEW OF ECONOMIC STUDIES 34 (April 1967): 98.

572. Hollond, M. Tappan. "Marshall on Rent: A Reply to Professor Ogilvie." THE ECONOMIC JOURNAL 40 (September 1930): 369-83.

573. Holmes, James M. "The Purchasing-Power-Parity Theory: In Defense of Gustav Cassel as a Modern Theorist." JOURNAL OF POLITICAL ECONOMY 75 (October 1967): 686-95.

574. Hotelling, Harold. "Edgeworth's Taxation Paradox and the Nature of Demand and Supply Functions." JOURNAL OF POLITICAL ECONOMY 40 (October 1932): 577-616.

575. Johnson, Shirley B., and Mayer, Thomas. "An Extension of Sidgwick's Equity Principle." QUARTERLY JOURNAL OF ECONOMICS 76 (August 1962): 454-63.

576. Kauder, Emil. "Genesis of the Marginal Utility Theory." THE ECONOMIC JOURNAL 63 (September 1953): 638-50.

577. Kemp, Murray C. "Note on a Marshallian Conjecture." QUARTERLY JOURNAL OF ECONOMICS 80 (August 1966): 481-84.

578. MacGregor, D.H. "Pareto's Law." THE ECONOMIC JOURNAL 46 (March 1936): 80-87.

579. Malmgren, H.B. "How Long Is the Long Run?" THE ECONOMIC JOURNAL 70 (June 1960): 412-15.

580. Maxwell, James A. "Some Marshallian Concepts, Especially the Representative Firm." THE ECONOMIC JOURNAL 68 (December 1958): 691-98.

581. Melitz, J. "Sidgwick's Theory of International Values." THE ECONOMIC JOURNAL 73 (September 1963): 431-41.

582. Mixter, Charles W. "Bohm-Bawerk on Rae." QUARTERLY JOURNAL OF ECONOMICS 16 (May 1902): 385-412.

583. Montgomery, Arthur. "Gustav Cassel: 1866-1945." THE ECONOMIC JOURNAL 57 (December 1947): 532-42.

584. Newman, Peter. "The Erosion of Marshall's Theory of Value." QUAR-TERLY JOURNAL OF ECONOMICS 74 (November 1960): 587-600.

585. Nichol, A.J. "Edgeworth's Theory of Duopoly Price." THE ECONOMIC JOURNAL 45 (March 1935): 51-66.

586. Niehaus, Jurg. "The Neoclassical Dichotomy as a Controlled Experiment." JOURNAL OF POLITICAL ECONOMY 77 (July/August 1969): 504-11.

587. Ogilvie, F.W. "Marshall on Rent." THE ECONOMIC JOURNAL 40 (March 1930): 1-24.

588. Ohlin, Bertil. "Tendencies in Swedish Economics." JOURNAL OF POLITICAL ECONOMY 35 (June 1927): 343-63.

589. Opie, Redvers. "Marshall's Time Analysis." THE ECONOMIC JOUR-NAL 41 (June 1931): 199-215.

590. Parsons, Talcott. "Economics and Sociology: Marshall in Relation to the Thought of His Time." QUARTERLY JOURNAL OF ECONOMICS 46 (February 1932): 316-47.

591. _____. "Wants and Activities in Marshall." QUARTERLY JOURNAL OF ECONOMICS 46 (November 1931): 101-40.

592. Patinkin, Don. "Wicksell's 'Cumulative Process'." THE ECONOMIC JOURNAL 62 (December 1952): 835-47.

593. Pigou, A.C. "The Burden of War and Future Generations." QUARTER-LY JOURNAL OF ECONOMICS 33 (February 1919): 242-55.

594. _____. "Producers' and Consumers' Surplus." THE ECONOMIC JOUR-NAL 20 (September 1910): 358-70.

595. _____. "The Value of Money." QUARTERLY JOURNAL OF ECO-NOMICS 32 (November 1917): 38-65.

596. Pole, David. "Pareto and the Compensating Principle--A Note." THE ECONOMIC JOURNAL 65 (March 1955): 156-57.

597. Pursell, G. "Unity in the Thought of Alfred Marshall." QUARTERLY

JOURNAL OF ECONOMICS 72 (November 1958): 588-600.

598. Robbins, Lionel. "The Economic Works of Philip Wicksteed." ECO-
NOMICA 10 (November 1930): 245-58.

599. Seligman, E.R.A. "Social Elements in the Theory of Value." QUAR-
TERLY JOURNAL OF ECONOMICS 15 (May 1901): 321-47.

600. Shove, G.F. "Varying Costs and Marginal Net Products." THE ECO-
NOMIC JOURNAL 38 (June 1928): 258-66.

601. Smith, J.G. "Some Nineteenth Century Irish Economists." ECONOMI-
CA n.s. 2 (February 1935): 21-32.

602. Stigler, George. "Production and Distribution in the Short Run." JOUR-
NAL OF POLITICAL ECONOMY 47 (June 1939): 305-27.

603. Taussig, F.W. "Alfred Marshall." QUARTERLY JOURNAL OF ECO-
NOMICS 39 (November 1924): 1-14.

604. Timberlake, Richard H., Jr. "Mr. Shaw and His Critics: Monetary
Policy in the Golden Era Reviewed." QUARTERLY JOURNAL OF ECO-
NOMICS 77 (February 1963): 40-54.

605. Walker, Donald A. "Leon Walras in the Light of His Correspondence
and Related Papers." JOURNAL OF POLITICAL ECONOMY 78 (July/
August 1970): 685-701.

606. Walsh, C.M. "Shaw's History of Currency." QUARTERLY JOURNAL OF
ECONOMICS 10 (July 1896): 431-54.

607. Wicksteed, Philip H. "On Certain Passages in Jevons's THEORY OF
POLITICAL ECONOMY." QUARTERLY JOURNAL OF ECONOMICS 3
(April 1889): 293-314.

608. Wieser, Friedrich von. "The Austrian School and the Theory of Value."
THE ECONOMIC JOURNAL 1 (March 1891): 108-21.

609. Wilson, E.B. "Generalization of Pareto's Demand Theory." QUARTERLY
JOURNAL OF ECONOMICS 49 (August 1935): 715-17.

Chapter 5

UNITED STATES ECONOMISTS

Chapter 5
UNITED STATES ECONOMISTS

A. INTRODUCTION

The U.S. economists working between 1800 and 1940 comprise a large and diversified group of writers. The two Careys, Henry and Mathew, were the principal representatives of early American economics, and their work, particularly that of Henry Carey, was the first generally analytical analysis produced in this country. Both the American Economics Association and a U.S. theoretical viewpoint were established during the 1880s. Although both the marginalists and the German historicists had significant impact on the development of economics in this country, a certain incipient independence emerged in the writings of the foremost American economists around the turn of the century.

There were many economists during this period and the annotated sources could not cover all of these writers, although an attempt has been made to treat quite thoroughly the better known writers of the period. Joseph A. Schumpeter is included in this group because he was as much an American scholar as he was European.

More than one school of thought is represented in this chapter: institutionalists, neoclassical theorists, and theorists of imperfect competition. There are some, like Henry George and Frank A. Fetter, who do not fit well into any of these three schools, but who did contribute greatly to the development of American as well as world economic theory.

Because of the time period covered here, many of the articles listed below concern topics related to depressions and economic crises. That is, in addition to the purely theoretical works, there were many attempts to prescribe cures for the economic woes of the country. Amongst pure theorists, there was extensive debate involving advocates of the various theories of imperfect competition as well as neoclassical theorists. The latter were actively debating various aspects of value and capital theory, as were economists in England and Europe. The next chapter is devoted to the post-Marshallian English economic theorists and will demonstrate the presence of heated argument in that group of theorists as well.

B. MAJOR CONTRIBUTIONS

610. Angell, James W. "Consumers' Demand." QUARTERLY JOURNAL OF ECONOMICS 39 (August 1925): 584–611.

   The focus of this essay is on the "standards-of-living" approach to consumers' demand price. Angell first examines the influence of standards of living on individual wants and then attempts to measure these wants. Finally, Angell discusses the actual relationship between these wants and the formation of market demand prices. This approach is then compared very generally with the marginal utility theory.

611. Ayers, C.E. "The Functions and Problems of Economic Theory." JOURNAL OF POLITICAL ECONOMY 26 (January 1918): 69–90.

   "The conception of economics as a purely descriptive science rests on a misconception of the history of economic thought." The author believes that economic thought proceeds through successive phases of a cycle which may reasonably be expected to repeat themselves. Examples of successive phases are drawn from a period extending back 150 years. The cycle entails "criticism, reconstruction, approbation, and renewed criticism of the institutional order." Ayers's teachings became the foundation for a school of economics still operative today.

612. Bullock, Charles Jesse. INTRODUCTION TO THE STUDY OF ECONOMICS. New York: Silver, Burdett, 1908. 619 p.

   This introductory text provides the student with an eighty-page summary of the economic history of the United States by way of introduction to economic theory. The economic principles throughout the book are discussed in terms of U.S. economic conditions and experience. When feasible, both sides of a controversy are presented (bimetallism and monopoly, for example). This is a good source for the person interested in an economist's interpretations of the economic environment at the turn of the century.

613. _____, ed. SELECTED READINGS IN ECONOMICS. New York: Ginn and Co., 1907. 705 p.

   This collection of works was designed to supplement the text cited above. Many of the contributors, most of whom were American, were the prominent economists of the time in the United States and Europe, and their essays here cover many aspects of economic theory.

614. Carey, Henry C. MISCELLANEOUS WORKS. Philadelphia: Henry Carey Baird, Industrial Publishers, 1873. 500 + p.

This volume collects a few of Carey's longer papers and many short papers and letters. The topics are many and varied, due to the diverse interests and prolific writings of this author, who is considered to be one of the first U.S. economists.

615. _____. THE PAST, THE PRESENT, AND THE FUTURE. Philadelphia: Henry Carey Baird, Industrial Publishers, 1872. 474 p.

In this work, Carey extolls the "golden rule" as the law of nature which governs man in all his efforts to maintain and improve his condition: "do unto others as ye would that others should do unto you." He criticizes the classical theory of Ricardo and Malthus. It is a work by an ardent individualist who argues for individual rights freedom.

616. Carey, Mathew. ESSAYS ON POLITICAL ECONOMY. Philadelphia: H.C. Carey and I. Lea, 1822. Reprint ed., New York: Augustus M. Kelley, 1968. 556 p.

This work contains six long and three shorter pieces, the latter being addresses and memorials. The collection was published as an attempt by Carey to direct the course of American economic policy. He believed that protection was bad and these works were written in an effort to convince people of the costs of protection.

617. Chamberlin, Edward H. "On the Origin of 'Oligopoly'." THE ECONOMIC JOURNAL 67 (June 1957): 211-18.

In response to a businessman's attack on the person, "whoever he was," who originated the word "oligopoly," the author seeks to clarify his position as the originator and to discuss at great length the various characteristics of oligopoly. The word denotes two classifications of characteristics--numbers and substitution--in addition to the behavioral characteristics concerning a firm's independence of action.

618. _____. TOWARDS A MORE GENERAL THEORY OF VALUE. New York: Oxford University Press, 1957. 318 p.

This is a collection of four new and twelve reprinted essays covering many aspects of the controversy generated by the theory of MONOPOLISTIC COMPETITION (1933). The general distinction between Robinson's approach (in THE THEORY OF IMPERFECT COMPETITION, 1933) and Chamberlin's still remains: Robinson is still concerned with industry classification, whereas Chamberlin emphasizes the activity of firms within the industry. This is an excellent group of articles on the topics.

619. _____, ed. MONOPOLY AND COMPETITION AND THEIR REGULA-

TION. London: Macmillan, 1954. 549 p.

This work contains the papers and proceedings of a conference held by the International Economic Association and thus includes work by prominent economists from several nations. There are, however, theoretical papers by Chamberlin and Joan Robinson on the measurement of degress of monopoly and competition.

620. Chamberlin, Edward H., et al. LABOR UNIONS AND PUBLIC POLICY. Washington, D.C.: American Enterprise Association, 1958. 177 p.

The author begins with the assertion that economic theory has not kept pace with the changing position of labor in the U.S. economy. This work is a response to the abuses on the part of unions that were revealed by the McClellan committee hearings in the late 1950s. It is predominantly a policy-oriented book and contains little pure theory.

621. Clark, John Bates. "Capital and Its Earnings." PUBLICATIONS OF THE AMERICAN ECONOMIC ASSOCIATION 3 (May 1888): 89-149.

Clark defines capital in terms of its nature, origin, and industrial function. The earnings of capital and the earnings of pure capital are distinguished and analyzed. The author regarded this work as an introduction to a much larger work on capital.

622. _____. THE CONTROL OF TRUSTS. New York: Macmillan, 1901. 88 p.

Intended as a policy statement only, this proposal "relies wholly on competition as the regulator of prices and wages and as the general protector of the interests of the public." Centralization is welcomed but freedom of entry is to be maintained. This freedom of entry (both foreign and domestic) would not only control the large trusts but would diminish the violence of commercial crises in the process. It is an excellent work for one interested in the economics of public policy.

623. _____. "Distribution as Determined by a Law of Rent." QUARTERLY JOURNAL OF ECONOMICS 5 (April 1891): 289-318.

Clark demonstrates how the rent theory may be used to describe or explain the distribution of final output. Rent is here presented as furnishing an "ultimate basis for the measurement of all values." Clark's article is preceded by J.A. Hobson's "The Law of the Three Rents," which exhibits a strikingly different viewpoint.

624. _____. THE DISTRIBUTION OF WEALTH. Reprint ed., New York: Kelley & Millman, 1956. 445 p.

Clark demonstrates that natural law controls the distribution of income and will, without friction, return to every agent of production the amount of wealth created by him. It is a static analysis in the sense that the author is interested in separating the static and dynamic forces of distribution in order to discover the static or "natural" standards towards which the economy tends to conform.

625. _____. ESSENTIALS OF ECONOMIC THEORY. New York: Macmillan, 1907. 566 p.

This work treats the nature, the causes, and the effects of: (1) population growth; (2) capital accumulation; (3) improved technology; and (4) improved organization of production. It is an attempt to formulate laws of dynamics in contrast to conventional comparative static analysis. The author also analyzes the timing relationships between various economic causes and effects. Big business and the role of government with respect to big business are also covered.

626. _____. "The Modern Appeal to Legal Forces in Economic Life." PUBLICATIONS OF THE AMERICAN ECONOMIC ASSOCIATION 9 (October and December 1894): 481-502.

In this assessment of the claims of socialists against modern society, Clark employs marginal productivity theory in an attempt to answer more precisely the allegations of socialists.

627. _____. "The Origin of Interest." QUARTERLY JOURNAL OF ECONOMICS 9 (April 1895): 257-78.

Responding to E. Bohm-Bawerk's THE POSITIVE THEORY OF CAPITAL, Clark chooses to analyze the concept of capital and the origin of interest in an economic system. A basic disagreement arises from their differing beliefs concerning the justification for paying interest and receiving interest payments. A reply by Bohm-Bawerk appears on pages 380-87 of the same journal.

628. _____. THE PHILOSOPHY OF WEALTH: ECONOMIC PRINCIPLES NEWLY FORMULATED. Boston: Ginn and Co., 1894. 236 p.

Clark believed that existing theoretical constructs presupposed a degrading opinion of human nature which vitiated the theory of the distribution of wealth. He attempts to construct a new theory of value and to "apply at all points the organic conception of society," which treats the economy as a mechanism comprising many interrelated parts. The book does not examine the topics of currency and protection.

629. _____. "Possibility of a Scientific Law of Wages." PUBLICATIONS

OF THE AMERICAN ECONOMIC ASSOCIATION 4 (March 1889): 37-69.

Clark here defines the prerequisites for a scientific law and states that an economic law is valid only if it remains true during changing social conditions. Although the bad effects of restriction had not yet affected labor because of the enlargement of social capital, the law of productivity still held ---and was in fact strengthened--by the establishment and interaction of trusts and unions.

630. _____. "The Theory of Economic Progress." ECONOMIC STUDIES 1 (April 1896): 1-22.

Presented as the presidential address to the American Economic Association meetings of December 1895, this essay is an expression of Clark's claim that the test of an economic system is the rate and direction of its movement. The author foresees an understanding between labor and capital and the role of legitimate capital accumulation to make wages higher and to ensure future progress.

631. _____. "A Universal Law of Economic Variation." QUARTERLY JOURNAL OF ECONOMICS 8 (April 1894): 261-79.

More commonly known as the "law of variable proportions," this law is considered by Clark not as a rule to apply in a given situation, but as a law which "governs individual and social action." It is suggested that the greatest gain might be had from a study of this law with respect to the social field. It is a good discussion of the applicability of marginal analysis to all facets of economic life.

632. Clark, John Maurice. ALTERNATIVE TO SERFDOM. New York: Alfred A. Knopf, 1948. 159 p.

This is a collection of five lectures delivered to the William W. Cook Foundation at the University of Michigan. The author compares the more technical economic inquires in this volume with his father's THE PHILOSOPHY OF WEALTH (see 628). From his position as an economist, albeit one who acknowledges the pervasiveness of all social activity, Clark attempts to approach the problems of freedom and responsibility, community and market mechanism, and political and economic agency. These essays are post-Keynesian and are, for that reason, of special interest.

633. _____. "Business Acceleration and the Law of Demand: A Technical Factor in Economic Cycles." JOURNAL OF POLITICAL ECONOMY 25 (March 1917): 217-35.

Clark here contends that, since the publication of Mitchell's

BUSINESS CYCLES, one can no longer explain cycles by reference to any one variable or factor. He does argue, however, that one factor—the relationship between final demand and derived demand—is predominant. He claims that the demand for more capital varies, not with the volume of demand for finished goods, but rather with the acceleration of that demand. That notion is the foundation of what was to become, years later, the accelerator principle in macroeconomic theory.

634. _____. ECONOMIC INSTITUTIONS AND HUMAN WELFARE. New York: Alfred A. Knopf, 1957. 295 p.

In this collection of essays the author examines the institutional setting in which the market system functions in order to understand more fully the verification of economic laws and principles. An attempt is made to define an acceptable concept of welfare and to determine whether existing welfare policies prohibit economic freedom. Clark concludes that the optimal system would be established at neither the laissez faire nor the collectivist extreme, but intermediate to both.

635. _____. GUIDEPOSTS IN TIME OF CHANGE. New York: Harper & Brothers, 1949. 210 p.

This is a collection of six lectures delivered at Amherst College in which Clark begins by delineating the threat of totalitarianism and then suggests an interpretation of this threat and ways of meeting it. The next lecture describes the objectives for our own economy and is followed by three lectures addressed to the problems of maintaining a high level of demand within the price, wage, and cost structure. The last lecture emphasizes need for change which confronts the members of the society if they are to maintain a free and viable system.

636. _____. "Imperfect Competition Theory and Basing-Point Problems." AMERICAN ECONOMIC REVIEW 33 (June 1943): 283-300.

In this response to two earlier articles by V.A. Lund and Arthur Smithies, Clark expresses his disagreement with Lund's proposition that "regular and habitual freight absorption" is a "monopolistic practice within the anti-trust laws and proof of collusion." Imperfect competition theory should be used to provide a "systematic analysis" of the effect of various trade practices on the operation of normal business motives. The issues center around the uses of various theories in the analysis. A "Reply" by Lund appears on page 612 and a "Rejoinder" by Clark follows on page 616 of this journal.

637. _____. "Inductive Evidence on Marginal Productivity." AMERICAN ECONOMIC REVIEW 18 (September 1928): 449-67.

In this study of the Cobb-Douglas essay (see 643), Clark attempts to assimilate both short- and long-run fluctuations into a more comprehensive formula, and to allow for factors such as technical progress not included in the Cobb-Douglas study. This article is reprinted in the author's PREFACE TO SOCIAL ECONOMICS, ESSAYS ON ECONOMIC THEORY AND SOCIAL PROBLEMS.

638. _____. "Investment in Relation to Business Activity and Employment." In STUDIES IN ECONOMICS AND INDUSTRIAL RELATIONS, prepared by University of Pennsylvania Bicentennial Conference, pp. 37-51. Philadelphia: University of Pennsylvania Press, 1941.

Advocating the study of dynamics as opposed to comparative statics, Clark contends that alternatives which appear illogical when examined in terms of comparative statics may well prove viable when studied in a dynamic frame of reference. The discussion covers income and spending, short cycles and chronic stagnation.

639. _____. "Overhead Costs in Modern Industry, Parts I, II, and III." JOURNAL OF POLITICAL ECONOMY 31 (February 1923): 47-64, (April 1923): 209-42, (October 1923): 606-36.

The first part serves to place overhead costs in their proper perspective with respect to direct cost analysis. The second part is addressed to problems related to variables governing efficiency of economic activity and overhead costs. The final part treats the relationship between overhead costs and the economies generated by larger plants. These three articles constitute the author's landmark studies on overhead costs and remain classic works on the topic today.

640. _____. PREFACE TO SOCIAL ECONOMICS, ESSAYS ON ECONOMIC THEORY AND SOCIAL PROBLEMS. Selected by Moses Abromovitz and Eli Ginzburg. New York: Farrar & Rinehart, 1936. 435 p.

This is a collection of fourteen essays by the author in which a variety of topics are covered under two general headings: (1) economic theory and social problems and (2) dynamics of the economic mechanism. There are many articles on other writers and theories in this well-rounded collection of the author's works.

641. _____. STRATEGIC FACTORS IN BUSINESS CYCLES. New York: National Bureau of Economic Research, 1934. 238 p.

This work does not focus on the depression of the 1930s but is an examination of business cycles in general. The task of the book was to apply theoretical analysis to an unusually

comprehensive array of concrete data. There are two parts to
the analysis, neither of which may be eliminated if one ex-
pects to have a strong science. The first part consists of
diagnosis; the second is more pragmatic, requiring the analyst
to question the ways in which one may control the variations
in economic activity.

642. _____. "Toward a Concept of Workable Competition." AMERICAN
ECONOMIC REVIEW 30 (June 1940): 241-56.

This article may well be a classic in the sense that it must be
one of the first considerations of the existence of second-best
solutions in economic theory. The situation considered is one
in which one of a set of required criteria is not fulfilled and
so the satisfaction of the remaining criteria may not produce
the best possible results. In fact, if one of the criteria for
competitive equilibria does not hold, then the next best solution may require that other conditions not hold either. This
theory has been quantified and rigorously developed and is
used extensively in cases where imperfect competition exists.

643. Cobb, Charles W., and Douglas, Paul H. "A Theory of Production."
AMERICAN ECONOMIC REVIEW 18, Supplement (March 1928): 139-65.

This is the classic article in which the now famous Cobb-Douglas production function was presented. The authors were attempting to analyze the changes in the amounts of labor and
capital that had been used to produce the existing volume of
goods and to determine what relationships existed between the
three variables--labor, capital, and product. Because of their
derivation of this production function, their results had lasting
impact.

644. Commons, John R. THE ECONOMICS OF COLLECTIVE ACTION. Edited
with an introduction by Kenneth H. Parsons. New York: Macmillan,
1951. 414 p.

This work, published posthumously, was the culmination of a
lifetime of work in economics. The book is generally an account of how Commons viewed worker groups and corporations
and their interaction. His ideas were grounded in his conception of social relationships and his postulate that the economy
was a social organization, rather than a mechanism or organ-
ism. The analysis centers on the production of wealth and the
distribution of income, as does most economic theory. The difference is that his investigations begin with the premise that
collective action is the "general and dominating fact of social
life."

645. _____. INSTITUTIONAL ECONOMICS. New York: Macmillan, 1934.
921 p.

The author has attempted to formulate very extensively the science of political economy. To explicate current concepts, Commons traced them back to their origins, sorting out the single correct interpretations of each. Dominant ideas are those that have emerged from what are described as "revolutionary cycles." The volume is an excellent example of institutional economics.

646. _____. LABOR AND ADMINISTRATION. New York: Macmillan, 1913. 431 p.

Commons addresses himself generally to the problem of preventing laws from becoming empty ideas and specifically to preventing the burst of enthusiasm generated by strikes from disintegrating into disorganization. These essays, beginning with the "Utilitarian Idealist," portray the new force in labor economics as seen by the author. One cannot be merely a "friend of labor" or a "curious collector of facts and statistics"; but rather one must "[measure] the facts and [build] them into a foundation and structure." Commons was such an economist.

647. _____. LEGAL FOUNDATIONS OF CAPITALISM. New York: Macmillan, 1924. 394 p.

From his work with the regulation and valuation of public utilities, Commons came to recognize the lack of a definition of reasonable value. A search through British and U.S. legal history, as well as the history of economic theory, revealed that what was needed was a statement of the legal foundations of capitalism. This is a theoretical work which should be studied by any scholar interested in public policy decision making.

648. _____, ed. TRADE UNIONISM AND LABOR PROBLEMS. New York: Ginn & Co., 1905. 628 p.

This collection of essays by various labor economists includes papers by Commons. The twenty-eight articles treat specific issues or problems involved with unions and labor economics. Five essays deal with minority problems in various industries and types of work. Each chapter or article is intended to "illustrate a single, definite, typical phase of the general subject."

649. Commons, John R., and Andrews, John B. PRINCIPLES OF LABOR LEGISLATION. 4th rev. ed. New York: Harper & Brothers, 1936. Reprint ed., New York: Augustus M. Kelley, 1967. 606 p.

This work, "intended to be both critical and constructive," is supposed to define the good and the bad features of labor-related statutes and to demonstrate from a historical perspective

how the "good is being strengthened and the bad remedied."
The coverage of the book is extremely broad and thorough.

650. Commons, John R., et al. HISTORY OF LABOR IN THE UNITED STATES.
2 vols. New York: Macmillan, 1918. Vol. I, 623 p.; vol. II,
620 p.

This set was sponsored by the Carnegie Institute as one of
their historical studies and Commons was the third director of
the group. The book is divided into sections, each written
by a prominent specialist in the field with which the section
is concerned. Volume I contains work on the colonial and
federal beginnings of unionism, the era of citizenship and
unionism, the rise of the trade union, humanitarianism, and
the growth of unionism. Volume II is devoted to the topic
of nationalization and unionism.

651. Davenport, H.J. "The Distributive Relations of Indirect Goods." QUAR-
TERLY JOURNAL OF ECONOMICS 32 (August 1918): 635-63.

Davenport is concerned with questions arising from the behavior of prices of inputs with respect to crises, and the resulting
effects of these price movements on final goods markets. Various types of inputs, such as labor versus materials, are discussed in terms of their effects on prices and cost during stages
of the cycle.

652. _____. THE ECONOMICS OF ALFRED MARSHALL. Ithaca, N.Y.:
Cornell University Press, 1935. 481 p.

Although the book was published posthumously, the body of
the work is virtually as the author left it. This study illustrates the views of a U.S. economist toward neoclassical, and
especially Marshallian, economics. Davenport attempted to
sort out the portions of the theory that are classical from those
that are Marshallian.

653. _____. "Interest Theory and Theories." AMERICAN ECONOMIC RE-
VIEW 17 (December 1927): 636-56.

This article begins by discussing the origin of interest and proceeds to an examination of various interest theories: time-preference and consumption, productivity theory, positive theory,
and the reformed perspective theory.

654. _____. "Non-Competing Groups." QUARTERLY JOURNAL OF ECO-
NOMICS 40 (November 1925): 52-81.

Davenport here examines the theory of noncompeting groups
by studying the benefits and disadvantages deriving from the
formation of labor groups. Cairne's presentation of the argu-

ment on these groups is discussed at length, along with the
works of Ricardo, Mill, Marshall, and Taussig. In conclusion,
Davenport advances three prerequisities for a labor theory of
value and demonstrates that they have not been satisfied.

655. _____. OUTLINES OF ECONOMIC THEORY. New York: Macmillan,
1896. 381 p.

This work served as a text and covers most areas of economic
theory, including value theory, production, distribution, capital theory, international trade, and population. The last
hundred or so pages are devoted to a discussion of economics
as an art. This section treats some of the previously discussed
topics from other viewpoints.

656. _____. "Proportions of Factors--Advantage and Size." QUARTERLY
JOURNAL OF ECONOMICS 23 (August 1909): 593-617.

The comparison made in this essay is a good one, for the two
concepts are frequently confused. First, the various social
static and dynamic senses of diminishing returns are discussed
along with concerns expressed by Malthus. The Law of Advantage, its applications, and its confusion with the law of
proportions are then considered.

657. _____. "Social Productivity versus Private Acquisition." QUARTERLY
JOURNAL OF ECONOMICS 25 (November 1910): 96-118.

The author traces various productivity doctrines back to the
mercantilists and Physiocrats, summarizes them, and then traces
the productivity theory of distribution in which productivity is
regarded as social service. Many of the various means of
characterizing capital are discussed and rejected in favor of
the pecuniary return, which is also applied to labor. The
closing sections discuss the necessary reformulations of doctrine
and the commonly accepted forms of the productivity theory of
distribution.

658. _____. VALUE AND DISTRIBUTION. Chicago: University of Chicago
Press, 1908. 582 p.

Davenport here attempts to put various aspects of the theory
of distribution into new perspective by emphasizing the entrepreneurial point of view in the computation of costs and in
the analysis of determining distributive shares. Much emphasis
is placed on the concept of opportunity cost and, given the
acceptance of the entrepreneurial point of view, rent is regarded as part of the cost of production. He attempts to rid
the science of many neoclassical concepts.

659. _____. "Velocities, Turnovers, and Prices." AMERICAN ECONOMIC

REVIEW 20 (March 1930): 9-19.

The complexity of this article is due in part to the author's use of various analogies. The problem appears to be that of determining which rate changes have an effect on prices. There is a distinction made among changes in the volumes of media or goods, changes in the rates (due to institutional changes) of turnover of media, and finally changes of the "ordinary sort" in the rate of turnover of media or goods. The latter two "ordinary" changes must move in the same direction. It is an interesting discussion of the intricacies of the quantity theory.

660. _____. "Wage Theory and Theories." QUARTERLY JOURNAL OF ECONOMICS 33 (February 1919): 256-97.

This treatment of the wages of laborers discusses wages fund theory, labor pain theory, and productivity theories, as well as surplus value theory. The predominant purpose appears to be the examination of the effects of advertising and other such "parasitisms" on the share left to labor. A theory of wages must account for the difference between competitive acquisition and social production.

661. Douglas, Paul H. THE THEORY OF WAGES. New York: Macmillan, 1934. 639 p.

An earlier draft of this work won the first Hart, Schaffner, and Marx international award in 1926 for the best treatise on the theory of wages. This work is an attempt to discover whether diminishing marginal product curves exist and, if so, what other curves the demand and especially the supply functions of factors resemble. Furthermore, Douglas asks, does the actual process of distribution corroborate the inductive tendencies discovered? Chapter 5 contains the application of the famous Cobb-Douglas production function to the problems of this work.

662. Dunbar, C.F. ECONOMIC ESSAYS. Edited by O.M.W. Sprague. Introduction by F.W. Taussig. New York: Macmillan, 1904. xvii, 372 p.

Many of these papers were found after the author's death, but they were sufficiently complete to be published as he left them. His primary areas of interest were banking, currency and gold, and public finance. Twenty of Dunbar's articles appear in this volume. They reflect the thinking of a man who had lived through the Civil War years and the subsequent recurrent monetary crises.

663. Ely, Richard T. FRENCH AND GERMAN SOCIALISM IN MODERN TIMES. New York: Harper & Brothers, 1883. 274 p.

Ely considered France and Germany to be the strongholds of

communism and socialism and this book is an extensive examination of the positions of several socialists and communists.
Particular political situations are also studied.

664. _____. THE LABOR MOVEMENT IN AMERICA. New ed. New York:
Thomas Y. Crowell, 1886. 399 p.

Ely did not intend to write a history of the labor movement,
but rather to illustrate that the data of the labor movement is
interesting and significant and could convince people of the
"vastness of our present opportunities." He asserts that there
is great potential for both good and bad outcomes in the fledg-
ling system. The topics covered treat both the economic and
social aspects of labor organizations.

665. _____. MONOPOLIES AND TRUSTS. New York: Macmillan, 1900.
278 p.

The author described this work as part of the larger study,
THE DISTRIBUTION OF WEALTH, upon which he had been
working for years. The topic of this volume is recurring and
important within the larger work and one of great concern to
economists and politicians of the time. The book is divided
into six chapters: "The Idea of Monopoly"; "Classification and
Causes of Monopoly"; "Law of Monopoly Price"; "Limits of
Monopoly and Permanency of Competition"; "The Concentration
of Production and Trusts"; and "Evils and Remedies."

666. _____. PROPERTY AND CONTRACT IN THEIR RELATIONS TO THE
DISTRIBUTION OF WEALTH. 2 vols. New York: Macmillan, 1914.
995 p.

In this work, the result of more than two decades of teaching
a course on this topic, Ely attempts to provide an economic
inquiry into the realm of property and contract. The difficulty
against which the author consciously guards is allowing the study
to become dominated by the legal questions and hence become
a law book. This is an interesting treatment of a topic only
recently reconsidered in economic theory.

667. _____. TAXATION IN AMERICAN STATES AND CITIES. New York:
Thomas Y. Crowell, 1888. 544 p.

This volume is a popular, or nontechnical, study of taxation in
which the incidence of the various taxes is analyzed and the
attempts of various groups to shift the burden to other less pow-
erful groups are examined. The book is broken into four main
portions: the rationale and history of taxation; taxation as it
existed; taxation as it should be; and a review of constitutional
provisions and statistical materials. The tax laws of several
states are employed in the analysis.

668. Ely, Richard T., and Wehrwein, George S. LAND ECONOMICS. New York: Macmillan, 1940. 512 p.

This work was originally published in two separate volumes, at separate times, by different publishers. The first five chapters develop the theoretical framework for the study of spatial relationships; the remaining nine chapters treat the application of the framework to various types of land and natural resources.

669. Ely, Richard T., et al. OUTLINES OF ECONOMICS. 4th ed. New York: Macmillan, 1923. 729 p.

Book I is concerned with the development of the current economic system and the economic history of the Unites States. Book II is addressed to the problems of general economic analysis: value and distribution theory, international trade, and monetary economics. Book III is a discussion of public finance. An appendix on the history of economic thought is included. The theoretical approach is primarily neoclassical or marginalist.

670. Fetter, Frank A. "The Economic Law of Market Area." QUARTERLY JOURNAL OF ECONOMICS 38 (May 1924): 520-29.

Fetter develops a theory of market areas in which he defines a method of dividing up territories between markets along lines which, unlike those utilized in other theories, are not straight. Although a very short piece, this essay is one of the first works on market areas and economic activity.

671. _____. "Interest Theories, Old and New." AMERICAN ECONOMIC REVIEW 4 (March 1914): 68-92.

This is an analysis of the controversy between psychological and productivity theories of interest. The work of Irving Fisher, THE RATE OF INTEREST (see 686), and the ensuing criticism by H.R. Seager are the focal points of Fetter's examination of both old and new versions of interest theory. These adversaries, along with Eugen Bohm-Bawerk, are categorized according to the nature of their explanations of interest theory: psychological explanations, enterpriser-productivity explanations, and combinations of the two. Bohm-Bawerk and Seager are viewed as eclectics using kinds of explanation, whereas Fisher is considered a productivity theorist in the market for money loans (although Fisher's approach to captialization theory is shown to utilize psychological explanations).

672. _____. "Interest Theory and Price Movements." AMERICAN ECONOMIC REVIEW 17, Supplement (March 1927): 62-105.

The author believes that there is much to be gained from a survey of interest history and theory and a statement of some of the newer speculative aspects. He acknowledges that agreement on theory and terminology does not exist on all aspects, but claims that a synthesis of existing theories may yield some "cross-fertilization." It is thus an excellent survey of interest theory and the relationship between interest and price.

673. _____. "The Passing of the Old Rent Concept." QUARTERLY JOUR-NAL OF ECONOMICS 15 (May 1901): 416-55.

Fetter examines those portions of Ricardo's theory considered as "difficulties" and points out the defects that must be recognized in the "newer form" of rent theory. The newer form is represented primarily by the work of Alfred Marshall. Five separate concepts are considered in the discussion of rent.

674. _____. "Price Economics versus Welfare Economics, Parts I and II." AMERICAN ECONOMIC REVIEW 10 (September 1920): 467-87, (December 1920): 719-37.

The first part sketches the "origins and main features of 'price economics' and various protests against it," developing the theory up to the last quarter of the nineteenth century when price economics seemed all but obsolete. Six different protesting groups are cited in the first article, but only one dissenting group--the liberal middle-class economists--is treated thoroughly in the second article. The second part starts with Alfred Marshall and then shifts to the United States, analyzing the neoclassical and psychological schools' viewpoints. It is an excellent treatment, still pertinent today.

675. _____. "Recent Discussion of the Capital Concept." QUARTERLY JOUR-NAL OF ECONOMICS 15 (November 1900): 1-45.

Fetter contends that "the circumstances and special problems of former generations have caused the grouping of unharmonized ideas under one term." The economist must sort out these ideas and form a consistent framework that fits the needs of social discussion. The author believes that the concept of capital is a prime example of a group of such terms requiring analysis. This is an extensive review of capital theory up to 1900.

676. _____. "The 'Roundabout Process' in the Interest Theory." QUARTERLY JOURNAL OF ECONOMICS 17 (November 1902): 163-80.

Bohm-Bawerk is criticized for having stated only that interest would exist under defined circumstances. Fetter alleges that Bohm-Bawerk had failed to produce an interest theory that would explain why such circumstances arise. The author examines only one of Bohm-Bawerk's reasons for the preference of present goods over future goods, citing the technical superiority of present goods when used in "roundabout" processes. It is a good discussion of interest theory.

677.   ____, ed. SOURCE BOOK IN ECONOMICS. New York: Century
Co., 1912. 385 p.

This is an extensive collection of essays by several authorities
on the main aspects of economic policy. Topics covered include population, wealth distribution, markets and prices,
monopoly, the state and industry, and others. It was compiled as a sourcebook of readings for college courses.

678. Fisher, Irving. BOOMS AND DEPRESSIONS, SOME FIRST PRINCIPLES.
London: George Allen & Unwin, 1933. 258 p.

This analysis is restricted to what the author considers to be
the most prominent nine factors related to business cycles. He
has attempted to isolate the most theoretically relevant variables in order to demonstrate that, given specific policies, depressions can usually be prevented. The specific policy was
the job of the Federal Reserve. Interestingly, Fisher calls for
international cooperation to counteract the depression of the
1930s.

679.   ____. ELEMENTARY PRINCIPLES OF ECONOMICS. New York: Macmillan, 1911. 476 p.

The aim of the book is to formulate some of the fundamental
principles of economics. The author has chosen to present the
material in a somewhat untraditional way, introducing the
student to the most familiar concepts first and then progressing
to less commonly encountered topics. He was the first to make
extensive use of graphics in a book of principles.

680.   ____. MATHEMATICAL INVESTIGATIONS IN THE THEORY OF VAL-
UE AND PRICE. New York: Augustus M. Kelley, 1965. 233 p.

To this publication of Fisher's dissertation has been added a
reprint of an article by Fisher entitled "Appreciation and Interest" (PUBLICATIONS OF THE AMERICAN ECONOMIC AS-
SOCIATION, vol. II, August 1896, pp. 1-100). The dissertation was an attempt to elaborate the foundations of value
theory in a very rigorous fashion. Fisher claimed that the relationship between monetary appreciation and the rate of Interest was not completely understood and that, consequently, the
monetary history of the years 1875 to 1895 had not been successfully interpreted. Both works are excellent examples of the
author's ability to render precise versions of economic concepts.

681.   ____. "The Mechanics of Bimetalism." THE ECONOMIC JOURNAL
4 (September 1894): 527-37.

Fisher attempts to ascertain the conditions necessary for the
proper function of bimetallism. The author maintains that a
fixed legal ratio between the two metals is necessary for the

system to be determinate. Otherwise, the two metals are "substitutes without a ratio of substitution." Some earlier works are discussed, and then both a static and a dynamic system are examined.

682. _____. THE MONEY ILLUSION. New York: Adelphi Co., 1928. 245 p.

Based on lectures presented at the Geneva School of International Studies, this volume is intended to demonstrate the instability in the buying power of all monetary units. The hidden causes of this instability, and the harm that results, are delineated and several implemented or proposed remedies are examined. A thirteen-page reading list is provided.

683. _____. THE NATURE OF CAPITAL AND INCOME. New York: Macmillan, 1906. 427 p.

Fisher here attempted to put the concepts and fundamental theorems of capital and income on a rational foundation. Claiming this to be one of the first rigorous treatments of income in the literature, Fisher emphasized that income was a crucial variable, one not to be neglected. A glossary of terms is included.

684. _____. 100% MONEY. 3rd ed. New Haven, Conn.: City Printing Co., 1945. 257 p.

Except for an addendum listing over twenty new sources and an extended discussion of the adverse articles, this edition is a reprint of the second edition (1936). The book is the expression of the concept that banks should keep 100 percent reserves against demand deposits. If this were required by law, control of inflation would be very much more effective. The first part is a general summary of the entire proposal; parts two and three are more detailed and technical discussions of how the system would work. This proposal still has many advocates today.

685. _____. THE PURCHASING POWER OF MONEY. New York: Macmillan, 1911. 503 p.

Fisher's objective is to "set forth the principles determining the purchasing power of money" and to examine the historical evidence of changes in the concept. The author states that the purchasing power of money depends on five factors: (1) volume of money in circulation; (2) its velocity of circulation; (3) the volume of demand deposits; (4) the velocity of demand deposits; and (5) the volume of trade. The book is presented as a reaffirmation of the quantity theory and is a very thorough derivation of each of the five factors as well as Fisher's version of the equation of exchange.

686.   _____. THE RATE OF INTEREST. New York: Macmillan, 1907.
442 p.

> The theory of interest proposed is an "agio" theory but differs
> from previous such theories because of the inclusion of an in-
> come concept that was developed in the author's THE NATURE
> OF CAPITAL AND INCOME (see 683). It is contended that the
> rate of interest depends upon the size, composition, probabil-
> ity, and, above all, the distribution in time of the income
> stream. He suggests that it might be called a "theory of pro-
> spective provision of income."

687.   _____. "The Role of Capital in Economic Theory." THE ECONOMIC
JOURNAL 7 (December 1897): 511-37.

> Capital "is not any particular kind of wealth, but a stock of
> wealth of any kind existing at an instant of time." This study
> is concerned with stocks and flows or "capital and income"
> and their interrelationship. Three important economic problems
> represent three primary areas of relationship: (1) the problem
> of saving; (2) the theory of interest; and (3) the problem of
> income and its distribution.

688.   _____. "Senses of Capital." THE ECONOMIC JOURNAL 7 (June
1897): 199-213.

> Fisher attempts to demonstrate that, especially for development
> of a theory of capital, classificatory economics is less fruitful
> than analytic economics. He acknowledges that classificatory
> problems are important in descriptive economics, but questions
> the potential of this method for promoting understanding of the
> economic environment. Fisher's conclusions are, however,
> generally favorable toward descriptive economics. He devotes
> the entire text of his essay to a study of the basic misconcep-
> tions inherent in definitions of capital. (See also 691.)

689.   _____. THE STOCK MARKET CRASH AND AFTER. New York: Macmillan, 1930. 286 p.

> Although Fisher predicted that the stock market was at a peak
> in September 1929, he had also predicted that the ensuing re-
> cession would not entail a serious crash and that the "new pla-
> teau of stock prices would survive any recession." At the
> time that he wrote this book, Fisher maintained this convic-
> tion. The viewpoints of many other authorities are also in-
> cluded in this book, whether or not they concurred with the
> views of the author. It is a good discussion of the economic
> atmosphere at that important time.

690.   _____. THE THEORY OF INTEREST, AS DETERMINED BY IMPATIENCE

TO SPEND INCOME AND OPPORTUNITY TO INVEST IT. New York: Macmillan, 1930. 566 p.

This work followed the author's THE RATE OF INTEREST (1907) (see 686) and incorporates new evidence and many revisions of the views expressed in the earlier volume. Chapter 1 contains a brief summary of the author's THE NATURE OF CAPITAL AND INCOME (see 683); chapters 2-18 deal with various situations that might affect interest rates. Chapter 19 presents a rigorous theoretical structure for the theory of interest outlined in previous chapters. The last two chapters contain a consideration of objections and a summary, respectively.

691.   _____. "What is Capital?" THE ECONOMIC JOURNAL 6 (December 1896): 409-534.

This article together with his essay, "Senses of Capital" (see 688), constitute Fisher's statement on the nature of capital. To answer the question proposed in the title, one must first find a definition that is scientific, one that designates "something which plays a real and important role" in the science. Practicality is the second requisite; the definition must replace and explain all primitive popular notions. Capital becomes a stock of wealth at any instant. The article analyzes attitudes toward capital expressed by former prominent economists.

692.   _____. WHY IS THE DOLLAR SHRINKING? New York: Macmillan, 1915. 233 p.

Assuming that most people do not understand the price mechanism and price structure and levels, the author attempts to state in a straightforward manner the principles which fix the scale of prices. He further intends to show the relationship between these principles and the "high cost of living" existing in 1915.

693.   Fisher, Irving, and Fisher, Herbert W. CONSTRUCTIVE INCOME TAXATION, A PROPOSAL FOR REFORM. New York: Harper & Brothers, 1942. 277 p.

Beginning with a definition of income, the authors pursued the problem of formulating a tax system that would tax income, but not savings. They allege that taxation of the latter would discourage the development and expansion of business enterprise. It is an interesting and different approach to taxation that may also be compared with proposals by such economists as J.S. Mill, A. Marshall, and A.C. Pigou.

694.   George, Henry. PROGRESS AND POVERTY. New York: Random House, 1929. 571 p.

This work was the culmination of many years of trying to sort out the root causes of the inequality that existed in the United

States in the 1870s. George's major emphasis was on the monopoly power derived from ownership of land. Some believe that editions of this work subsequent to the first treated wages and capital in the marginalist manner. George presents a remedy for the maldistribution of wealth and income.

695. _____. THE SCIENCE OF POLITICAL ECONOMY. New York: Doubleday, 1898. 545 p.

This work, left unfinished at the time of George's death, was intended to "recast political economy and examine and explicate terminology as well as principles." The five parts deal with the meaning of political economy, the nature of wealth, the production of wealth, the distribution of wealth, and money --the medium of exchange and measure of value. The aim of the work was to trace the development of the science both inside and outside academic institutions.

696. Graham, Frank D. "Partial Reserve Money and the 100 Percent Proposal." AMERICAN ECONOMIC REVIEW 26 (September 1936): 428-40.

Graham asks who should have the right to issue money and defines the principles that should govern the issue. The position of the commercial banks is examined with respect to their issuing activity and the 100 percent reserve remedy. Graham concludes that what is needed is socialization of the supply of money and laissez faire among the commercial banks.

697. _____. "The Primary Functions of Money and Their Consummation in Monetary Policy." AMERICAN ECONOMIC REVIEW 30, Supplement (March 1940): 1-16.

Graham combines the functions of money into two broad classes in order to analyze monetary policy. The discussion is dominated by the problem of how one might best conduct monetary policy-making in a growing economy in which it is necessary to determine whether prices should fall or the money supply grow.

698. _____. THE THEORY OF INTERNATIONAL VALUES. Princeton, N.J.: Princeton University Press, 1948. 349 p.

In this attempt to formulate a new theory of international values, Graham breaks with traditional Ricardo-Mill treatments. The book is nonmathematical and uses no geometry, but it is a rigorous theoretical treatment and is considered a classic in international trade theory.

699. Graham, Frank D., and Whittlesey, Charles R. "Fluctuating Exchange Rates, Foreign Trade and the Price Level." AMERICAN ECONOMIC REVIEW 24 (September 1934): 401-16.

The authors were in favor of floating exchange rates and drew
analogies between free prices and free exchange rates. They
contend that, because prices would not be fixed to promote
efficiency, exchange rates should also be unfixed. Historical
and theoretical justifications of their opposition to fixed rates
of exchange among world currencies, and the internal versus
external balance question are also discussed.

700. Hadley, Arthur Twining. ECONOMIC PROBLEMS OF DEMOCRACY.
New York: Macmillan, 1923. 162 p.

This nontheoretical work was originally presented as a series of
lectures on the interrelationship of economic freedom and political freedom in the twentieth century, as compared with the
nineteenth century, in the United States and Great Britain.

701. _____. ECONOMICS: AN ACCOUNT OF THE RELATIONS BETWEEN
PRIVATE PROPERTY AND PUBLIC WELFARE. New York: G.P. Putnam's
Sons, 1896. 496 p.

This is an attempt to cope with the relatively new problem of
concentration of power and wealth in the hands of the few.
Hadley believes that one may no longer use the competitive
theory to explain economic activity because the capital structure and corporate power are noncompetitive by nature.

702. Hawley, Frederick Barnard. ENTERPRISE AND THE PRODUCTIVE PRO-
CESS. New York: G.P. Putnam's Sons, 1907. 467 p.

Hawley attributed the rejection of economic theory by practi-
tioners to "scholastic" elements, citing the misunderstanding
of one or more underlying premises. This rendering of economic
theory, presented from the viewpoint of the entrepreneur, was
designed to command assent from all who understood it. He
discusses the question of state interference in the productive
process as well as the effect of unions.

703. Hoxie, Robert F. "Fetter's Theory of Value." QUARTERLY JOURNAL
OF ECONOMICS 19 (February 1905): 210-30.

Hoxie claims that Fetter, unlike many writers, regarded the
Austrians as "unemancipated" from classical theory. Fetter is
said to have developed Austrian theory beyond and away from
its classical elements. The article is a critical review of Fetter's value theory and resulting distribution theory.

704. _____. TRADE UNIONISM IN THE UNITED STATES. Edited and
selected by Lucy Hoxie and Nathan Fine. New York: D. Appleton,
1928. 468 p.

Lucy Hoxie and Nathan Fine gathered Hoxie's notes and lec-

tures on trade unionism and added some material published
elsewhere. The notes, made just before Hoxie's death, docu-
ment his investigation of relations between labor and scientific management. Unions are separated into classes and types,
several of which are discussed thoroughly.

705. Knight, Frank H. "Capital, Time, and the Interest Rate." ECONOMICA
n.s. 1 (August 1934): 257-86.

Knight wishes to eliminate from his theoretical framework "all
notions of any definite relation between quantity of capital
and the 'length of the production process,' or 'time' in any
form except the basic one of a dimension in summating any
process." In Knight's opinion, the production process may
have any determinate time length under the ordinary conditions
of capitalistic industry. Theories rejected by Knight include
those of Jevons, Wicksell, and Bohm-Bawerk.

706. _____. "The Concept of Normal Price in Value and Distribution."
QUARTERLY JOURNAL OF ECONOMICS 32 (November 1917): 66-100.

Knight intended to "examine, clarify, and make precise the
meaning of normal price." The two particular uses of the
term--for primary valuation (consumption goods) and secondary
valuation (distribution)--form the basis of the discussion. The
works of A. Marshall and J.B. Clark are compared, contrasted,
and criticized in terms of their usefulness for the purposes at
hand.

707. _____. THE ECONOMIC ORGANIZATION. New York: Harper &
Row, Publishers, 1965. 179 p.

The author discusses the place of economic science in the
activity of society as a whole. The structure of the economic
system is developed from the incipient price system and discussed with respect to supply and demand and the theory of
distribution. The volume includes a useful article entitled
"Notes on Utility and Cost."

708. _____. THE ETHICS OF COMPETITION AND OTHER ESSAYS. New
York: Harper & Brothers, 1935. 363 p.

This collection of Knight's essays was put together by some of
his colleagues in order to make his work more readily available to students of the social sciences. The collection, in
addition to two articles on ethics in economics, includes three
articles on utility and value theory, two on methodology,
and one each on statics and dynamics, interest theory, long-
and short-run costs and pricing, interpretations of social costs,
and economic theory and nationalism.

709. _____ . "Neglected Factors in the Problem of Normal Interest." QUAR-
TERLY JOURNAL OF ECONOMICS 30 (February 1916): 279-310.

This systematic treatment of interest is presented in four parts:
(1) the nature of capital; (2) the supply; (3) the demand; and
(4) the equilibrium of the supply and demand for capital. The
fourth part is a discussion of the static theoretical concept versus the actual market environment. It is an excellent study
of some of the fallacious arguments regarding capital theory.

710. _____ . ON THE HISTORY AND METHOD OF ECONOMICS, SELECTED
ESSAYS. Chicago: Phoenix Books, University of Chicago Press, 1956.
309 p.

This collection, gathered without the aid of the author, was
prepared for students of economics and economic method. The
twelve articles deal with economics in general, particular problems of production and distribution theory, points of interest
in the philosophy of the social sciences, and the role of political considerations in economics. The volume is an excellent
sampling of the author's work on methodological issues.

711. _____ . "The Place of Marginal Economics in a Collectivist System."
AMERICAN ECONOMIC REVIEW 26, Supplement (March 1936): 255-66.

Knight's intent is to demonstrate that marginal economics plays
approximately the same role in a collectivist state as in an
economy of competitive individualism. The problems of a collectivist society are political and essentially irrelevant for the
economic theorist. Knight's analysis begins with a discussion
of the "role of abstract economic principles" and proceeds to
a study of the economics of collectivism with respect to the
stationary state and to change.

712. _____ . "Professor Hayek and the Theory of Investment." THE ECO-
NOMIC JOURNAL 45 (March 1935): 77-94.

Unconcerned with the technical problems of the "structure of
investment" discussed by Hayek, Knight directs his attention
to Hayek's assertion that "a change in the amount of capital
in society is identical with a change in the investment structure." Knight contends that time, in the sense of length of
the production process, is not directly related to changes in
capital. (See also 705.)

713. _____ . "The Quantity of Capital and the Rate of Interest, Parts I and
II." JOURNAL OF POLITICAL ECONOMY 44 (August 1936): 433-63,
(October 1936); 612-4?

The objective of the first part is to demonstrate that, under
real world conditions, the psychological theory of interest is
invalid and the interest rate is a productivity ratio. The in-

terest rate concept "does not involve a quantity of capital at
all, but only a relation between an instantaneous rate of investment and a resultant instantaneous rate of growth in potential income." The second part is a study of the process of
growth in investment and, more specifically, whether this
growth tends toward equilibrium under any "tenable and useful set of ceteris paribus assumptions." The analysis is conducted "under the form of price analysis in terms of supply
and demand."

714. _____. RISK, UNCERTAINTY AND PROFIT. Introduction by George
Stigler. Chicago: University of Chicago Press, 1971. 381 p. Paperbound.

This study in "pure theory" is an attempt to refine, rather than
reconstruct, existing theory. One must first know what economic classification the system has and only then may he commence toward discovering what such a system can and cannot
accomplish. Only from this vantage point may one answer
the questions as to what may reasonably be expected from the
particular method of organization. The author stated that "no
one mode of organization is adequate or tolerable for all purposes in all fields." One must study other systems in the manner in which the author has studied the free enterprise system,
and finally compare all of them.

715. _____. "Some Issues in the Economics of Stationary States." AMERICAN
ECONOMIC REVIEW 26 (September 1936): 393-411.

In this response to A.C. Pigou's THE ECONOMICS OF STA-
TIONARY STATES (London: Macmillan, 1935), Knight expresses particular disagreement with Pigou's notion of stationary
equilibrium and the foundations necessary to produce such a
situation.

716. _____. "A Suggestion for Simplifying the Statement of the General
Theory of Price." JOURNAL OF POLITICAL ECONOMY 36 (June 1928):
353-70.

This is a detailed study of pricing and cost structures in several types of industry. Knight chose a historical perspective,
noting that one often finds that supposedly new ideas were in
fact advanced much earlier by theorists who remain essentially
unknown. The controversy concerning cost versus utility as
the basis of price is discussed along with the general shape of
cost curves, and a simplified distribution theory is offered.
This is a wide-ranging article covering most aspects of pricing
in an attempt to ascertain which points have, and which have
not, been discussed in the literature.

717. Laughlin, J. Laurence. THE HISTORY OF BIMETALISM IN THE UNITED STATES. New York: D. Appleton, 1886. 257 p.

Although his inquiry was intended to be a historical analysis, Laughlin includes some theoretical discussion, particularly concerning the changing value of gold with respect to its quantity. Interestingly, the author suggests tying the value of a "legal unit of payment" to the prices of a number of staple items in order to provide repayment of long contracts with the original purchasing power, a concept similar to indexing.

718. _____. "The Quantity Theory of Money." JOURNAL OF POLITICAL ECONOMY 32 (June 1924): 265-81.

This is an attack on the quantity theorists for their neglect of the supply factors in "determining prices" and their concentration on the stock of money as the "determinant of prices." It is a classic article by a metalist who has failed to see the distinction between real and nominal income and the difference between "prices" and the "price level." As a metalist, Laughlin does not wish the banking system to manipulate the economy by creating demand with note issues.

719. _____, ed. BANKING REFORM. Chicago: National Citizens League, 1912. 428 p.

This work, which appeared two years before the establishment of the Federal Reserve System, advances an argument against the formation of such a system. The proposal here is for some type of decentralized national reserve agency. The functions and the proper position of this banking reform structure are discussed in great detail. The modern student would find this a useful expression of a viewpoint seldom encountered today.

720. Mitchell, Wesley C. THE BACKWARD ART OF SPENDING MONEY AND OTHER ESSAYS. Selected by Joseph Dorfman. New York: McGraw-Hill, 1937. 421 p.

Topics covered by the seventeen essays include money and monetary policy, and statistics and quantitative methods. There are also several articles on contemporary and earlier writers. It is an excellent source of information about Mitchell's economic thought.

721. _____. "Business Cycles as Revealed by Business Annals." In BUSINESS ANNALS, by Willard Long Thorp, pp. 15-100. New York: National Bureau of Economic Research, 1926.

Mitchell's essay is the introductory chapter to Thorp's book and explains, among other things, the uses, scope, and reliability of business annals. The last three sections, and the last two-thirds of the chapter, are devoted to a discussion of the character, duration, and international comparison of business cycles.

722. _____. BUSINESS CYCLES, THE PROBLEM AND ITS SETTING. New York: National Bureau of Economic Research, 1927. 48 p.

This is the first of two planned volumes which were to appear as close together as possible. These were to serve as an updating of the author's 1913 work on business cycles. This one is subtitled "The Problem of Business Activity." This is, indeed, a refinement and advancement of the knowledge of business cycles since the author's first work which appeared in 1913. The methods of analysis had not changed since 1913; therefore, the present work is neither shorter nor easier than its predecessor.

723. _____. "The Crisis of 1920 and the Problem of Controlling Business Cycles." AMERICAN ECONOMIC REVIEW 12, Supplement (March 1922): 20-32.

This is a detailed discussion of the proper method of approach to analysis of business cycles. Mitchell advocates a cooperative effort by the theorist and the data gatherers and analysts.

724. _____. "Economic Resources in Economic Theory" In STUDIES IN ECONOMICS AND INDUSTRIAL RELATIONS, prepared by University of Pennsylvania Bicentennial Conference, pp. 1-23. Philadelphia: University of Pennsylvania Press, 1941.

In this paper read at the bicentennial celebration at the University of Pennsylvania, Mitchell speaks of resources and resource use, emphasizing that one cannot examine production and distribution in isolation. If we expect individuals to endorse the system, we must insure that, as individuals, they gain from it. One must work constantly to make the principles of the economic system functional for all and the greatest resource for that effort is thorough knowledge.

725. _____. GOLD PRICES AND WAGES UNDER THE GREENBACK STANDARD. Berkeley: University of California Press, 1908. Reprint ed., New York: Augustus M. Kelley, 1966. 627 p.

Mitchell had intended to extend the study begun in A HISTORY OF THE GREENBACKS, 1862-1865 (see 726) up to the resumption of specie payments in 1879. This work, however, is limited to presentation of his data on gold prices and wages. The methods of gathering the data as well as the means by which it was marshalled are explained in five chapters.

726. _____. A HISTORY OF THE GREENBACKS, 1862-1865. Chicago: University of Chicago Press, 1903. 577 p.

Mitchell analyzes the history and consequences of the legal tender acts during this period. The effects of the acts on wages, prices, rent, interest, profits, the specie value of

paper money, and the production and consumption of wealth
are considered. The book contains over 140 pages of statistical appendices and is an excellent source of data on this topic
and period.

727. _____. WHAT HAPPENS DURING BUSINESS CYCLES? Studies in
Business Cycles, no. 5. New York: National Bureau of Economic Research, 1951. 386 p.

This progress report on a work only half finished by Mitchell
was published posthumously. It was to have been a comprehensive study of business cycles, but is still useful for anyone
desiring to understand more fully the workings and vicissitudes
of the U.S. economy.

728. _____, ed. INCOME IN THE UNITED STATES, ITS AMOUNT AND
DISTRIBUTION, 1909-1919. New York: National Bureau of Economic
Research, 1922. 440 p.

Income generation and distribution are examined from the standpoint of sources of production and incomes. The personal distribution of income is analyzed from income tax returns, wage
distribution, and several other nontax sources. The use of
Pareto's Law to describe mathematically the frequency distribution of income is discussed but not encouraged. This is a
detailed report of the study of income, which had been conducted by W.I. King, O.W. Krauth, and F.R. Macaulay.

729. Mitchell, Wesley C., and Burns, Arthur F. MEASURING BUSINESS CY-
CLES. Studies in Business Cycles, no. 2. New York: National Bureau
of Economic Research, 1946. 560 p.

This is an application of a modification of the system for measuring business cycles first presented in 1927 in BUSINESS CY-
CLES, THE PROBLEM AND ITS SETTING (see 722). This text
is primarily work by Burns utilizing Mitchell's tools and assis-
tance. It is an excellent presentation of the National Bureau's
approach to business cycle analysis.

730. Mitchell, Wesley C., et al. INCOME IN THE UNITED STATES, ITS
AMOUNT AND DISTRIBUTION. New York: Harcourt, Brace, 1921.
152 p.

This volume is a summary of the later volume by the same
authors. This is also the first publication of the National
Bureau of Economic Research. It is a fairly aggregated set
of data that was soon to be disaggregated and presented in
a more explicit manner. A few different breakdowns of the
income distribution are given in this volume that are not in
the more detailed volume that appeared the next year.

731. Patten, Simon N. THE PREMISES OF POLITICAL ECONOMY. Philadelphia: J.B. Lippincott, 1885. Reprint ed., New York: Augustus M. Kelley, 1968. 244 p.

Patten expresses dissatisfaction with the classical, and especially the Ricardian, treatment of economic theory, especially distribution theory. The viewpoint presented here is interesting, although it does not extend work by others on the classical theory. The work does demonstrate that, in 1885, marginalism had not yet permeated U.S. economic theory.

732. _____. "The Stability of Prices." PUBLICATIONS OF THE AMERICAN ECONOMIC ASSOCIATION 3 (January 1889): 369-428.

The author begins by discussing the physical conditions that keep prices stable and then moves to the topics of zero-rent lands and the margin of cultivation. The author discusses the law of distribution regarding the income shares of factors, relative to the fixity of their endowment as well as the relationship between shares of varying fixity. The place of surplus revenue and the social conditions that stabilize prices are also discussed.

733. Patton, Jacob Harris. POLITICAL ECONOMY FOR AMERICAN YOUTH. New York: A. Lovell, 1892. 297 p.

This analysis of the fundamentals of economics, "written from an American standpoint," was intended to enable young people to consider more knowledgeably contemporary issues. Because of the emphasis on an American perspective, topics not usually included in an economics text are also explored here.

734. Schumpeter, Joseph A[lois]. BUSINESS CYCLES: A THEORETICAL HISTORICAL, AND STATISTICAL ANALYSIS OF THE CAPITALIST PROCESS. 2 vols. New York: McGraw-Hill, 1939. 1095 p.

This is a classic analysis of what Schumpeter considers the crucial role of business cycles. The subtitle informs the reader of the attempted approach. He recommends no policy, limiting his study to scientific analysis of the economic process. Schumpeter's theory of business cycles is consistent with his theory of economic development and presents some alternatives to Mitchell's approach, which was different in many ways.

735. _____. CAPITALISM, SOCIALISM AND DEMOCRACY. New York: Harper & Row, Publishers, 1950. 431 p.

In this monumental work Schumpeter studies the relationship between the three systems of the world from 1942 to 1949. He concluded that capitalism was destroying itself by its own success. The book discusses at great length all types of socialism, historical and contemporary, and compares them with capitalism and democracy.

736. _____. ECONOMIC DOCTRINE AND METHOD. Translated by R. Avis. New York: Oxford University Press, 1967. 207 p.

This book first appeared in German in 1912 and was translated into English in 1954. Topics are: (1) "Development of Economics as a Science"; (2) "Discovery of the Circular Flow of Economic Life: The Physiocrats"; (3) "Classical System and Its Offshoots"; and (4) "Historical School and the Theory of Marginal Utility." The volume is highly recommended.

737. _____. "On the Concept of Social Value." QUARTERLY JOURNAL OF ECONOMICS 23 (February 1909): 213-32.

Schumpeter examines the use of the concept of social value in economic theory as a purely methodological question. He concludes that the concept of social value and social wants corresponds to no reality in a noncommunist state, although it is indispensable for the study of a communistic state.

738. _____. THE THEORY OF ECONOMIC DEVELOPMENT. Translated by Redvers Opie. New York: Oxford University Press, 1961. 255 p.

Originally published in German in 1911, this work was translated in 1934 and published as volume 46 of the Harvard Economic Studies. This theoretical presentation of the author's views on development should be read by any serious student of economic development. The first chapter would benefit any reader interested in the functioning of a complete economic system.

739. Seligman, E.R.A. THE SHIFTING AND INCIDENCE OF TAXATION. 4th ed. New York: Columbia University Press, 1921. 431 p.

The first part of this work, originally published in 1899, is devoted to a historical survey of the taxation theory. It presents extensive information on incidence theory and covers nearly all earlier writers and viewpoints. In the second part, the "doctrine of incidence" is examined. After defining principles, the author discusses every major type of tax. It is an excellent book by one of the foremost authorities on taxation.

740. Simons, Henry C. ECONOMIC POLICY FOR A FREE SOCIETY. Chicago: University of Chicago Press, 1948. 353 p.

The first six essays are general statements of Simons's economic viewpoint. The next four emphasize monetary, fiscal, and financial considerations, and include his famous article on "rules only." The last three articles concentrate on international commercial policy. This work contains most of Simons's major writings except those on taxation.

741. Sumner, W.G. A HISTORY OF AMERICAN CURRENCY. New York: Henry Holt, 1884. 391 p.

This is an expanded version of an earlier group of essays on U.S. currencies. Papers on "English Bank Restriction," "Austrian Paper Money," and an edited version of the "Bullion Report" are included. It is an early work on a topic relatively unexplored at that time.

742. _____. LECTURES ON THE HISTORY OF PROTECTION IN THE UNITED STATES. New York: G.P. Putnam's Sons, 1877. 64 p.

Sumner endeavors to delineate the weakness and ignorance characteristic of U.S. tariff history. He then presents arguments for free trade based on historical evidence. Various arguments against free trade are also examined in their historical setting. The last lecture is an attempt to draw conclusions from the evidence. The author is an ardent free trader and proposes four rules for trade and four for general taxation.

743. Sweezy, Paul M. "Demand under Conditions of Oligopoly." JOURNAL OF POLITICAL ECONOMY 47 (August 1939): 568-73.

This is the classic article in which Sweezy introduced the concept of the "kinked" demand curve. Oligopoly is assumed to prevail and the oligopolists are assumed to react to actions of the other members of the industry. A distinction is made, however, between their responses to price rises and price declines. The distinction yields the "kinked" demand curve.

744. Taussig, F.W. "Capital Interest, and Diminishing Returns." QUARTERLY JOURNAL OF ECONOMICS 22 (May 1908): 333-63.

Taussig studies the effects of increasing capital in situations in which all other variables are held constant and in situations in which variables are changing. The works of Carver, Clark, Bohm-Bawerk, and Ricardo are discussed. Static and dynamic conditions are considered and the author draws some conclusions regarding qualitative changes versus quantitative changes in capital.

745. _____. "The Employer's Place in Distribution." QUARTERLY JOURNAL OF ECONOMICS 10 (October 1895): 67-94.

This examination of the old wages fund concept is an attempt to ascertain what if any relation exists between wages and capital. The author is basically interested in the extant distribution process and how various sectors obtain their shares.

746. _____. INTERNATIONAL TRADE. New York: Macmillan, 1927.
425 p.

>This was a very early work of excellent quality and thorough-
ness. Taussig included here some discussion of protection and
free trade, topics he examined more extensively in other works.
The first part of this volume is theoretical; the second part
contains the empirical verification of the theoretical work.
Part three deals with trade among countries with "dislocated
exchanges."

747. _____. "Is Market Price Determinate?" QUARTERLY JOURNAL OF
ECONOMICS 35 (May 1921): 394-411.

>According to Taussig, "no one supposes that economics is an
accurate science"; it only informs the practitioner of the trend
of the variable(s) studied. Many of the more likely disturbances of the market system are analyzed in terms of their
effects on market prices. The intent of the paper is to explain
the effects of market disturbances on actual life.

748. _____. "Minimum Wages for Women." QUARTERLY JOURNAL OF
ECONOMICS 30 (May 1916): 411-42.

>Accepted economic principles are applied to legislative mea-
sures for regulating women's wages. A distinction is drawn
between minimum wages for women and minimum wages for
men, and the latter case is not discussed. Taussig's study
considers the effect of this legislation on management and
employee efficiency and the expected results of a high minimum for women.

749. _____. PRINCIPLES OF ECONOMICS. 2 vols. 3rd ed. New York:
Macmillan, 1922. Vol. I, 545 p.; vol. II, 576 p.

>Taussig's PRINCIPLES was the basic text for many of the promi-
nent economists of the 1950s and 1960s who had begun their
work in economics between 1910 and 1930. The volumes were
intended for those seriously engaging in the study of economics.
The first volume contains the material on the organization of
production, value and exchange, money and the exchange
mechanism, and international trade (an area in which Taussig
was expert). The second volume deals with distribution, labor,
economic organization, and taxation. It was and is a rigorous
treatment of the fundamentals of economics.

750. _____. SOME ASPECTS OF THE TARIFF QUESTION. 3rd ed., continued to 1930 with the cooperation of Harry D. White. Cambridge,
Mass.: Harvard University Press, 1931. Reprint ed., New York: Augustus M. Kelley, 1972. 497 p.

>The first three chapters state some questions of principle and

summarize major conclusions. The remaining four parts provide evidence from several industries--sugar, iron and steel, and textiles. The last part discusses each of the industries from 1910 to 1930. This is an excellent supplement to the author's TARIFF HISTORY OF THE UNITED STATES (see 751).

751. _____. THE TARIFF HISTORY OF THE UNITED STATES. 8th ed. New York: G.P. Putnam's Sons, 1892. Reprint ed., New York: Augustus M. Kelley, 1967. 536 p.

All of the articles in this work were originally published elsewhere, but were revised and expanded for this volume. A detailed history of tariff legislation in the United States from 1789 to 1930 is included. Part I develops the study to 1861; part II deals with the years from 1861 to 1930. Each subsequent edition after 1887 included a supplementary chapter to bring the history up to date. The author recommends that one also read his SOME ASPECTS OF THE TARIFF QUESTION (see 750).

752. _____. WAGES AND CAPITAL. London and New York: Macmillan, 1896. 329 p.

As an attempt to reexamine the wages fund controversy and the quantity theory, the author has traced earlier and, in his view, probably more accurate, writings. The five chapters of part I present Taussig's theory and views on these topics. Part II is a critical history of other work on the two topics. The last chapter is a summary of the material in both parts. (Also cited in Chapter 4, entry 525.)

753. Triffin, Robert. MONOPOLISTIC COMPETITION AND GENERAL EQUILIBRIUM THEORY. Cambridge, Mass.: Harvard University Press, 1940. 197 p.

Triffin wishes to bridge the long-existing gap between Walrasian general equilibrium theory and the modern version of Marshallian particular equilibrium analysis, utilizing the theory of monopolistic competition. Excellent reviews of work by Chamberlin, Robinson, Pareto, and von Stackelberg are included. The analysis is focused on prominent areas of difficulty in economic theory and market imperfections.

754. Veblen, Thorstein. ABSENTEE OWNERSHIP AND BUSINESS ENTERPRISE IN RECENT TIMES. New York: B.W. Huebsch, 1923. 445 p.

The first half of the essay deals with England and is a summary of the range of economic circumstances and growth and change which led up to the twentieth century. The last half of the period is studied in terms of situations existing in the United States. The second part of the book is an objective theoretical analysis of the economic situation as it has taken shape during the twentieth century. Absentee ownership and the use of credit in the United States are emphasized.

755. _____. THE ENGINEERS AND THE PRICE SYSTEM. New York: Viking, 1933. 169 p.

These essays, first published in the magazine DIAL, predicted that a deparession would result from the post-war situation of 1919. Veblen's articles anticipate various fundamental problems, the seriousness of which would become evident during the the depression of the 1930s.

756. _____. ESSAYS IN OUR CHANGING ORDER. Edited by Leon Andzrooni. New York: Viking, 1943. 472 p.

This book contains many of Veblen's important essays. The works are divided into three groups: essays in economics, miscellaneous papers, and war essays, the last group being by far the most numerous. There are also some excellent studies of other economists and their theories in the first section. Some of the miscellaneous papers are concerned with philosophy.

757. _____. ESSAYS, REVIEWS, AND REPORTS. Edited with an introduction by Joseph Dorfman. Clifton, N.J.: Augustus M. Kelley, 1973. 690 p.

Dorfman's essay, "New Light on Veblen," occupies the first 330 pages; the remainder of the volume contains about seven essays, over forty reviews on many social science topics, and a few reports. The four-part appendix includes obituaries, reviews of Veblen's work, and some personal data.

758. _____. THE HIGHER LEARNING IN AMERICA: A MEMORANDUM ON THE CONDUCT OF UNIVERSITIES BY BUSINESS MEN. New York: B.W. Huebsch, 1918. 286 p.

This is an examination of governing boards, academic administration, prestige, material equipment, academic personnel, and other topics. Most of Veblen's information is based on his study of the University of Chicago.

759. _____. AN INQUIRY INTO THE NATURE OF PEACE AND THE TERMS OF ITS PERPETUATION. New York: B.W. Huebsch, 1919. 367 p.

In this work, Veblen searched for the terms by which peace at large may be installed and maintained. He asked what, in the present situation, would allow the realization of the necessary conditions for peace in the foreseeable future. Finally, he projected and examined the consequences that would ensue from the establishment of a general peace. The answers are sought in "terms of those known factors of human behavior that can be shown by analysis of experience to control the conduct of nations in conjectures of this kind."

760. _____. THE INSTINCT OF WORKMANSHIP AND THE STATE OF THE INDUSTRIAL ARTS. New York: B.W. Huebsch, 1922. 355 p.

The author is attempting to analyze the relationship between industrial practice and other institutional facts that define any given phase of civilization. He assumes that technological practices influence the scope and direction of civilization in nontechnological ways. He does not, however, disregard the effects that these other areas, in turn, might have on the state of the industrial arts. It is a detailed study of technology, culture, and society.

761. _____. THE PLACE OF SCIENCE IN MODERN CIVILIZATION, AND OTHER ESSAYS. New York: B.W. Huebsch, 1919. 509 p.

These fourteen essays, first published in journals, examine such topics as why economics is not an evolutionary science, the economics of J.B. Clark, G. Schmoller, Karl Marx, and many other subjects related to economics and political economy. It is a very important work for one who is interested in the issues of Veblen's time.

762. _____. THE THEORY OF BUSINESS ENTERPRISE. New York: Charles Scribner's Sons, 1904. 400 p.

This work is an inquiry into the "nature, causes, utility, and further drift of business enterprise" away from the traditional concept of business enterprise and toward materialism-dominated industry. Veblen has chosen to discuss this situation from the businessman's viewpoint, considering "the aims, motives, and means that condition current business traffic."

763. _____. THE THEORY OF THE LEISURE CLASS. Introduction by C. Wright Mills. New York: New American Library, 1953. 261 p.

This was Veblen's first book (1899) and is probably his best known work. Veblen demonstrates his superior skills as an economist and as a social and political polemicist. It is an attack on the activities and values of a particular group of the very wealthy in the United States. Many link this book with the more recent work of John Kenneth Galbraith, THE AFFLUENT SOCIETY. Although written before the turn of the century, it is a worthwhile book for anyone interested in social and/or economic criticism.

764. _____. THE VESTED INTERESTS AND THE COMMON MAN. New York: B.W. Huebsch, 1919. Reprint ed., New York: Augustus M. Kelley, 1964. 183 p.

This is a collection of papers originally written for the magazine DIAL. In these papers Veblen examines the apparent shift in the underlying principles of business behavior since the late eighteenth century. He appears to draw a distinction between business enterprise and industry, the latter characterized by materialistic factors.

765. Viner, Jacob. "Angell's THEORY OF INTERNATIONAL PRICES." JOURNAL OF POLITICAL ECONOMY 34 (October 1926): 597-623.

In this detailed review of Angell's book, Viner considers only those historical and constructive doctrines with which he disagrees. The author criticizes Angell's appraisal of the works of other writers and the way in which Angell presents his own theory in terms that make it appear both new and in direct opposition to earlier work. After spending over twenty pages critizing the book, Viner calls it "a distinguished, stimulating, and valuable addition to the literature."

766. _____. "The Prevalence of Dumping in International Trade, Parts I and II." JOURNAL OF POLITICAL ECONOMY 30 (October 1922): 655-80, (December 1922): 796-826.

The first part is concerned with instances of dumping before 1880 and with specific German instances since 1880. Part II deals with dumping by the remaining developed countries, and includes a short section on monopolies and dumping. The author has approached his topic cautiously, believing that conservative judgments would cause less harm.

767. _____. "Taxation and Changes in Price Levels." JOURNAL OF POLITI-CAL ECONOMY 31 (August 1923): 494-520.

Dissatisfied with available treatments of the relationship between taxation and price, Viner attempts in this article to "open up the subject in the hope that it will lead to further discussion of the general problem and its detailed manifestations." Assuming the practical difficulties of stabilizing prices to be very great, the author defines the problems of price instability that arise from the initiation of tax laws and makes a few suggestions that would be "capable of practical application."

768. _____. "The Utility Concept in Value Theory and Its Critics, Parts I and II." JOURNAL OF POLITICAL ECONOMY 33 (August 1925): 369-87, (December 1925): 638-59.

In response to extant criticism of utility theory, Viner examines the utility concept in the price system (part I) and in welfare economics (part II). Utility theory has made positive contributions to knowledge in price economics and Viner claims that failure to examine cases thoroughly has engendered much of the criticism. Part II contains an extensive discussion of difficulties in welfare economics. Viner's conclusion concerning the mobility of the subjective calculus for measurement of absolute quantities is that "the imperfect measurement of variations in welfare may serve as a better guide to action than the perfect measurement of something which has something to do with welfare."

769. Walker, Francis A. DISCUSSIONS IN ECONOMICS AND STATISTICS. 2 vols. New York: Henry Holt, 1899. 454 p. Reprint ed., with an introduction by Joseph Dorfman, New York: Augustus M. Kelley, 1971. 481 p.

Dorfman's introduction to the reprint edition is a study of Walker as a revisionist. The first volume contains essays on finance

and taxation, money and bimetallism, and economic theory.
Most major topics in domestic and European economics are represented in these articles. The essays in volume II concern
statistics, national growth, and social economics, and are of
a less theoretical nature. They are more useful as a source
of factual information about the United States during the last
quarter of the nineteenth century.

770. _____. POLITICAL ECONOMY. New York: Henry Holt, 1886.
415 p.

This is an abridged version of the third edition of Walker's
MANUAL OF POLITICAL ECONOMY (Boston: Little, Brown,
1874). The book treats in a formal manner production, exchange, distribution, and consumption, and concludes with a
group of applications of the theory to problems of the day,
many of which still concern economists today. For its time,
this work was quite theoretical.

771. _____. "The Source of Business Profits." QUARTERLY JOURNAL OF
ECONOMICS 1 (April 1887): 265-88.

In this answer to Henry Sidgwick's criticism of Walker's treatment of the wages fund controversy, Walker here presents a
residual theory of wages in which the laborers get what is left
after profits, which are kept at the "normal" level by competition. This approach is especially interesting for its implications for socialist challenges.

C. COMMENTARIES ON THE MAJOR CONTRIBUTIONS

772. Bennion, E.G. "Unemployment in the Theories of Schumpeter and
Keynes." AMERICAN ECONOMIC REVIEW 33 (June 1943): 336-47.

One of the purposes of this article was to show that cyclical
unemployment was an integral part of Schumpeter's theory.
Keynes's theory attempts to explain involuntary unemployment,
whereas Schumpeter's formulation is a dynamic theory in which
changing production functions are essential. Bennion's second
purpose was to create a synthesis of the two theories in order
to explain secular stagnation.

773. Boulding, Kenneth. "Institutional Economics: A New Look at Institutionalism." AMERICAN ECONOMIC REVIEW 47 (May 1957): 1-12.

Institutionalism is viewed as "a movement of dissent" that has
created no establishment. Institutionalists oppose both the or-
thodoxy of classical and academic economic theory and the
customs, habits, and motivations of those who run economic
institutions. These dissenters are distinguished from challengers

who attempt to supply new alternatives. European as well as
U.S. institutionalists are discussed. Comments by other
noted economists follow this article in the journal.

774. Dewey, Donald. MODERN CAPITAL THEORY. New York: Columbia
University Press, 1965. 238 p.

This is a systematic revision and reconstruction of capital theory. Dewey exhibits the same basic attitudes toward capital
theory developed by Irving Fisher, contending that the basic
determinants of capital accumulation are the marginal productivity of investment and the taste for investment. Part of
Dewey's purpose is to counter the preoccupation of modern
capital theorists with money.

775. Johnson, E.A.J. THE FOUNDATIONS OF AMERICAN ECONOMIC
FREEDOM. Minneapolis: University of Minnesota Press, 1973. 335 p.

This work is an examination of the roots of the free enterprise
system. The discussion covers early policy makers and relates
their economic beliefs to the system that ensued. The volume
contains nearly as much economic as intellectual history.

776. Kuznets, Simon. "Schumpeter's Business Cycles." AMERICAN ECO-
NOMIC REVIEW 30 (June 1940): 257-71.

This is a very detailed review of Schumpeter's BUSINESS CY-
CLES: A THEORETICAL, HISTORICAL, AND STATISTICAL
ANALYSIS OF THE CAPITALIST PROCESS (see 734). Kuznets
limits his address to three aspects of Schumpeter's vast topic:
(a) "the relation between distribution of entrepreneurial
ability and the cyclical character of economic change; (b) the
four-phase scheme of the business cycle and its bearing upon
statistical analysis; and (c) the three types of cycles distinguished." Kuznets's analysis elicits some definite shortcom-
ings in Schumpeter's presentation of these three topics.

777. Oser, Jacob. HENRY GEORGE. New York: Twayne Publishers, 1974.
130 p.

George's PROGRESS AND POVERTY is the focus for this biography in which Oser traces George's life and career up to his
conception of PROGRESS AND POVERTY and then analyzes
the entire work. A critical chapter and one on the public
reception of the work are included, along with a chapter on
his other works and subsequent career. It is a good study of
an interesting man and his work.

778. Post, Louis F. THE PROPHET OF SAN FRANCISCO: PERSONAL MEMO-
RIES AND INTERPRETATIONS OF HENRY GEORGE. New York: Van-

guard Press, 1930. 335 p.

This work is a study of many of the ideas and activities in which Henry George was engaged, written by a personal friend. Post also examines George's influence on later scholars.

779. Seligman, Ben B. MAIN CURRENTS IN MODERN ECONOMICS: ECO-NOMIC THOUGHT SINCE 1870. New York: The Free Press, 1963. 887 p.

This general text contains approximately a hundred pages on the U.S. institutionalist school and its members. This school had a very significant impact on the evolution of U.S. economic thought. Their methodology was similar to that of their European counterparts, the German historicists. (Also cited in Chapter 3, entry 312.)

780. Warriner, Doreen. "Schumpeter and the Conception of Static Equilibrium." THE ECONOMIC JOURNAL 41 (March 1931): 38-50.

In his preface to THE THEORY OF ECONOMIC DEVELOPMENT (see 738), Schumpeter noted that he had eschewed the use of the terms "static" and "dynamic" out of deference for Frisch. Warriner here contends that Schumpeter's altered terminology engendered his synthesis of British neoclassical and German historical thought. The author discusses at great length the role of static equilibrium in in Schumpeter's model of cycles, illustrating the necessary function of the opposing forces.

D. CONTRIBUTIONS OF LESSER IMPORTANCE

781. Anderson, Karl L. "The Unity of Veblen's Theoretical System." QUAR-TERLY JOURNAL OF ECONOMICS 47 (August 1933): 598-626.

782. Angell, James W. "The Components of the Circular Velocity of Money." QUARTERLY JOURNAL OF ECONOMICS 51 (February 1937): 224-72.

783. _____. "Equilibrium in International Trade: The United States, 1919-26." QUARTERLY JOURNAL OF ECONOMICS 42 (May 1928): 388-433.

784. _____. "The General Dynamics of Money." JOURNAL OF POLITICAL ECONOMY 45 (June 1937): 289-346.

785. _____. "International Trade under Inconvertible Paper." QUARTERLY JOURNAL OF ECONOMICS 36 (April 1920): 359-412.

786. _____. "Money, Prices and Production: Some Fundamental Concepts." QUARTERLY JOURNAL OF ECONOMICS 48 (November 1933): 39-76.

787. _____. "The 100 Per Cent Reserve Plan." QUARTERLY JOURNAL OF ECONOMICS 50 (November 1935): 1-35.

788. Armstrong, W.E. "Uncertainty and the Utility Function." THE ECONOMIC JOURNAL 58 (March 1948): 1-10.

789. Brown, Harry. "Capital Valuation and the 'Psychological School'." AMERICAN ECONOMIC REVIEW 19 (September 1929): 357-62. (See also Vol. 20, March 1930, p. 78 and June 1930, p. 248.)

790. _____. "The Marginal Productivity versus the Impatience Theory of Interest." QUARTERLY JOURNAL OF ECONOMICS 27 (August 1913): 630-50.

791. Burns, E.M. "Does Institutionalism Complement or Compete with 'Orthodox Economics'?" AMERICAN ECONOMIC REVIEW 21 (March 1931): 80-87.

792. Carey, Henry C. PRINCIPLES OF SOCIAL SCIENCE. 3 vols. New York: Augustus M. Kelley, 1963. Vol. I, 474 p.; vol. II, 480 p.; vol. III, 511 p.

793. Chamberlin, Edward H. "Duopoly: Value Where Sellers Are Few." QUARTERLY JOURNAL OF ECONOMICS 44 (November 1929): 63-100.

794. _____. "Monopolistic or Imperfect Competition?" QUARTERLY JOURNAL OF ECONOMICS 51 (August 1937): 557-80.

795. _____. "The Origin and Early Development of Monopolistic Competition Theory." QUARTERLY JOURNAL OF ECONOMICS 75 (November 1961): 515-43.

796. Clark, John Bates. "Concerning the Nature of Capital: A Reply." QUARTERLY JOURNAL OF ECONOMICS 21 (May 1907): 351-70.

797. _____. "The Future of Economic Theory." QUARTERLY JOURNAL OF ECONOMICS 13 (October 1898): 1-14.

798. Clark, John Maurice. "An Appraisal of the Workability of Compensatory Devices." AMERICAN ECONOMIC REVIEW 29 (March 1939): 194-208.

799. _____. "The Concept of Value." QUARTERLY JOURNAL OF ECONOMICS 29 (August 1915): 663-73.

800. Coase, R.H. "The Nature of the Firm." ECONOMICA n.s. 4 (Novem-

ber 1937): 386-405.

801. Coats, A.W. "The Influence of Veblen's Methodology." JOURNAL OF
POLITICAL ECONOMY 62 (December 1954): 529-37.

802. Commons, John R. "Political Economy and Business Economy: Comments on Fisher's Capital and Income." QUARTERLY JOURNAL OF
ECONOMICS 22 (November 1907): 120-25.

803. _____. "Protection and Natural Monopolies." QUARTERLY JOURNAL
OF ECONOMICS 6 (July 1892): 279-84.

804. Cummings, John. "The Theory of the Leisure Class." JOURNAL OF PO-
LITICAL ECONOMY 7 (September 1899): 425-55.

805. Davenport, H.J. "Capital as a Competitive Concept." JOURNAL OF
POLITICAL ECONOMY 13 (December 1904): 31-47.

806. _____. "Cost and Its Significance." AMERICAN ECONOMIC REVIEW
1 (December 1911): 724-52.

807. _____. "A New Text; Seligman: 'Social Value'." JOURNAL OF
POLITICAL ECONOMY 14 (March 1906): 143-69.

808. _____. "Proposed Modifications in Austrian Theory and Terminology."
QUARTERLY JOURNAL OF ECONOMICS 16 (May 1902): 355-84.

809. Demsetz, Harold. "The Nature of Equilibrium in Monopolistic Competition." JOURNAL OF POLITICAL ECONOMY 67 (February 1959): 21-
30.

810. Dunbar, C.F. "The Reaction in Political Economy." QUARTERLY
JOURNAL OF ECONOMICS 1 (October 1886): 113-33.

811. Durand, David. "Some Thoughts on Marginal Productivity, with Special
Reference to Professor Douglas' Analysis." JOURNAL OF POLITICAL
ECONOMY 45 (December 1937): 740-58.

812. Fetter, Frank A. "Davenport's Competitive Economics." JOURNAL OF
POLITICAL ECONOMY 22 (June 1914): 550-65.

813. _____. "The Definition of Price." AMERICAN ECONOMIC REVIEW
2 (December 1912): 783-813.

814. _____. "The Nature of Capital and Income." JOURNAL OF POLITI-

CAL ECONOMY 15 (March 1907): 129-48.

815. Fisher, Irving. "Cournot and Mathematical Economics." QUARTERLY JOURNAL OF ECONOMICS 12 (January 1898): 119-38, 238-44.

816. _____. "Davenport's VALUE AND DISTRIBUTION." JOURNAL OF POLITICAL ECONOMY 16 (December 1908): 661-79.

817. _____. "The Impatience Theory of Interest." AMERICAN ECONOMIC REVIEW 3 (September 1913): 610-18. (See also the "comment" on p. 618.)

818. _____. "Precedents for Defining Capital." QUARTERLY JOURNAL OF ECONOMICS 18 (May 1904): 386-408.

819. Friedman, Milton. "Wesley C. Mitchell as an Economic Theorist." JOURNAL OF POLITICAL ECONOMY 58 (December 1950): 465-93.

820. Gordon, Barry J. "Aristotle, Schumpeter, and the Metallist Tradition." QUARTERLY JOURNAL OF ECONOMICS 75 (November 1961): 608-14.

821. Graham, Frank D. "Achilles' Heels in Monetary Standards." AMERICAN ECONOMIC REVIEW 30 (March 1940): 16-32.

822. _____. "Relation of Wage Rates to the Use of Machinery." AMERICAN ECONOMIC REVIEW 16 (September 1926): 434-42.

823. Gruchy, Allan G. "John R. Commons' Concept of Twentieth-Century Economics." JOURNAL OF POLITICAL ECONOMY 48 (December 1940): 823-49.

824. Hamilton, Earl J. "American Treasure and the Rise of Capitalism." ECONOMICA 9 (November 1929): 338-57.

825. Hardy, Charles Oscar. "Liberalism in the Modern State: The Philosophy of Henry Simons." JOURNAL OF POLITICAL ECONOMY 56 (August 1948): 305-14.

826. Harris, Abram L. "Types of Institutionalism." JOURNAL OF POLITICAL ECONOMY 40 (December 1932): 721-49.

827. Harrod, R.F. "Doctrines of Imperfect Competition." QUARTERLY JOURNAL OF ECONOMICS 48 (May 1934): 442-70.

828. Heweth, William W. "Professor Irving Fisher on Income, in the Light of

Experience." AMERICAN ECONOMIC REVIEW 19 (June 1929): 217-26.

829. Homan, Paul T. "John Bates Clark: Earlier and Later Phases of His Work." QUARTERLY JOURNAL OF ECONOMICS 42 (November 1927): 39-69.

830. Johnson, Alvin S. "Davenport's Economics and the Present Problems of Theory." QUARTERLY JOURNAL OF ECONOMICS 28 (May 1914): 417-46.

831. Johnson, Edgar H. "The Economics of Henry George's PROGRESS AND POVERTY." JOURNAL OF POLITICAL ECONOMY 18 (November 1910): 714-35.

832. Kaldor, Nicholas. "Professor Chamberlin on Monopolistic and Imperfect Competition." QUARTERLY JOURNAL OF ECONOMICS 52 (May 1938): 513-29. (See also the "reply" on p. 530.)

833. Knight, Frank H. "Cost of Production and Price over Long and Short Periods." JOURNAL OF POLITICAL ECONOMY 29 (April 1921): 304-35.

834. _____. "Professor Fisher's Interest Theory: A Case in Point." JOURNAL OF POLITICAL ECONOMY 39 (April 1931): 176-212.

835. _____. "Some Fallacies in the Interpretation of Social Cost." QUARTERLY JOURNAL OF ECONOMICS 38 (August 1924): 582-606.

836. _____. "What is 'Truth' in Economics?" JOURNAL OF POLITICAL ECONOMICS 48 (February 1940): 1-32. (See also Vol. 50, December 1942, pp. 732, 750.)

837. Knight, Frank H., and Clark, John Maurice. "A Note on Professor Clark's Illustration of Marginal Productivity." JOURNAL OF POLITICAL ECONOMY 33 (October 1925): 550-53.

838. Laughlin, J. Laurence. "The Gold-Exchange Standard." QUARTERLY JOURNAL OF ECONOMICS 41 (August 1927): 644-63.

839. _____. "Hobson's Theory of Distribution." JOURNAL OF POLITICAL ECONOMY 12 (June 1904): 305-26.

840. Leontief, Wassily. "Stackelberg on Monopolistic Competition." JOURNAL OF POLITICAL ECONOMY 44 (August 1936): 554-59.

841. MacDonald, Ronan. "Schumpeter and Max Weber--Central Visions and Social Theories." QUARTERLY JOURNAL OF ECONOMICS 79 (August 1965): 373-96.

842. Machlup, Fritz. "Evaluation of the Practical Significance of the Theory of Monopolistic Competition." AMERICAN ECONOMIC REVIEW 29 (June 1939): 227-36.

843. _____. "Professor Knight and the 'Period of Production'." JOURNAL OF POLITICAL ECONOMY 43 (October 1935): 577-624, (December 1935): 808.

844. Mitchell, Wesley C. "The Quantity Theory of the Value of Money." JOURNAL OF POLITICAL ECONOMY 4 (March 1896): 139-65.

845. _____. "The Real Issues in the Quantity-Theory Controversy." JOURNAL OF POLITICAL ECONOMY 12 (June 1904): 403-8.

846. Nichol, A.J. "Professor Chamberlin's Theory of United Competition." QUARTERLY JOURNAL OF ECONOMICS 48 (February 1934): 317-37.

847. Padan, R.S. "J.B. Clark's Formulae of Wages and Interest." JOURNAL OF POLITICAL ECONOMY 9 (March 1901): 161-90.

848. Patten, Simon N. "President Walker's Theory of Distribution." QUARTERLY JOURNAL OF ECONOMICS 4 (October 1889): 34-49.

849. Rimmer, Douglas. "Schumpeter and the Underdeveloped Countries." QUARTERLY JOURNAL OF ECONOMICS 75 (August 1961): 422-50.

850. Roberts, Paul Craig. "Oskar Lange's Theory of Socialist Planning." JOURNAL OF POLITICAL ECONOMY 79 (July/August 1971): 562-77.

851. Robinson, Austin. "Monopoly and Imperfect Competition." THE ECONOMIC JOURNAL 47 (March 1937): 169-72.

852. Rogin, Leo. "Davenport on the Economics of Alfred Marshall." AMERICAN ECONOMIC REVIEW 26 (June 1936): 248-57.

853. Rosenstein-Rodan, P.N. "The Role of Time in Economic Theory." ECONOMICA n.s. 1 (February 1934): 77-97.

854. Rothschild, K.W. "Price Theory and Oligopoly." THE ECONOMIC JOURNAL 57 (September 1947): 299-320.

855. Ruttan, Vernon W. "Usher and Schumpeter on Invention, Innovation, and Technological Change." QUARTERLY JOURNAL OF ECONOMICS 73 (November 1959): 596-606. (See also the "comment" in Vol. 75, February 1961, p. 152.)

856. Schlesinger, James R., and Phillips, Almavin. "The Ebb Tide of Capitalism? Schumpeter's Prophecy Re-Examined." QUARTERLY JOURNAL OF ECONOMICS 73 (August 1959): 448-65.

857. Schumpeter, Joseph Alois. "The Explanation of the Business Cycle." ECONOMICA 7 (December 1927): 286-311.

858. _____. "The Instability of Capitalism." THE ECONOMIC JOURNAL 38 (September 1928): 361-86.

859. Shafer, Joseph E. "Institutional Economics of Professor Commons." AMERICAN ECONOMIC REVIEW 22 (June 1932): 261-64. (See also p. 264 and vol. 23, March 1933, p. 87.)

860. Sowell, Thomas. "The 'Evolutionary' Economics of Thorstein Veblen." OXFORD ECONOMIC PAPERS n.s. 19 (July 1967): 177-98.

861. Stigler, George J. "The Kinky Oligopoly Demand Curve and Rigid Prices." JOURNAL OF POLITICAL ECONOMY 55 (October 1947): 432-49.

862. _____. "Notes on the Theory of Duopoly." JOURNAL OF POLITICAL ECONOMY 48 (August 1940): 521-41.

863. Taussig, F.W. "A Contribution to the Study of Cost Curves." QUARTERLY JOURNAL OF ECONOMICS 38 (November 1923): 173-76.

864. _____. "A Contribution to the Theory of Railway Rates." QUARTERLY JOURNAL OF ECONOMICS 5 (July 1891): 438-65.

865. _____. "Employment and the National Dividend." QUARTERLY JOURNAL OF ECONOMICS 51 (November 1936): 198-203.

866. _____. "Exhaustion of the Soil and the Theory of Rent." QUARTERLY JOURNAL OF ECONOMICS 31 (February 1917): 345-48.

867. _____. "International Trade under Depreciated Paper: A Contribution to Theory." QUARTERLY JOURNAL OF ECONOMICS 31 (May 1917): 380-403. (See also Vol. 32, May 1918, pp. 404, 410, and October 1918, pp. 674, 690; Vol. 33, February 1919, p. 368.)

868. _____. "The Plan for a Compensated Dollar." QUARTERLY JOURNAL OF ECONOMICS 27 (May 1913): 401-16.

869. _____. "Reciprocity." QUARTERLY JOURNAL OF ECONOMICS 7 (October 1892): 26-39.

870. _____. "Wages and Prices in Relation to International Trade." QUARTERLY JOURNAL OF ECONOMICS 20 (August 1906): 497-522.

871. Turner, John Roscoe. "Henry C. Carey's Attitude toward the Ricardian Theory of Rent." QUARTERLY JOURNAL OF ECONOMICS 26 (August 1912): 644-72.

872. Veblen, Thorstein. "Credit and Prices." JOURNAL OF POLITICAL ECONOMY 13 (June 1905): 460-72.

873. _____. "Limitations of Marginal Utility." JOURNAL OF POLITICAL ECONOMY 17 (November 1909): 620-36.

874. _____. "On the Nature of Capital: Investment, Intangible Assets, and the Pecuniary Magnate." QUARTERLY JOURNAL OF ECONOMICS 23 (November 1908): 104-36.

875. _____. "The Preconceptions of Economic Science." QUARTERLY JOURNAL OF ECONOMICS 13 (January 1899): 121-50, (July 1899): 396-426; 14 (February 1900): 240-69.

876. _____. "Professor Clark's Economics." QUARTERLY JOURNAL OF ECONOMICS 22 (February 1908): 147-95.

877. Walker, Francis A. "The Doctrine of Rent, and the Residual Claimant Theory of Wages." QUARTERLY JOURNAL OF ECONOMICS 5 (July 1891): 417-37.

878. _____. "Protection and Protectionists." QUARTERLY JOURNAL OF ECONOMICS 4 (April 1890): 245-75.

879. _____. "The Quantity Theory of Money." QUARTERLY JOURNAL OF ECONOMICS 9 (July 1895): 372-79.

880. _____. "A Reply to Mr. MacVane: On the Source of Business Profits." QUARTERLY JOURNAL OF ECONOMICS 2 (April 1000): 263-96.

881. Walsh, Robert M. "Empirical Tests for Price Theories: Fisher, Foster

and Catchings, Keynes." QUARTERLY JOURNAL OF ECONOMICS 48 (May 1934): 546-58.

882. Weston, N.A. "The Ricardian Epoch in American Economics." AMERICAN ECONOMIC REVIEW 23 (March 1933): 27-34.

883. White, Horace G. "A Review of Monopolistic and Imperfect Competition Theories." AMERICAN ECONOMIC REVIEW 26 (December 1936): 637-49.

884. Young, Allyn A. "Increasing Returns and Economic Progress." THE ECONOMIC JOURNAL 38 (December 1928): 527-42.

Chapter 6

TWENTIETH-CENTURY
BRITISH ECONOMIC THOUGHT

Chapter 6

TWENTIETH-CENTURY BRITISH ECONOMIC THOUGHT

A. INTRODUCTION

Twentieth-century British economics is so dominated by the work of J.M. Keynes that students are sometimes surprised to learn that there are many other notable and prolific economists whose books must be considered major contributions to the literature. Because these modern writers also scrutinized carefully the work of their colleagues, the criticism of the major works--particularly after 1936 when Keynes's GENERAL THEORY OF EMPLOYMENT, INTEREST AND MONEY appeared--is essential reading for the serious student. Value and exchange theory, along with trade cycle theory, were issues of importance during this period.

Because numerous sources of information about Keynes and his work are readily available, few are listed here. During the past decade or so, scholars have come to believe that current "Keynesian" interpretations may in fact be antithetic to Keynes's own theoretical approach. Several of the works in this chapter present this argument.

Because this chapter documents the development of economic analysis to 1940, many writers listed here--J.R. Hicks and Joan Robinson are two--are still alive and productive. But it has not been possible to list as many of their books published after 1940 as might be desired.

The beginning of the era covered in this chapter includes such writers as A.C. Pigou, whose work exhibits characteristics of both marginalist and twentieth-century thinking. Considering the predominance of neoclassical theory until the late 1930s, however, the presence of firmly transitional theorists should not surprise.

Finally, it should be noted that many of the individual essays cited here have been collected and published as books by their authors. The popularity of this approach to publication benefits both libraries and students wishing to own their materials.

B. MAJOR CONTRIBUTIONS

885. Allen, R.G.D. "The Foundations of a Mathematical Theory of Exchange." ECONOMICA 12 (May 1932): 197-226.

This rigorous treatment of the theory of exchange begins with an examination of the actions of individuals as consumers and concludes with a study of the market and mutual interaction of consumers. The last section is a discussion of the assumptions necessary for the development--but not the construction-- of an equilibrium position. The essay requires thorough knowledge of calculus.

886. _____. "On the Marginal Utility of Money and Its Application." ECONOMICA 13 (May 1933): 186-209.

This is an attempt to provide a rigorous theoretical basis for the problems considered by R. Frisch in his NEW METHODS OF MEASURING MARGINAL UTILITY (Verlag von J.C.B. Mohr, 1932). The first section is a study of money utility and its possible statistical measurement; the second part is an application of this notion to the labor supply curve. The final section is an examination of a theoretical price index. This paper, like others by the author, requires an extensive background in mathematics.

887. Beveridge, W.H. "Mr. Keynes' Evidence for Overpopulation." ECONOMICA 4 (February 1924): 1-20.

Beveridge refers to evidence presented by Keynes in a reply to an earlier article by Beveridge. (Both essays appeared in the ECONOMIC JOURNAL for December 1923. See 888.) The two are arguing about European population levels before and after the war. They disagree not only on the nature of the problem, but on how to solve it as well.

888. _____. "Population and Unemployment." ECONOMIC JOURNAL 33 (December 1923): 447-75.

Beveridge here examines the relationship between unemployment and the rate of population growth. Unlike many of his critics, he thinks that the rate of unemployment is basically unaffected by changes in population growth. A "Reply" by J.M. Keynes follows this article.

889. _____. "Unemployment in the Trade Cycle." ECONOMIC JOURNAL 49 (March 1939): 52-65.

Two factors about the relationship between unemployment and the trade cycle were stated briefly in this article. The first concerns the principal characteristic of industries that rely

heavily on exports. The second factor is the seasonal tendency evident in the British trade cycle. He does present some
evidence in support of his findings, but poses many questions
regarding the relationship between these two and between these
and other factors.

890. Bowley, A.L. "The Theoretical Effects of Rationing on Prices." ECO-
NOMIC JOURNAL 30 (September 1920): 340-47.

This mathematical essay concerns an issue that is plaguing
many countries today. The treatment utilizes geometry and
algebra, but little or no calculus. Seven different cases are
examined and discussed.

891. _____. "Wages and the Mobility of Labour." ECONOMIC JOURNAL
22 (March 1912): 46-52.

Possible differential wage rates between trade unions and the
Labour Exchanges is the subject of this article. The author
is interested only in the effects that increased mobility engendered by the exchanges would have on wages. Mathematical
analysis is restricted to the last section.

892. Dobb, Maurice H. "Economic Theory and the Problems of a Socialist
Economy." ECONOMIC JOURNAL 43 (December 1933): 588-98.

Acknowledging the prevalence of economic forces in a socialist
system, as most scholars do, Dobb attempts to explore their
implications with respect to altered property rights and distribution systems.

893. _____. "A Note on Saving and Investment in a Socialist Economy."
ECONOMIC JOURNAL 49 (December 1939): 713-28.

The author rejects the "trial and error" method of determining
the equilibrium price in a socialist system advocated by O.
Lange, A.P. Lerner, and R.L. Hall. Dobb claims that their
approach necessarily would produce the same instability present in capitalist systems. In Dobb's opinion, instability is
present when neither the marginal efficiency of capital, nor
the relationship between the price level of finished goods and
money wages, is independent of the rate of investment. It
is an interesting analysis.

894. _____. "A Skeptical View of the Theory of Wages." ECONOMIC
JOURNAL 39 (December 1929): 506-19.

This critical analysis of the methodology of British economists
is concerned with the wage-theory portion of the distribution
theory. The theory is criticized as logically inconsistent and
incompletely defined and derived. Other aspects of distribution

are also examined.

895. Gregory, T.E. "Rationalisation and Technological Unemployment." ECO-
NOMIC JOURNAL 40 (December 1930): 551-67.

This is a study of two new terms--"nationalization" and "technological unemployment"--in economic vocabulary. The former
denotes the process of altering the production process in such
a manner as to reduce the quantity of labor necessary to produce the existing quantum of welfare. The latter may ensue
from the function of the former. It is an interesting analysis
of a very relevant topic.

896. Hahn, F.H., and Brechling, F.P.R., eds. THE THEORY OF INTEREST
RATES. London: Macmillan, 1965. 365 p.

This is a collection of papers from a conference convened to
reexamine money and interest theory in the light of theoretical
developments since the GENERAL THEORY. Topics include
"theories of asset preference," "equilibrium models," and "growth
and intertemporal allocation." Some of the articles employ
advanced mathematics.

897. Harrod, R.F. ECONOMIC DYNAMICS. London: Macmillan, 1973. 195 p.

Although undertaken as a revision of his earlier work, TO-
WARDS A DYNAMIC ECONOMICS (see 904), this volume
contains very little of the original material. New ideas and approaches to the subject have precluded reusing that material
in this far more complete treatment of the subject of dynamics.

898. _____. ECONOMIC ESSAYS. New York: Harcourt, Brace, 1952.
301 p.

Some of these essays are new, others are reprinted; all were
prepared for the general economist who specialized in none of
the fields studied here: population and labor, lack of competition, Keynesian employment theory, and von Hayek's concept of individualism. A new edition of this work appeared in
1972 and included an essay, "Increasing Returns," which should
be read along with the eight articles on imperfect competition.

899. _____. "An Essay in Dynamic Theory." ECONOMIC JOURNAL 49
(March 1939): 14-33.

On the basis of three propositions which unite the multiplier
and acceleration principle, Harrod attempts to build a dynamic theory of economic activity. This concept became very
important in growth theory during the 1950s and 1960s, especially in the United States. The author considers actual, war-
ranted, and natural rates of growth.

900. _____. "The Law of Decreasing Costs." ECONOMIC JOURNAL 41 (December 1931): 566-76.

Using conditions specified by Sraffa ("The Laws of Returns under Competitive Conditions," ECONOMIC JOURNAL, Vol. 36, December 1926, pp. 42-53; see 997), Harrod examines four different aspects of decreasing costs, including both long- and short-term variations. The reader is also referred to R.G.D. Allen's "Decreasing Costs: A Mathematical Note," (ECONOMIC JOURNAL, Vol. 42, June 1932, pp. 323-26); R.F. Harrod's "Decreasing Costs: An Addendum," (ECONOMIC JOURNAL, Vol. 42, September 1932, pp. 490-92); and R.F. Kahn's "Decreasing Costs: A Note on the Contributions of Mr. Harrod and Mr. Allen," (ECONOMIC JOURNAL, Vol. 42, December 1932, pp. 657-61). These essays extend the debate on decreasing costs and their implications.

901. _____. MONEY. London: Macmillan, 1969. 355 p.

The first of four parts deals with various forms of money, both domestic and international. The third and fourth parts are concerned with the institutions and policies of today and the future. The second part is devoted to monetary theory, classical and Keynesian, as well as growth theory and external equilibrium theory. The work deals with international theory almost as much as domestic.

902. _____. "Scope and Method of Economics." ECONOMIC JOURNAL 48 (June 1938): 383 p.

Harrod analyzes the way in which one should study economics. One should commence with the necessary economic criterion (nature and authority of prescriptions given on the basis of the analytical map); secondly, one should consider the theory of value and distribution (scope and validity of casual knowledge); and thirdly, one must consider the fields of dynamic and empirical analysis. It is not a study purporting the attributes of deduction and the importance of observation of the facts.

903. _____. TOPICAL COMMENT. London: Macmillan, 1961. 265 p.

These essays on the world economic situation are designed to acquaint the reader with the successive phases of economic development since the war. Most of the studies deal with international monetary problems and related domestic policies, past, present, and future. A bibliography of Harrod's work on this topic is included.

904. _____. TOWARDS A DYNAMIC ECONOMICS. London: Macmillan, 1966. 169 p.

First published in 1948, this book has been reprinted numerous times. Harrod here confronts the problem of stagnation, in his opinion the ultimate economic crisis. The dynamic theory employed in his analysis of the problem has as its basis the propensity to save. It has become one of the classic growth models, widely known as the Harrod-Domar Model. His later work, ECONOMIC DYNAMICS (see 897), is a more thorough study of the problems inherent in dynamic analysis.

905. Hawtrey, R.G. "Mr. Robertson on Banking Policy." ECONOMIC JOURNAL 36 (September 1926): 417-33.

In this critical analysis of D.H. Robertson's BANKING POLICY AND THE PRICE LEVEL, Hawtrey expresses his favor with Robertson's notion that prices cannot be stabilized through credit control. The work anticipates the monetarist-Keynesian debates of today.

906. _____. "Monetary Analysis and the Investment Market." ECONOMIC JOURNAL 44 (December 1934): 631-49.

This is an attempt to explain the activity of the investment market with monetary analysis, using algebraic notation to avoid ambiguities inherent in prose analysis. Hawtrey's thinking was in some respects similar to Keynes's; for that reason, this article is of interest to the scholar.

907. _____. "Public Expenditures and the Demand for Labor." ECONOMICA 5 (March 1925): 38-48.

This is an examination of the controversy surrounding the use of public expenditures to decrease unemployment. A major issue was whether borrowed funds merely exchange employers for labor or create net new jobs. Hawtrey concludes that informed credit management would affect public expenditures in such a way as to reduce unemployment.

908. Hayek, F.A. von. "The Maintenance of Capital." ECONOMICA n.s. 2 (August 1935): 241-76.

The concept of a "constant amount of capital" is analyzed. According to the author, economists had neglected the implications of this concept when utilizing it in theory construction. Many issues are raised and left unanswered in this article, but the examination of the constant amount of capital concept was accomplished. It is a good essay on capital theory.

909. _____. MONETARY NATIONALISM AND INTERNATIONAL STABILITY. Reprint ed., New York: Augustus M. Kelley, 1964. 94 p.

This work was based on a series of five lectures presented to the Graduate Institute of International Studies at Geneva in 1936. The topics covered are: "National Monetary Systems," "Function and Mechanism of International Flows of Money," "Independent Currencies," "International Capital Markets," and "Problems of a Really International Standard," all of which are relevant to the current world monetary situation.

910. _____. "On the Relationship between Investment and Output." ECONOMIC JOURNAL 44 (June 1934): 207-31.

This is a demonstration of the proposition that neither of the two definitions of "capital stock"--"the discounted value of the expected future products" and "the result of investing factors of production for definite periods"--is sufficient without the other, although they are not equally valid. The coordination of these two concepts by application of the "time structure of production" is the essential chore to which the author addresses himself.

911. _____. "The 'Paradox' of Saving." ECONOMICA 11 (May 1931): 125-69.

Hayek attempts to illustrate the error of Foster's and Catchings's approach to saving and consumption, which was to develop a theory of crises from their ideas on underconsumption.

912. _____. PRICES AND PRODUCTION. New York: Augustus M. Kelley, 1966. 162 p.

Originally a series of lectures presented at the University of London in 1930-31, the volume has been improved but not substantially changed for later editions. Hayek's thesis is developed within the framework of Mises's monetary theory, but his emphasis is on production and concomitant capital accumulation. An appendix contains replies to some of his critics.

913. Hicks, J.R. CRITICAL ESSAYS IN MONETARY THEORY. London: Oxford University Press, 1967. 219 p.

The first three essays provide a foundation for the explication of monetary theory; subsequent papers clarify certain issues in the controversy between the currency school and the banking schools. Work by Keynes and others, especially Thornton and Hayek, is examined.

914. _____. ESSAYS IN WORLD ECONOMICS. London: Oxford University Press, 1959. 274 p.

Free trade, the dollar problem, and world price and wage fluctuations are studied for British and world economic situations. Part II concerns the problems of the underdeveloped

countries: population, financing, and others. The work
exhibits the same superior theoretical system employed in the
author's earlier works.

915. _____. "The Foundation of Welfare Economics." ECONOMIC JOUR-
NAL 49 (December 1939): 696-712.

Here Hicks rejects the premises from which Pigou's prescription
was derived in THE ECONOMICS OF WELFARE. The intent
of this paper is to synthesize work by R.F. Harrod, N. Kaldor,
and H. Hotelling to provide alternative bases for the three weak
areas of Pigou's work. It is a rigorous but nonmathematical
work.

916. _____. A REVISION OF DEMAND THEORY. London: Oxford University Press, 1959. 198 p.

This small theoretical work is a "revision" of the first three
chapters of the author's VALUE AND CAPITAL (see 919).
The author has sought to incorporate concepts that had appeared
in the literature since 1939. Hicks continues to favor his essentially marginalist approach over the revealed preference
theory developed by Samuelson and others. It is, as usual, a
nonmathematical presentation.

917. _____. "The Theory of Uncertainty and Risk." ECONOMICA 11 (May
1931): 170-89.

Acknowledging the work of F.H. Knight, Hicks asserts that
it is not enough to know in what economic phenomena one
might find an explanation of profit. One must learn exactly
what profit is and what determines its magnitude. The author
accuses Knight of having built his theory of profit on meta-
physics. It is an interesting and informative article on profit
and its relation to uncertainty.

918. _____. THE THEORY OF WAGES. 2nd ed. London: Macmillan,
1966. 388 p.

First published in 1932, this work became a classic in the
field and is still widely recognized as a useful source. The
first section of the book is an exact reprint of the first edition and treats the problems of wage theory in both competitive and imperfectly competitive situations, including, in the
latter group, those arising from regulation. The effects of
hours and conditions and the distribution of economic progress
are also examined. Section II contains three articles, the
last two written soon after publication of the first edition and
the first a review by G.F. Shove. Section III contains a
history of the book and reviews of each chapter.

919. _____. VALUE AND CAPITAL. London: Oxford University Press, 1968. 340 p.

This classic text is one of the finest advanced works on value theory and capital theory in a general equilibrium framework. Nearly every aspect of an economic system is discussed in this work, some at great length. It is essential reading for every serious student.

920. _____. "Wages and Interest: The Dynamic Problem." ECONOMIC JOURNAL 45 (September 1935): 456–68.

Hicks rejects the theories of capital formulated by J.B. Clark and Bohm-Bawerk and Wicksell as suitable only for comparative static analysis and inadequate for analysis of the dynamic situation. Hicks then propounds a theory in which transactions do not occur in a continuous manner. A very simple economy is hypothesized and the theory is examined within the realm of that economy.

921. Hicks, J.R., and Allen, R.G.D. "A Reconsideration of the Theory of Value, Parts I & II." ECONOMICA n.s. 1 (February 1934): 52–76, (May 1934): 196–219.

Hicks and Allen endeavor to determine what adjustments in the marginal theory of value were necessitated by Pareto's discovery of the immeasurability of utility. Part I was written by J.R. Hicks, part II by R.G.D. Allen. The first part utilizes geometry to develop the marginal theory of value. The second part is "A Mathematical Theory of Individual Demand Functions" and requires a background in calculus. These two articles are considered classics in value theory literature.

922. Hobson, J.A. THE ECONOMICS OF DISTRIBUTION. New York: Macmillan, 1907. 361 p.

In an attempt to cope with the problems of monopoly power in labor and capital markets, the author has formulated a new theory of distribution. Hobson's intent is to develop an "intelligible, self-consistent theory of distribution by extending the analysis that had been used for land to the other factors of production." The opinion of the author is that "all processes of bargaining and competition, by which prices are attained and the distribution of wealth achieved, are affected by certain elements of force which assign 'forced gains' . . . to the buyers or the sellers."

923. _____. GOLD PRICES AND WAGES. London: Methuen, 1913. 181 p.

This is a discussion of the relationship between money and the demand and supply of credit. Hobson examines some of the traditional views on the effects of credit expansion on prices; but he examines many variables not usually considered, such as growth of the large development projects in unsettled areas, which produce nonconsumer goods. Hobson treats the issue as a short-run problem, a temporary disequilibrium, rather than inflation.

924. _____. "Underconsumption, an Exposition and a Reply." ECONOMICA 13 (November 1933): 402-17.

This is an extended reply to E.F.M. Durbin's comments on Hobson's earlier work and is followed by a "Reply" by Durbin and a rejoinder by the author. Hobson was one of the more prominent advocates of the underconsumptionist view during this period.

925. Kahn, R.F. "The Problem of Duopoly." ECONOMIC JOURNAL 47 (March 1937): 1-20.

The Cournot solution and the Bertrand solution are both discussed, and a variation on each is proposed. Both original solutions contain positive characteristics, but neither is totally satisfactory as an explanation of duopoly or oligopoly behavior in the market.

926. _____. "The Relation of Home Investment to Unemployment." ECONOMIC JOURNAL 41 (June 1931): 173-98.

This is an examination of the effects on the domestic economy of public works expenditures. All of the usual objections to such expenditure are considered in an effort to comprehend the full net effect of public expenditure. The author then describes the expansionary effect of such government expenditures as road building. Study of this paper enables one to understand why Keynes chose Kahn's theoretical framework for the marginal propensity to consume.

927. Kaldor, Nicholas. "A Case against Technical Progress?" ECONOMICA 12 (May 1932): 180-96.

This is an examination of the argument that technological development produces greater unemployment. Although technical progress might cause dislocation of labor, increasing unemployment and technical progress are simultaneous rather than related as cause and effect. Monopolistic factors in either business or labor are considered the primary cause of unemployment.

928. _____. "The Equilibrium of the Firm." ECONOMIC JOURNAL 44 (March 1934): 60-76.

Asserting that economists have never questioned whether the

"assumptions of a determinate cost-schedule can be derived from the premises upon which static analysis, in general, is based," the author attempts to demonstrate that there are unforeseen difficulties involved in the derivation. Assuming perfect competition and the existence of a functional relationship between cost and output, one must produce a functional form that is consistent with both assumptions. Difficulty is encountered, however, even after the assumption of perfect competition is abandoned. It is a very interesting and important discussion.

929. _____. ESSAYS ON ECONOMIC STABILITY AND GROWTH. London: Gerald Duckworth & Co., 1963. 302 p.

These studies derived from Keynes's method of analysis in which a few strategic aggregates were employed to analyze economic activity. Topics covered include "Speculation, Liquidity Preference and the Theory of Employment," "Theory of Economic Fluctuations," and "Theory of Economic Growth." The works of many other theorists--Pigou, Hicks, Hayek, and Hawtrey-- are discussed.

930. _____. ESSAYS ON VALUE AND DISTRIBUTION. London: Gerald Duckworth & Co., 1966. 238 p.

Most of the articles in this collection were written in the 1930s and deal with issues in value and distribution theory that prevailed during those years. There are ten articles in the five parts: "Theory of Equilibrium," "Theory of Imperfect Competition," "Theory of Welfare Economics," "Theory of Capital," and the "Theory of Distribution." This collection provides the reader with an excellent overview of the theoretical problems of that very important era.

931. _____. "Stability and Full Employment." ECONOMIC JOURNAL 48 (December 1938): 642-57.

This is an examination and classification of the problems accompanying policies designed to promote full employment. Provided full employment could be achieved, the maintenance of a stable economy at a reasonable level of prosperity would become a major problem. Certain factors, present during full employment, produce inherent instability.

932. Kalecki, M. "The Principle of Increasing Risk." ECONOMICA n.s. 4 (November 1937): 440-47.

The object of the paper is the determination of the size of investment an entrepreneur should make, given a set of prevailing conditions. The rate of investment was found to depend on the entrepreneur's capital accumulation and on the "velocity of change of marginal net profitability."

933. _____ . "A Theory of Commodity, Income, and Capital Taxation."
ECONOMIC JOURNAL 47 (September 1937): 444-50.

Using Keynes's concept of "effective demand," Kalecki utilizes
a simple model to examine the influences of taxes on effective
demand. Some surprising conclusions about which taxes should
be utilized are obtained: the tax on capital is found to induce
income growth!

934. _____ . "A Theory of Profits." ECONOMIC JOURNAL 52 (June-
September 1942): 258-67.

This is a short- and long-period analysis of profits. Short-
period analysis is conducted in terms of factors operative in
previous periods; long-period analysis employs the relationship
between the level of the rate of profit and the rate of interest.

935. Keynes, J[ohn] M[aynard]. "Alternative Theories of the Rate of Interest."
ECONOMIC JOURNAL 47 (June 1937): 241-52.

This article follows one by B. Ohlin and is an attempt to clarify some definite misunderstandings on Ohlin's part. Keynes
elaborately distinguishes between his own description of the
determination of interest rates through liquidity preference
and Ohlin's description. Ohlin's work was intended as a
break with traditional credit market theory, but proved to be
merely a restatement of that theory. This is a good discussion
of Keynes's liquidity preference theory. Rejoinders by Ohlin,
Robertson, and Hawtrey, and Keynes's replies to these, appear
in the same volume of the JOURNAL.

936. _____ . ESSAYS IN PERSUASION. New York: W.W. Norton & Co.,
1963. 376 p.

These essays, first published in 1931, include "Treaty of Peace,"
"Inflation and Deflation," "Return to the Gold Standard,"
"Politics," and "The Future." The author felt that these articles were more like prophecies than persuasive arguments,
since the predictions generally were substantiated by empirical
evidence. They are the works of a man urgently trying to
persuade his audience.

937. _____ . THE GENERAL THEORY OF EMPLOYMENT, INTEREST AND
MONEY. London: Macmillan, 1936. 403 p. (Paperbound ed.,
New York: Harcourt, Brace & World, 1965.)

This well-known classic was first published in 1936 and has
generated widespread reassessment of economics during the
ensuing forty years. This is the work from which all of the
"Keynesian" models are supposedly derived. Often alleged to
represent Keynes's break with neoclassical tradition, the work
in fact may not have been such a marked shift. It is interest-

ing but difficult reading, containing few equations and no
mathematics. It is highly recommended for any serious student
of economics. (Also cited in Chapter 1, entry 36.)

938. _____. HOW TO PAY FOR THE WAR, A RADICAL PLAN FOR THE
CHANCELLOR OF THE EXCHEQUER. New York: Harcourt, Brace,
1940. 88 p.

In this essay, Keynes proposed a method of payment for World
War II which also satisfied the claims of the private consumer.
The proposal included universal family cash allowances, accumulation of working class wealth under working class control,
a cheap ration of necessaries, and a capital levy after the
war. Many of the topics are relevant for current exigencies.

939. _____. INDIAN CURRENCY AND FINANCE. Vol. 1 of THE COL-
LECTED WRITINGS OF JOHN MAYNARD KEYNES. London: Macmillan,
1971. 185 p.

This was Keynes's first book and was published in 1913 before
he took a seat on the Royal Commission on Indian Finance and
Currency. Keynes discusses every aspect of currency and banking policy as it might best be conducted in India. Some of
the British domestic situations directly related to the Indian
currency issues are also considered.

940. _____. LAISSEZ-FAIRE AND COMMUNISM. New York: New Repub-
lic, 1926. 144 p.

The problems of a laissez faire economy and the alternative of
communism are examined. Economic individualism and its role
in determining economic activity are also studied. The second
part of the book is a fifty-page discussion of Russia and the
peculiarities of its system with respect to the individual.

941. _____. "A Note on the Long-Term Rate of Interest in Relation to the
Conversion Scheme." ECONOMIC JOURNAL 42 (September 1932):
415-23.

Keynes advocates reduction of the long-term rate of interest
as a method of recovery from the recession. Rates on the war
debt were to be converted by issuing government debts of varying maturities, thus relieving the pressure on the long-term market and allowing its rates to decline.

942. _____. "Relative Movements of Real Wages and Output." ECONOMIC
JOURNAL 49 (March 1939): 34-51.

In response to questions raised by Dunlop and Tarshis, Keynes
reconsiders a particular aspect of his GENERAL THEORY OF
EMPLOYMENT. Although two questions are cited, only one
is considered here: Do changes in effective demand which

change employment in the same direction consequently cause both real and money wages to move together? The question may well be: What was the impetus for the change in money and real wages, and does that determine whether the two move together?

943. _____. A REVISION OF THE TREATY. New York: Harcourt, Brace, 1922. 242 p.

Instead of revising THE ECONOMIC CONSEQUENCES OF THE PEACE (Harcourt, Brace and Howe, 1920), Keynes chose to publish this "Sequel," which contains corrections and additional thoughts on the topic. The intent is to provide the reader with sufficient information to intelligently review the reparations problem. Most of the major issues are covered in some detail and are examined critically. There is also an appendix of documents.

944. _____. A TREATISE ON MONEY. 2 vols. New York: Harcourt, Brace, 1930. Vol. I, 363 p.; vol. II, 424 p.

These volumes were written by Keynes in what most have called his transitional period from one theoretical base to another. Some writers have indicated that one can find evidence here of Keynes's approaching "split" with neoclassical theory. Others see in the work only traditional economic theory. The first volume contains the "Pure Theory of Money"; the second is the "Applied Theory of Money." Each volume is a very thorough and detailed examination of its topic.

945. Meade, J.E. "The Amount of Money and the Banking System" ECONOMIC JOURNAL 44 (March 1934): 77-83.

Examining three types of banking systems characterized by varying degrees of gold coverage, Meade attempts to analyze the effects on the quantity of money that result from given changes in the banking system. It is a rigorous article which also attempts to illustrate the English banking system between 1925 and 1930.

946. Pigou, A.C. "An Analysis of Supply." ECONOMIC JOURNAL 38 (June 1928): 238-57.

Pigou assumes that the industry supply price is the price that determines the regular flow of a good when the industry is fully adjusted to producing that quantity. The intent of the analysis is to examine the effects on price and output, "all other things not remaining equal." The concepts of increasing, decreasing, and constant costs are instantiated with particular cost-altering occurrences.

947. _____. "A Contribution to the Theory of Credit." ECONOMIC JOURNAL 36 (June 1926): 215-27.

> In an effort to explicate two chapters of D.H. Roberton's BANKING POLICY AND THE PRICE LEVEL, Pigou formulated a simplified version of "The Kinds of Saving" and "Shot Locking in the Trade Cycle." Although he praised Robertson's work, he claimed that it was so highly condensed that the average reader could not fully understand the material. This is a systematic treatment of the relationship between credit and money and the remainder of the economy. A comment by R.A. Lehfeldt appears on page 657 of the same JOURNAL.

948. _____. "Disturbances in Equilibrium in International Trade." ECONOMIC JOURNAL 39 (September 1929): 344-56.

> Two sets of criteria are dictated as conditions for exchange equilibrium, and two additional criteria are defined for full equilibrium. The author then examines cases in which equilibrium situations are disturbed by some shock or temporary "accident." Both barter and money economies are discussed.

949. _____. "The Elasticity of Substitution." ECONOMIC JOURNAL 44 (June 1934): 232-41.

> Pigou offers some "general considerations" regarding elasticity of substitution, basing his discussion on work by J.R. Hicks, J. Robinson, and R.F. Kahn, the originators of the concept. Although Pigou employs algebra, patient readers will be able to grasp the essence of his argument.

950. _____. EMPLOYMENT AND EQUILIBRIUM, A THEORETICAL DISCUSSION. London: Macmillan, 1941. 283 p.

> Pigou attempts to provide theoretical answers to many of the questions posed by Keynes in GENERAL THEORY. After dealing with definitions and other preliminaries, the conditions for a short-run flow equilibrium are explained. Two types of systems are examined along with various kinds of "multiplier," and, finally, disequilibrium is studied.

951. _____. "Inflation." ECONOMIC JOURNAL 27 (December 1917): 486-94.

> Pigou first defines inflation, then examines the proportion of price changes due to local causes in England. "Local," in this sense, means "domestic," and the paper is a study of the effect on England's prices of the large world trade position occupied by that nation.

952. _____. "The Interdependence of Different Sources of Demand and Supply in a Market." ECONOMIC JOURNAL 23 (March 1913): 19-24.

> Since it may not always be possible to define individual demand

and supply schedules, Pigou wishes to discover which alternative assumptions regarding the derivation of the aggregate curve
must be made, and under what circumstances.

953. _____. "Interest after the War and the Export of Capital." ECO-
NOMIC JOURNAL 26 (December 1916): 413-24.

The article considers the possible real rate of interest in Great
Britain after World War I, both with and without prohibitions
of capital exports. Secondly, the question of the wisdom of
prohibition or other interference with capital flows is posed
and discussed.

954. _____. "The Laws of Diminishing and Increasing Cost." ECONOMIC
JOURNAL 37 (June 1927): 188-97.

This is an analytical discussion of the relation between the
quantity of output and the costs of production of particular
commodities. This is a long-run relation, but the discussion
assumes a static situation. In other words, Pigou is examining
the "normal" relationship between cost and output under a particular production function with no technological change. This
is part of the continuing controversy regarding decreasing costs
and diminishing returns.

955. _____. "The Monetary Theory of the Trade Cycle." ECONOMIC
JOURNAL 39 (June 1929): 183-94.

The author is commenting on R.G. Hawtrey's use of the equation of exchange and the trade cycle. He maintains that the
trade cycle is not merely a monetary phenomenon, and not
merely a rise in credit availability, but also the situation of
business and/or government. On pages 636-43 there is a reply
by R.G. Hawtrey and a rejoinder by Pigou.

956. _____. "Net Income and Capital Depletion." ECONOMIC JOURNAL
45 (June 1935): 235-41.

This short paper distinguishes between the method of calculation
of net income in a stationary state and in a dynamic state.
"Capital depletion" is the term applied to the concept in the
dynamic state. Difficulty arises when one tries to decide what
may be included in this depletion allowance. Pigou compares
the economist's and the businessman's ideas on the subject.

957. _____. PROTECTIVE AND PREFERENTIAL IMPORT DUTIES. London:
Macmillan, 1906. Reprint ed., New York: Augustus M. Kelley, 1968.
117 p.

This is an analysis of the effects of various trade restrictions
on the domestic economy. The first part of the book deals

with the effect of protective duties on the national dividend and welfare. The second part studies the effects of preferential trade agreements between the mother country and her colonies. The last part is divided into two sections, one dealing with the effects on business, and one with the effects on the economy as a whole.

958. _____. "Real and Money Wage Rates in Relation to Unemployment." ECONOMIC JOURNAL 47 (September 1937): 405-22.

In response to doubts that have recently been raised regarding the expansionary effects on employment of cuts in money and/or real wage rates, Pigou constructed a simple model to analyze the short-run consequences of "all-round cuts in wage rates." This article is a classic in employment theory and in "theoretical" means of increasing employment.

959. _____. "The Statistical Derivation of Demand Curves." ECONOMIC JOURNAL 40 (September 1930): 384-400.

This is an excellent discussion of variables that affect demand in general, and those which specifically affect the construction of a demand curve. Pigou elaborates a method for statistical estimation of demand curves and provides several examples of his procedure.

960. _____. "Wage Policy and Unemployment." ECONOMIC JOURNAL 37 (September 1927): 355-68.

An an approach to the problem of unemployment, Pigou examines the prewar and postwar wage rate unemployment data. The condition of high real wages, maintained by the unions, and of high unemployment is here analyzed. Because of ever higher minimum wages, this problem also exists today.

961. Robbins, Lionel. AUTOBIOGRAPHY OF AN ECONOMIST. London: Macmillan, 1971. 301 p.

Concerned by the turmoil and campus unrest that plagued the London School of Economics in 1968-69, the author began this work as a distraction from "these squalid happenings." It is a narrative account of his life and experiences, including those at L.S.E., before and after World War II.

962. _____. "Consumption and the Trade Cycle." ECONOMICA 12 (November 1932): 413-30.

Robbins examines the underconsumptionist theories of the trade cycle downturn and attempts to illustrate a more correct view of the relationship between consumption and the downturn. The author concludes that one possible reason for the duration of the current (1932) recession may be the effort made to main-

tain purchasing power. It is an interesting analysis that utilizes work by several other writers.

963. _____. "The Economic Effects of Variations of Hours of Labour." ECO-
NOMIC JOURNAL 39 (March 1929): 25–40.

Assuming that the subjective components of work-leisure decisions are outside the realm of scientific inquiry, the author
examines the objective consequences of any variation in the
work-leisure choice. He plots output, income, and distribu-
tional factors against variations in working hours.

964. _____. ECONOMIC PLANNING AND INTERNATIONAL ORDER. London: Macmillan, 1937. 330 p.

Various types of planned economic development are evaluated
in terms of their implications for the welfare of mankind, rather than for one country. Conflicts between the requirements
of an international order and those of individual national groups
are studied.

965. _____. THE ECONOMIST IN THE TWENTIETH CENTURY AND OTHER
LECTURES IN POLITICAL ECONOMY. London: Macmillan, 1954.
225 p.

This collection of essays, prepared since World War II, deals
primarily with finance and commercial policy. Domestic and
international problems are compared with both older and current policy measures and issues. Many problems of continuing
interest are studied.

966. _____. "The Elasticity of Demand for Income, in Terms of Efforts."
ECONOMICA 10 (June 1930): 123–29.

This is an analysis of the effects of taxes and other factors on
the marginal utility of income relative to the marginal utility
of work. The work of Pigou is examined and the author concludes that one cannot predict on an a priori basis the response
of labor to an imposed tax.

967. _____. AN ESSAY ON THE NATURE AND SIGNIFICANCE OF ECO-
NOMIC SCIENCE. 2nd ed. London: Macmillan, 1969. 160 p.

Robbins's purpose was to define more clearly the subject matter
and logical method of economics and to explain the ways in
which political practices impose limitations on economics. Topics include relativity of economic quantitites, generalizations,
and the place of economic science amongst related disciplines.
This is an excellent book with which to begin study of methodology.

968. _____. THE GREAT DEPRESSION. London: Macmillan, 1935.
238 p.

Utilizing orthodox economics, Robbins has attempted to provide
a commentary on the more obvious features of the economic
slump and its antecedents. An excellent work to read in conjunction with J.M. Keynes's THE ECONOMIC CONSEQUENCES
OF THE PEACE and A REVISION OF THE TREATY, this work is
broader in scope than Keynes's and provides more detail concerning the conditions of, and the remedies for, the depression.

969. _____. "On a Certain Ambiguity in the Conception of Stationary Equilibrium." ECONOMIC JOURNAL 40 (June 1930): 194-214.

The intent of this article was to clarify certain assumptions integral to the theory of the stationary state. The discussion
begins with an examination of the historical uses of the concept, and then ambiguities are noted. The works of Schumpeter and J.B. Clark are discussed and compared, and it is demonstrated that there are really two different conceptions of stationary equilibrium. The works of Marshall, Wicksteed, Bohm-
Bawerk, and others are also discussed.

970. _____. "Remarks upon Certain Aspects of the Theory of Costs." ECO-
NOMIC JOURNAL 44 (March 1934): 1-18.

Assuming that most points of argument arise from subtle differences between object and assumption, the author attempts to
clarify and adequately state these characteristics. He discusses
the fundamental nature of costs and the relationship between
this conception and the Marshallian supply curve. The last
two sections concern costs and productivity and variations in
costs over time.

971. _____. "The Representative Firm." ECONOMIC JOURNAL 38 (September 1928): 387-404.

Not satisfied with the definition of the representative firm provided by Marshall, and the interpretations resulting from its
use, Robbins attempted to clarify the concept by examining
and comparing several different methods of ascertaining the
representative firm. The results are of significant importance
for economic theory.

972. _____. THE THEORY OF ECONOMIC DEVELOPMENT IN THE HISTORY
OF ECONOMIC THOUGHT. London: Macmillan, 1968. 185 p.

A "selective discussion of famous propositions," this work is
an excellent source for the person interested in the background
of economic development from the time of the mercantilists.
Topics of the many quotations presented and discussed include
population, accumulation and effective demand, education, or-

ganization, money, and the desirability of growth. The work
is an exercise in comparative statics, not dynamics, and is
nonmathematical.

973. Robertson, D.H. BRITAIN IN THE WORLD ECONOMY. London: George
Allen & Unwin, 1954. 92 p.

Originally presented as the Page-Barbour Lectures for 1953 at
the University of Virginia, these four essays were intended for
a nonspecialist audience. The essays are entitled "The
Mother Country," "The Sterling Area," "Dollar Shortage," and
"Discrimination." The volume is a comment on the situation
in 1953 by a very astute British economist.

974. _____. THE CONTROL OF INDUSTRY. New York: Harcourt, Brace,
1923. 171 p.

Disregarding the problems of production and distribution in a
growing world, the author addresses the problem of governmental control: How shall men and women, given certain economic circumstances, retain the character of self-directing
human beings? Nearly every aspect of "industrial" activity
is examined, including the effects of size, organization, and
control. "Industry" is correctly defined as including all forms
of economic activity, not just manufacturing. It is an excellent study of various forms of control and organization in an
industrial society.

975. _____. ESSAYS IN MONEY AND INTEREST. Manchester: C. Nich-
olls, 1966. 256 p.

This collection of eighteen articles represents many of the
author's major contributions. Examples are: "Theories of Banking Policy"; "Effective Demand and the Multiplier"; "Creep-
ing Inflation"; and ". . . Notes on the Theory of Interest."
A memoir by Sir John Hicks is also included.

976. _____. "The Future of International Trade." ECONOMIC JOURNAL
48 (March 1938): 1-14.

In his general consideration of the future of international trade,
Robertson asks whether or not it will ever resume its nineteenth-
century level of importance. The first step in the analysis is
to examine the necessary conditions for trade and determine
whether these conditions have changed. Secondly, noneco-
nomic conditions must be assessed. Robertson concludes with
six propositions for foreign trade.

977. _____. "Industrial Fluctuation and the Natural Rate of Interest." ECO-
NOMIC JOURNAL 44 (December 1934): 650-56.

Robertson here integrated his concept of saving with attempts

to analyze "cyclical fluctuations" in terms of divergence between "natural" and "market" rates of interest. The article
does not provide a survey of the literature, but merely examines
the issues raised in recent literature, with frequent reference
to the work of Adarkar.

978. _____. "Mr. Keynes' Theory of Money." ECONOMIC JOURNAL 41
(September 1931): 395–411.

In this critical analysis of Keynes's A TREATISE ON MONEY,
Robertson concentrates on Books III and IV in an attempt to
shed some light on "what remains a field of appalling intellectual difficulty." Keynes knew that his equations would
not yield the desired results and Robertson hoped to provide a
"harmonious synthesis" for the ideas embodied in the equations
and writing. A "Rejoinder" by Keynes follows this article in
the same JOURNAL.

979. _____. "Saving and Hoarding." ECONOMIC JOURNAL 43 (September 1933): 399–413.

The intent of this essay is to clarify the definitions of hoarding and saving so that analysis of the latter may be more
fruitfully conducted. A comment by Keynes appears on page
699 of the same JOURNAL.

980. _____. "Those Empty Boxes." ECONOMIC JOURNAL 34 (March 1924):
16–30.

This is a response to an article by A.C. Pigou and to his book,
THE ECONOMICS OF WELFARE. The purpose is to criticize
certain mechanisms elaborated by Pigou for dealing with
diminishing and increasing returns. Robertson contends that
the mechanism renders the "filling of the boxes" unnecessarily
difficult and leads to a use of the boxes which, under certain conditions of political and economic development, might
become misleading and dangerous. The author prefers to
speak of decreasing and increasing cost industries. The article is followed by comment by Pigou.

981. _____. UTILITY AND ALL THAT, AND OTHER ESSAYS. London:
George Allen & Unwin, 1952. Reprint ed., New York: Augustus M.
Kelley, 1966. 207 p.

Written between 1945 and 1951, these sixteen articles represent
the author's views on fundamental concepts, capital and interest
theory, international economics, and monetary economics.

982. Robinson, E.A.G. THE STRUCTURE OF INDUSTRY. New York: Harcourt, Brace, 1932. 184 p.

This book was part of a series, edited by J.M. Keynes, intended to present the elements of economics in a lucid, accurate, and illuminating way. Topics covered include those of interest to one concerned with firm structure, size location, and growth.

983. Robinson, Joan. "Disguised Unemployment." ECONOMIC JOURNAL 46 (June 1936): 225-37.

The concept of disguised unemployment, or underemployed labor, is succinctly described. Robinson explains why, in the industrialized capitalistic worlds, employment fluctuates with effective demand, whereas in less developed and communistic states, complete idleness does not exist for the worker. The worker is thus not unemployed, although he may be employed to work at less than maximum productivity. It is an interesting analysis, especially in light of current government income maintenance programs.

984. _____. ECONOMICS, AN AWKWARD CORNER. Introduction by Robert Lekachman. New York: Pantheon Books, 1967. 86 p.

This essay treats the issues surrounding the problems of the 1960s: incomes and prices, balance of payments, employment and economic growth, monopoly power, and others. There is also a postscript on the "crisis of 1966." The discussion concerns England, but the plight of the world is also considered with respect to the British situation.

985. _____. THE ECONOMICS OF IMPERFECT COMPETITION. 2nd ed. London: Macmillan, 1969. 352 p. Paperbound.

This classic work in economic theory was first published in 1933 and has since been reprinted numerous times. It was an attempt to examine the spectrum of economic concepts in the context of imperfect competition. The relatively new concept of the marginal revenue curve was utilized extensively. A considerable amount of attention was also given to determining the optimum size firm.

986. _____. ESSAYS IN THE THEORY OF ECONOMIC GROWTH. New York: St. Martin's Press, 1962. 138 p.

Prepared as a companion to the ACCUMULATION OF CAPITAL, the volume contains four essays dealing with (a) the "normal" prices controversy between Walrasian and Marxian theory; (b) capital accumulation; (c) technical progress; and (d) the neoclassical theorem treating the analysis of the technical frontier. This group of essays covers many of the problems that continue to plague modern industrial economics.

987. _____ ESSAYS IN THE THEORY OF EMPLOYMENT. London: Mac-millan, 1937. 255 p.

This collection is an attempt to apply the principles of Keynes's GENERAL THEORY to various problems. Topics include labor employment, saving and investment, foreign exchange policies, and the indeterminacy of economic systems. The last essay presents "Some Relfections in Marxism."

988. _____. EXERCISES IN ECONOMIC ANALYSIS. London: Macmillan, 1960. 242 p.

This textbook is intended for the student working with others to do the exercises and discuss the answers. The author cautions the reader to distinguish the units of measurement of quantities, one from another, static from dynamic analysis, and technical or physical relations from social relations. All of the traditional neoclassical topics are covered, and the socialist economy is considered in the section on production and accumulation.

989. _____. FREEDOM AND NECESSITY. New York: Pantheon Books, 1970. 128 p.

In an attempt to stimulate thought regarding economic society, Robinson described the evolution of the modern industrial state from the origin of society to the modern system. The fourteen chapters treat topical areas in an interesting, succinct, and thought-provoking manner.

990. _____. "Imperfect Competition and Falling Supply Price." ECONOMIC JOURNAL 42 (December 1932): 544-54.

This is another article on the possibility of downward sloping supply curves. Earlier essays by P. Sraffa and R. Harrod dealt with most of the issues, but Robinson here hopes to show that, whereas the possibility of falling average costs is greater than the others supposed, the possibility of downward sloping supply curves is far less than they had supposed. Study of the problem is limited to its implications in an imperfectly competitive economy.

991. _____. INTRODUCTION TO THE THEORY OF EMPLOYMENT. London: Macmillan, 1938. 126 p.

This elementary work is addressed to students who have had difficulty assimilating Keynes's GENERAL THEORY OF EM-PLOYMENT, INTEREST AND MONEY with the literature that has appeared since its publication. It is a very complete treat-ment of the ways in which economic activity affect employment.

992. _____. "A Parable on Savings and Investment." ECONOMICA 13 (February 1933): 75-84

The classical and the Keynesian (from A TREATISE ON MONEY) views on price changes resulting from monetary or other dis-turbances are studied. The author points out many of the problems that result from overlooking some essential, but not commonly considered, variables. It is an attempt to clarify the position taken by Hayek vis-a-vis that of Keynes.

993. Shackle, G.L.S. "Expectations and Employment." ECONOMIC JOURNAL 49 (September 1939): 442-52.

This is a cursory examination of the valuation process that businessmen perform with respect to the business future. This, the author feels, is an essential point in Keynes's GENERAL THEORY. The study of the businessman's "attitude to his ignorance of the future, and those changes of this attitude which may be supposed to occur in a regular way" is still a primary area of economic inquiry today. The intent is to establish some generalizations about these attitudes and employment.

994. _____. UNCERTAINTY IN ECONOMICS AND OTHER REFLECTIONS. Cambridge: At the University Press, 1955. 267 p.

The first nine essays dealt with the problem of expectations and uncertainty as the theory had evolved between 1949 and 1955. Part II contains two articles on interest rates, and part IV includes four articles on investment and employment. The last part contains three articles on the philosophy of economics, a topic which Shackle believes to be of considerable importance, given the implicit or explicit role of the economist as prophet.

995. _____. THE YEARS OF HIGH THEORY: INVENTION AND TRADITION IN ECONOMIC THOUGHT 1926-1939. Cambridge: At the University Press, 1967. 328 p.

Shackle considers the development of economic theory from P. Sraffa's work in 1926 to the "landslide of invention" after Leontief's initiation of input-output analysis. The works of Robinson, E.H. Chamberlin, Myrdal, Keynes, and the post-Keynesians are studied as intermediate between the positions of Sraffa and Leontief. It is an excellent source from which to obtain an understanding of the occurrence of events and the flow of economic theory.

996. Sraffa, Piero. "Dr. Hayek on Money and Capital." ECONOMIC JOURNAL 42 (March 1932): 42-53.

In this critique of Hayek's PRICES AND PRODUCTION, Sraffa contends that Hayek has not considered adequately views on money theory alternative to his own and that, as a result of his failure to recognize accepted distinctions between real and money values, Hayek has committed significant errors.

997. _____. "The Laws of Returns Under Competitive Conditions." ECONOMIC JOURNAL 36 (December 1926): 535-50.

In this study of the concept of competitive price determination by supply and demand, Sraffa contends that evidence for a viable notion of "supply" is considerably weaker than that for "demand." His intent here is to sort out the body of literature on concept of supply, distinguishing dead materials from living. This article is also relevant to the problem of increasing and diminishing returns.

998. Webb, Sidney. "The End of Laissez-Faire." ECONOMIC JOURNAL 36 (September 1926): 434-41.

This is a short study of the masterful work of J.M. Keynes as a pamphleteer, and is especially concerned with Keynes's THE END OF LAISSEZ-FAIRE. Referring to the coal strike and other problems, Keynes implied that the necessary conditions for laissez faire no longer existed in the British economy. To Webb's disappointment, Keynes did not give much attention to "protectionism, on the one hand, and Marxian Socialism on the other." The author was one of the principals of the Fabian society.

C. COMMENTARIES ON THE MAJOR CONTRIBUTIONS

999. Cassel, Gustav. FUNDAMENTAL THOUGHTS IN ECONOMICS. New York: Harcourt, Brace, 1925. 153 p.

An attempt is made to "expound the leading ideas" in Cassel's economic works. The four chapters were originally lectures given at the University of London. Topics covered are: "Aims and Methods of Economic Theory"; "Economics as a Theory of Price"; "Principle of Scarcity and the Conception of Cost"; and the "Scarcity Theory of Money." The author has included footnote references to his other more detailed works.

1000. _____. ON QUANTITATIVE THINKING IN ECONOMICS. Oxford: At the University Press, 1935. 181 p.

Cassel believes that a reconstruction of economics as a science is necessary and that it should aim at presenting "actual facts and problems of economic life in the most distinct forms," which should be measurable whenever possible. The title notwithstanding, the volume contains few equations and no geometric figures. It is a discussion of quantitative analysis and deals with the usage of quantitative data.

1001. _____. THE THEORY OF SOCIAL ECONOMY. Translated by S.L. Barron. New York: Harcourt, Brace, 1932. 708 p.

A theory of social economy, the work is addressed to the "economic relations of a whole social body as far as possible irrespective of its extensions, its organization, its laws of property, etc." The traditional theory of value is replaced by a theory of prices, rendering a theory of money an essential part of the study. The author also regards his business cycle theory as superior to existing theories.

1002. Cassels, John M. "A Critical Consideration of Professor Pigou's Method for Deriving Demand Curves." ECONOMIC JOURNAL 43 (December 1933): 575-85.

Cassels regards Pigou's derivation as a procedure of considerable importance and devotes this article to the defects of the method. He finds one error of a fundamental nature that does alter significantly Pigou's results. Pigou's response (pages 586-87 of the same issue) amounts to an acknowledgement of the difficulty.

1003. Harrod, R.F. THE LIFE OF JOHN MAYNARD KEYNES. New York: Harcourt, Brace, 1951. 674 p.

This is a definitive work on a great economist, by a great economist. The work covers in detail the development of the man who was to alter greatly both international politics and economic theory. There is also a "Note on TREATISE ON PROBABILITY," which concerns one of Keynes's more obscure works. There are many plates of Keynes and his close friends and family.

1004. Klein, Lawrence R. THE KEYNESIAN REVOLUTION. 2nd ed. New York: Macmillan, 1966. 288 p.

The first edition, which appeared in 1947, is essentially reprinted for this second edition with two new chapters, the first of which is a reconsideration of Keynesian analysis and the second an empirical model and econometric materials illustrating measurability in the Keynesian system. The first seven chapters discuss the Keynesian system and compare it with the neoclassical system and Keynes's earlier works.

1005. Kurihara, Kenneth K. THE KEYNESIAN THEORY OF ECONOMIC DEVELOPMENT. New York: Columbia University Press, 1959. 219 p.

Kurihara wishes to distinguish Keynesian analysis from neoclassical and Marxian and to "elucidate the operationally significant mechanisms of economic development in given socio-cultural conditions." The author sometimes differs with the way in which Keynes's two students, Harrod and Robinson, have extended Keynes's short-run analysis technique. Kurihara believes that a model should be both verifiable with statistical data and consistent with Keynesian tradition. This is a thorough treatment of the development problem.

1006. Lekachman, Robert. THE AGE OF KEYNES. New York: Random House, 1966. 110 p.

This short but well-done biography of Keynes covers enough of the formative years to allow the student to understand the forces that influenced Keynes's development as an economist. Keynes is described as a man of many talents who, through his thinking and writing and his government service, was able to make his mark on the industrialized Western world.

1007. _____, ed. KEYNES' GENERAL THEORY: REPORTS OF THREE DE-CADES. New York: St. Martin's Press, 1964. 347 p.

This group of essays was gathered to celebrate the twenty-fifth anniversary of Keynes's GENERAL THEORY. The first section presents papers on Keynes and his theory. The second section offers for comparison and contrast articles written by the contributors just before Keynes published his great work, and others written by the same economists just after. The final section presents for comparison articles written in the 1940s and 1960s. The collection is an excellent supplement for study of GENERAL THEORY.

1008. Lange, Oscar. "The Rate Interest and the Optimum Propensity to Consume." ECONOMICA n.s. 5 (February 1936): 12-32.

The intent of the paper is to demonstrate the cooperative roles of the liquidity preference with the marginal efficiency of investment and the propensity to consume in determining the rate of interest. Furthermore, Lange wishes to show that traditional theory and Keynes's theory are but special cases of a more general theory. The author treats the topic of underconsumption in an attempt to apply Keynes's analytical framework.

1009. Leijonhufrud, Axel. ON KEYNESIAN ECONOMICS AND THE ECO-NOMICS OF KEYNES: A STUDY IN MONETARY THEORY. New York: Oxford University Press, 1968. 431 p.

This work is probably one of the best treatments of analysis and theory after Keynes. Some economists have asked: "Would Keynes be an anti-Keynesian today?" The basic argument is that Keynes's own departure from neoclassical theory was not as dramatic as were the extensions of his work by his interpreters. Even if one does not agree with the approach, the work demands thoughtful consideration.

1010. Lutz, Friedrich A. THE THEORY OF INTEREST. Chicago: Aldine Publishing Co., 1968. 336 p.

> Many approaches to the theory of interest are presented. Those such as von Hayek's, which deal with the stationary state, and Keynes's and others are relevant for this chapter. The book concludes with more than a hundred pages on the "Positive Theory of Interest," which is not an interpretation of the work of any particular twentieth-century British theorist. (Also cited in Chapter 4, entry 480.)

1011. Robinson, Joan, ed. AFTER KEYNES. Oxford: Basil Blackwell, 1973. 202 p.

> These papers were presented to Sections F and D of the British Association for the Advancement of Science. Those presented to Section F concern economic issues to which Keynes addressed his many talents. The six articles for Section D deal with environmental issues. The papers on economics represent a broad treatment of many issues that remain unsettled.

1012. Schumpeter, Joseph Alois. TEN GREAT ECONOMISTS, FROM MARX TO KEYNES. New York: Oxford University Press, 1965. 305 p.

> In the thirty-one pages on Keynes the author provides not only an analysis of the theories, but a fairly complete study of his life as well. The coverage comes up to, but does not include, the GENERAL THEORY and so is primarily an examination of Keynes's more classical ideas on economics. (Also cited in Chapter 4, entry 508.)

1013. Tinbergen, J. "Statistical Evidence on the Acceleration Principle." ECONOMICA n.s. 5 (May 1938): 164-76.

> This is a precise statement of the acceleration principle and the necessary conditions for its valid application. The principle is tested against data for the United Kingdom, France, Germany, and the United States. Tinbergen's conclusion is that the principle is not very useful for explaining economic activity.

1014. Townshend, Hugh. "Liquidity-Premium and the Theory of Value." ECONOMIC JOURNAL 47 (March 1937): 157-69.

> This is an attempt to settle the difference of opinion between Keynes and J.R. Hicks on the role of the interest rate. Hicks said that interest is a price determined by the supply and demand condition for new money loans. It was contended that Keynes's interest rate depended on the rates for previously sold loans as well as for new loans. Most of the article deals with the effects on prices of various monetary actions.

D. CONTRIBUTIONS OF LESSER IMPORTANCE

1015. Beveridge, William. "An Analysis of Unemployment." ECONOMICA n.s. 3 (November 1936): 357-86.

1016. Bowley, A.L. "Bilateral Monopoly." THE ECONOMIC JOURNAL 38 (December 1928): 651-59.

1017. Clower, Robert. "Keynes and the Classics: A Dynamical Perspective." QUARTERLY JOURNAL OF ECONOMICS 74 (May 1960): 318-23.

1018. Davidson, Paul. "A Keynesian View of the Relationship between Accumulation, Money and the Money Wage-Rate." THE ECONOMIC JOURNAL 79 (June 1969): 300-23.

1019. _____. "Keynes's Finance Motive." OXFORD ECONOMIC PAPERS n.s. 17 (March 1965): 47-65.

1020. Edwards, Edgar O. "Classical and Keynesian Employment Theories: A Reconciliation." QUARTERLY JOURNAL OF ECONOMICS 73 (August 1959): 407-28.

1021. Ellsworth, P.T. "Mr. Keynes on the Rate of Interest and the Marginal Efficiency of Capital." JOURNAL OF POLITICAL ECONOMY 44 (December 1936): 767-90.

1022. Fellner, William, and Ellis, Howard S. "Hicks and the Time-Period Controversy." JOURNAL OF POLITICAL ECONOMY 48 (August 1940): 563-78.

1023. Ferger, Wirth F. "Notes on Pigou's Method of Deriving Demand Curves." THE ECONOMIC JOURNAL 42 (March 1932): 17-26. (See also p. 26.)

1024. Friedman, Milton. "Professor Pigou's Method for Measuring Elasticities of Demand from Budgetary Data." QUARTERLY JOURNAL OF ECONOMICS 50 (November 1935): 151-63.

1025. Hahn, F.H. "The Rate of Interest and General Equilibrium Analysis." THE ECONOMIC JOURNAL 65 (March 1955): 52-66. (See also Vol. 65, December 1955, p. 626.)

1026. Harrod, R.F. "The Equilibrium of Duopoly." THE ECONOMIC JOURNAL 44 (June 1934): 335-37.

1027. _____. "Progressive Taxation and Equal Sacrifice." THE ECONOMIC

JOURNAL 40 (December 1930): 704-7.

1028. Hart, Albert G. "An Examination of Mr. Keynes's Price-Level Concepts." JOURNAL OF POLITICAL ECONOMY 41 (October 1933): 625-38.

1029. Hawtrey, R.G. "The Gold Standard." THE ECONOMIC JOURNAL 29 (December 1919): 428-42.

1030. _____. "Mr. Harrod on the British Boom." THE ECONOMIC JOURNAL 66 (December 1956): 610-20.

1031. _____. "The Nature of Profit." THE ECONOMIC JOURNAL 61 (September 1951): 489-504.

1032. Hayek, F.A. von. "Economics and Knowledge." ECONOMICA n.s. 4 (February 1937): 33-54.

1033. _____. "The Mythology of Capital." QUARTERLY JOURNAL OF ECONOMICS 50 (February 1936): 199-228.

1034. _____. "A Note on the Development of the Doctrine of 'Forced Saving'." QUARTERLY JOURNAL OF ECONOMICS 47 (November 1932): 123-33.

1035. _____. "Reflection on the Pure Theory of Money of Mr. J.M. Keynes." ECONOMICA 11 (August 1931): 270-95. (See also Vol. 11, November 1931, pp. 387, 398, and Vol. 12, February 1932, p. 22).

1036. _____. "The Trend of Economic Thinking." ECONOMICA 13 (May 1933): 121-37.

1037. _____. "Utility Analysis and Interest." THE ECONOMIC JOURNAL 46 (March 1936): 44-60.

1038. Hicks, J.R. "Growth and Anti-Growth." OXFORD ECONOMIC PAPERS 18 (November 1966): 257-69.

1039. _____. "Liquidity." THE ECONOMIC JOURNAL 72 (December 1962): 787-802.

1040. _____. "Marginal Productivity and the Principle of Variation." ECONOMICA 12 (February 1932): 79-88.

1041. _____. "A Neo-Austrian Growth Theory." THE ECONOMIC JOURNAL 80 (June 1970): 257-81.

1042. _____. "A Rehabilitation of 'Classical' Economics?" THE ECONOMIC JOURNAL 67 (June 1957): 278-89.

1043. _____. "A Suggestion for Simplifying the Theory of Money." ECONOMICA n.s. 2 (February 1935): 1-19.

1044. Holden, G.R. "Mr. Keynes Consumption Function and the Time-Preference Postulate." QUARTERLY JOURNAL OF ECONOMICS 52 (February 1938): 281-96.

1045. Hoover, Calvin B. "Keynes and the Economic System." JOURNAL OF POLITICAL ECONOMY 56 (October 1948): 392-402.

1046. Jong, F.J. de. "Supply Functions in Keynesian Economics." THE ECONOMIC JOURNAL 64 (March 1954): 3-24. (See also Vol. 64, December 1954, pp. 834, 840; Vol. 65, September 1955, pp. 474, 479; and Vol. 66, September 1956, pp. 482, 488.)

1047. Kakfa, Alexander. "Professor Hicks's Theory of Money Interest." AMERICAN ECONOMIC REVIEW 31 (June 1941): 327-29.

1048. Kahn, R.F. "Some Notes on Ideal Output." THE ECONOMIC JOURNAL 45 (March 1935): 1-34. (See also Vol. 48, June 1938, p. 336.)

1049. _____. "Two Applications of the Concept of Elasticity of Substitution." THE ECONOMIC JOURNAL 45 (June 1935): 242-45.

1050. Kaldor, Nicholas. "Market Imperfection and Excess Capacity." ECONOMICA n.s. 2 (February 1935): 33-50.

1051. _____. "A Model of the Trade Cycle." THE ECONOMIC JOURNAL 50 (March 1940): 78-92.

1052. Kemp, Murray C. "Professor Pigou on the Efficiency of the Competitive Capital Market." THE ECONOMIC JOURNAL 64 (June 1954): 405-7.

1053. Keynes, J[ohn] M[aynard]. "The 'Ex-Ante' Theory of the Rate of Interest." THE ECONOMIC JOURNAL 47 (December 1937): 663-69. (See also Vol. 48, June 1938, pp. 314, 318, and September 1938, p. 555.)

1054. _____. "Fluctuations in Net Investment in the United States." THE ECONOMIC JOURNAL 46 (September 1936): 540-47.

1055. _____. "The General Theory of Employment." QUARTERLY JOURNAL

OF ECONOMICS 51 (February 1937): 209-23.

1056. Klein, Lawrence R. "Theories of Effective Demand and Employment." JOURNAL OF POLITICAL ECONOMY 55 (April 1947): 108-32.

1057. Leontief, Wassily. "The Fundamental Assumption of Mr. Keynes' Monetary Theory of Unemployment." QUARTERLY JOURNAL OF ECONOMICS 51 (November 1936): 192-97.

1058. Lerner, A.P. "Professor Hicks' Dynamics." QUARTERLY JOURNAL OF ECONOMICS 54 (February 1940): 298-306.

1059. MacDougall, G.D.A. "The Definition of Prime and Supplementary Costs." THE ECONOMIC JOURNAL 46 (September 1936): 443-61.

1060. Machlup, Fritz. "Professor Hicks' Statics." QUARTERLY JOURNAL OF ECONOMICS 54 (February 1940): 277-97.

1061. Marglin, S.A. "Investment and Interest: A Reformulation and Extension of Keynesian Theory." THE ECONOMIC JOURNAL 80 (December 1970): 910-31.

1062. Marty, Alvin L. "A Geometrical Exposition of the Keynesian Supply Function." THE ECONOMIC JOURNAL 71 (September 1961): 560-65.

1063. Millar, J.R. "The Social Accounting Basis of Keynes' Aggregate Supply and Demand Functions." THE ECONOMIC JOURNAL 82 (June 1972): 600-611.

1064. Morgenstern, Osker. "Professor Hicks on Value and Capital." JOURNAL OF POLITICAL ECONOMY 49 (June 1941): 361-93.

1065. Patinkin, Don. "Friedman on the Quantity Theory and Keynesian Economics." JOURNAL OF POLITICAL ECONOMY 80 (July/August 1972): 883-905.

1066. _____. "Involuntary Unemployment and the Keynesian Supply Function." THE ECONOMIC JOURNAL 59 (September 1949): 360-83.

1067. Pigou, A.C. "The Foreign Exchanges." QUARTERLY JOURNAL OF ECONOMICS 37 (November 1922): 52-74.

1068. _____. "A Method of Determining the Numerical Value of Elasticities of Demand." THE ECONOMIC JOURNAL 20 (December 1910): 636-40.

1069. _____. "Mr. J.M. Keynes' General Theory of Employement, Interest and Money." ECONOMICA n.s. 3 (May 1936): 115-32.

1070. Pigou, A.C., Friedman, Milton, and Georgesu-Roegen, Nicholas St. "Marginal Utility of Money and Elasticities of Demand." QUARTERLY JOURNAL OF ECONOMICS 50 (May 1936): 532.

1071. Robbins, Lionel. "Economic Notes on Some Arguments for Protection." ECONOMICA 11 (February 1931): 45-62.

1072. Robertson, D.H. "Economic Incentive." ECONOMICA 1 (October 1921): 231-45.

1073. _____. "A Note on the Theory of Money." ECONOMICA 13 (August 1933): 243-47.

1074. _____. "Some Notes on Mr. Keynes' General Theory of Employment." QUARTERLY JOURNAL OF ECONOMICS 51 (November 1936): 168-91.

1075. _____. "A Word for the Devil." ECONOMICA 3 (November 1923): 203-8.

1076. Robinson, Austin. "John Maynard Keynes: 1883-1946." THE ECONOMIC JOURNAL 57 (March 1947): 1-68.

1077. Robinson, Joan. "The Concept of Hoarding." THE ECONOMIC JOURNAL 48 (June 1938): 231-36.

1078. _____. "A Fundamental Objection to Laissez-Faire." THE ECONOMIC JOURNAL 45 (September 1935): 580-82. (See also Vol. 46, March 1936, p. 163.)

1079. _____. "The Model of an Expanding Economy." THE ECONOMIC JOURNAL 62 (March 1952): 42-53.

1080. _____. "Own Rates of Interest." THE ECONOMIC JOURNAL 71 September 1961): 596-600.

1081. _____. "What Is Perfect Competition?" QUARTERLY JOURNAL OF ECONOMICS 49 (November 1934): 104-20.

1082. Rosenstein-Rodan, P.N. "The Coordination of the General Theories of Money and Price." ECONOMICA n.s. 3 (August 1936): 257-80.

1083. Samuelson, Paul A. "D.H. Robertson (1890-1963)." QUARTERLY JOUR-

NAL OF ECONOMICS 77 (November 1963): 517-36.

1084. Shackle, G.L.S. "The Breakdown of the Boom: A Possible Mechanism." ECONOMICA n.s. 3 (November 1936): 423-35.

1085. _____. "Twenty Years On: A Survey of the Theory of the Multiplier." THE ECONOMIC JOURNAL 61 (June 1951): 241-60.

1086. Sweezy, Paul M. "Professor Pigou's THEORY OF UNEMPLOYMENT." JOURNAL OF POLITICAL ECONOMY 42 (December 1934): 800-811.

1087. Viner, Jacob. "Mr. Keynes on the Causes of Unemployment." QUARTERLY JOURNAL OF ECONOMICS 51 (November 1936): 147-67.

1088. Wells, Paul. "Keynes' Aggregate Supply Function: A Suggested Interpretation." THE ECONOMIC JOURNAL 70 (September 1960): 536-42.

1089. Williams, John H. "The Monetary Doctrines of J.M. Keynes." QUARTERLY JOURNAL OF ECONOMICS 45 (August 1931): 547-87.

1090. Wright, A.L. "The Genesis of the Multiplier Theory." OXFORD ECONOMIC PAPERS n.s. 8 (June 1956): 181-93.

APPENDIXES AND INDEXES

Appendix A
JOURNALS

AMERICAN ECONOMIC REVIEW, 1313 Twenty-First Avenue, South, Nashville, Tenn. 37212. 1911- . Quarterly.

ECONOMICA, General Secretary, Economica Publishing Office, London School of Economics, Houghton Street, London WC2 2AE, England. 1921- . Quarterly.

ECONOMIC JOURNAL, Secretary, Royal Economic Society, The Marshall Library, Sidgewick Avenue, Cambridge CB3 9DB, England. 1891- . Quarterly.

HISTORY OF POLITICAL ECONOMY, Duke University Press, Durham, N.C. 27706. 1969- . Quarterly.

JOURNAL OF ECONOMIC ISSUES, Harry M. Trevling, Secretary-Treasurer, Department of Economics, Michigan State University, East Lansing, Mich. 48823. 1967- . Quarterly.

JOURNAL OF POLITICAL ECONOMY, University of Chicago Press, 5750 Ellis Avenue, Chicago, III. 60637. 1892- . Bimonthly.

OXFORD ECONOMIC PAPERS, Oxford University Press, Press Road, Neasden, London NW10 0DD, England. 1938- . 3/year.

QUARTERLY JOURNAL OF ECONOMICS, Harvard University Press, 79 Garden Street, Cambridge, Mass. 02138. 1886- . Quarterly.

Appendix B

PROFESSIONAL ORGANIZATIONS SPECIALIZING IN THE HISTORY OF ECONOMIC THOUGHT

Although a multitude of associations are concerned directly or indirectly with the history of economic thought, only a few devote a considerable amount of time and effort to promoting this field. Consequently, I have chosen to list only the four major associations that deal with history of economic thought. The interested reader is referred to the ENCYCLOPEDIA OF ASSOCIATIONS published by Gale Research Company.

1. American Economics Association
   Rendigs Fels, Secretary
   1313 21st Avenue South
   Nashville, TN 37212

2. Association for Evolutionary
   Economics
   Harry M. Trebling, Secretary-
   Treasurer
   Department of Economics
   Michigan State University
   East Lansing, MI 48823

3. History of Economics Society
   James L. Cochrane, Secretary
   Department of Economics
   University of South Carolina
   Columbia, SC 29208

4. Royal Economic Society
   The Marshall Library
   Sidgewick Avenue
   Cambridge CB3 9DB
   England

AUTHOR INDEX

Included in the Author Index are all authors, editors, compilers, and translators whose works are cited in the bibliography. Additional references appear in the Subject Index for authors who are the subject of biography, or whose works are the subject of analysis. Except when preceded by "p." all numbers refer to entry numbers, not page numbers.

A

Abbott, Leonard Dalton 1, 89
Abramovitz, Moses 640
Adams, Herbert B. 304
Allen, R.G.D. 885-86, 921
Allen, William R. 61
Amano, Akihivo 537
Anderson, B.L. 115
Anderson, Karl L. 781
Andrews, John B. 649
Andzrooni, Leon 756
Angell, James W. 610, 782-87
Aoki, Masahiko 538
Aquinas, St. Thomas 6
Arkin, Marcus 14
Armstrong, W.E. 788
Ashley, Sir William J. 13, 104, 267-71, 277, 315-18
Ashton, T.S. 116
Aveling, Edward 98
Ayers, C.E. 611

B

Bagehot, Walter 117, 365
Bailey, Martin J. 422-23
Balassa, Bela A. 118
Balogh, T. 62

Barnett, Harold J. 119
Barrington, Donald 200
Barucci, Piero 424
Bastable, C.F. 366-67
Bauer, Stephen 63
Baur, P.T. 425
Beach, Frank H. 88
Beer, M. 15
Bennion, E.G. 772
Berle, Adolf A. 201
Bernardelli, H. 426
Beveridge, W.H. 887-89, 1015
Bhaduri, Amit 202
Bharadwaj, Krishna 427
Birck, L.V. 203
Bitterman, Henry J. 204
Black, J. 539
Black, R.D. Collison 205, 395, 397, 428-29, 532
Blaug, Mark 120-21, 206-7, 430
Bloch, Henri-Simon 431
Bloom, Solomon F. 208
Bloomfield, Arthur I. 16
Bober, M.M. 122
Bodin, Jean 6
Bohm-Bawerk, Eugen 123, 337-40, 368, 432, 627
Bonar, James 124, 209-13, 290, 368, 432

Author Index

Hoxie, Lucy 704
Hoxie, Robert F. 703-4
Hull, Charles Henry 5, 33
Huncke, George D. 123
Hume, David 6
Hunter, L.C. 155
Hutchison, T.W. 76, 232-33, 465-66
Hutton, Richard Holt 117

I

Ingram, John Kells 275

J

Jaffe, William 354-55, 467-68
Jevons, W. Stanley 365, 391-97, 495
Johnson, Alvin S. 830
Johnson, E.A.J. 34, 775
Johnson, Edgar H. 831
Johnson, Harry G. 469
Johnson, Jerah 35
Johnson, Shirley B. 575
Jones, J.H. 77
Jones, Richard 300
Jong, F.J. de 1046

K

Kafka, Alexander 1047
Kahn, R.F. 359, 925-26, 1048-49
Kaldor, Nicholas 832, 927-31, 1050-51
Kalecki, M. 932-34
Kapp, K. William 6, 300
Kapp, Lore L. 6, 300
Kauder, Emil 470-71, 576
Kemp, Murray C. 234, 577, 1052
Keynes, Geoffrey 156, 472-74
Keynes, John Maynard 36, 140, 156, 401, 457, 472-74, 497, 935-44, 950, 968, 978, 982, 987, 991-93, 998, 1007, 1053-55, p. 173
Keynes, John Neville 301
Kiker, B.F. 326
Klein, Lawrence R. 1004, 1056
Kleindorfer, Paul 549
Knapp, G.F. 290
Knight, Frank H. 157, 287, 475,

705-16, 833-37
Konekamp, Rosamond 395
Krupp, Sherman Roy 476
Kuczynski, Marguerite 7
Kuenne, Robert E. 477-78
Kuhn, W.E. 479
Kurihara, Kenneth K. 1005
Kuznets, Simon 776

L

Labor, John J. 278
Laidler, David 158
Lange, Oscar 446, 1008
Laughlin, J. Laurence 717-19, 838-39
Leigh, Arthur H. 78, 327
Leijonhufrud, Axel 1009
Lekachman, Robert 302, 1006-7
Leontief, Wassily 235, 840, 1057
Lerner, A.P. 1058
Leslie, Thomas Edward Cliffe 328-29
Letwin, William 37
Levy, S. Leon 159
Lindahl, Erik 345, 361
Lindgren, J. Ralph 236
Link, Robert G. 160
List, Frederick 276
Lowe, Adolph 161
Lutz, Friedrich A. 480-81, 1010
Lutz, Vera 481
Luxemburg, Rosa 162

M

McArthur, Ellen A. 274
McCulloch, J.R. 8, 38, 95
Macdonald, Robert A. 163
MacDonald, Ronan 841
MacDougall, G.D.A. 1059
Macfie, A.L. 164
MacGregor, D.H. 570
Machlup, Fritz 165, 842-43, 1060
McLellan, David 100
Macvane, S.M. 482-83
Majumdar, Tapas 484
Malloch, Christian A. 363
Malmgren, H.B. 579
Malthus, Thomas Robert 96-97, 124, 173, 183

TITLE INDEX

The Title Index includes titles of books, monographs, and pamphlets. Some titles have been shortened. Periodicals, articles, and individual chapter or essay titles are not included. Except when preceded by "p." all numbers refer to entry numbers, not page numbers.

Title Index

Title Index

Title Index

SUBJECT INDEX

Numbers in this index refer to <u>entry</u> <u>numbers</u>. References to authors indicate that they are the <u>subject</u> of discussion. The subentry "welfare" shown under "Pareto, Vilfredo," for example, shows that Pareto's theories of welfare are analyzed by another author. To consult Pareto's theories on welfare directly, see the Author Index for Pareto as a primary author.

Subject Index

Subject Index